The Literate Classroom

Edited by
Prue Goodwin

David Fulton Publishers
London

David Fulton Publishers Ltd
Ormond House, 26–27 Boswell Street, London WC1N 3JD

First published in Great Britain by David Fulton Publishers 1999

Note: The right of Prue Goodwin to be identified as the editor of this work has been asserted by her in accordance with the Copyright, Designs and Patents Act 1988.

Copyright © David Fulton Publishers Ltd 1999

British Library Cataloguing in Publication Data

A catalogue record for this book is available from the British Library

ISBN 1–85346–566–6

Typeset by FSH Print & Production Ltd
Printed by The Cromwell Press Ltd, Trowbridge, Wilts.

Contents

Contributors   v

The literate classroom: an introduction   ix
Prue Goodwin

Part I   **Starting points for literacy**   1
1   Shared reading and shared writing at Key Stage 1   1
    Liz Laycock
2   Developing phonic skills in the early years   11
    Lesley Clark
3   The struggle to punctuate: a case study of two children learning   18
    Nigel Hall
4   'This is my reading writing and this is my writing writing'   30
    Liz Slater

Part II   **Becoming readers**   37
5   Responding to fiction   37
    Tony Martin
6   Reading silently   45
    Geoff Fenwick
7   A sense of time and place: literature in the wider curriculum   52
    Gillian Lathey
8   Reading the pictures: children's responses to *Rose Blanche*   58
    Catriona Nicholson
9   The creation of readers, or Mr Magnolia meets the Literacy Hour.
    Will he survive?   65
    Judith Graham

Part III   **Becoming writers**   73
10   Writers' workshops in action   73
    Anne Rowe and Prue Goodwin
11   Developing children's narrative writing using story structures   79
    Maureen Lewis
12   The problems and possibilities of non-fiction writing   91
    David Wray and Maureen Lewis
13   In their own write: word processing in Urdu   99
    Urmi Chana, Viv Edwards and Sue Walker

Part IV The world of literacy 107

14 Working with words: vocabulary development in the primary school 107
    George Hunt

15 Opening the wardrobe of voices: standard English and
    language study at Key Stage 2 115
    Michael Lockwood

16 Who's afraid of the big bad verse? 124
    Chris Powling, with Sean O'Flynn

17 The role of drama in the literate classroom 134
    Suzi Clipson-Boyles

Index 142

Contributors

Urmi Chana, **Viv Edwards** and **Sue Walker** all work at The University of Reading. Urmi Chana, a former advisory teacher, is currently a research officer at the Reading and Language Information Centre (RALIC); Viv Edwards is Professor of Language in Education and Director of RALIC; and Sue Walker is Head of the Department of Typography and Graphic Communication. Together they have worked on a number of research projects, including the Multilingual Resources for Children Project and the Multilingual Word processing in the Primary School.

Lesley Clark is a Lecturer in Language and Education at the Reading and Language Information Centre, The University of Reading. She was previously a teacher in primary schools in England and Singapore, working with all ages of pupils particularly with early-years and special educational needs pupils. Her book *Help Your Child with Reading* (1994, Hodder & Stoughton) offers guidance to parents on supporting their children's literacy learning.

Suzi Clipson-Boyles is a Senior Lecturer in Primary English at Oxford Brookes University where she directs the Catch Up Project, a literacy intervention programme for struggling readers in Year 3. Her drama work has featured on radio and television, and she has written several publications including *Drama in Primary English Teaching* (1997, David Fulton Publishers).

Geoff Fenwick works in the Education Department of John Moores University, Liverpool, where he specialises in the teaching of language and literature. One of his interests is sustained silent reading, a subject on which he has researched and published widely.

Prue Goodwin taught in primary and middle schools before becoming a Lecturer in Reading and Language and Director of INSET at the Reading and Language Information Centre, The University of Reading. Her research has been into reluctance to read. She teaches a module on picture books in the MA course in Children's Literature at Roehampton Institute, London.

Judith Graham has been a Principal Lecturer at Roehampton Institute, London since 1994, lecturing in language, literacy and children's literature. Her early teaching experience was in inner-city schools; she has also been a lecturer at The University of Greenwich. Her publications include *Pictures on the Page*, (1990, National Association for the Teaching of English) an exploration of the role of picture books in children's developing literacy, *Cracking Good Books – Teaching Literature at Key Stage 2* (1997, National Association for the Teaching of English); and as editors with Alison Kelly, *Reading under control* (1997, David Fulton Publishers).

Nigel Hall is Reader in Literacy Education at the Didsbury School of Education, Manchester Metropolitan University. He has written or been an editor of a large number of books in the field of language and literacy, has contributed many chapters in other books and lectures extensively throughout the UK and the rest of the world. He is codirector of The Punctuation Project.

George Hunt has taught in several London primary schools and has worked on literacy programmes in Dominica and Mongolia. He is currently a Lecturer in Language in Education at The University of Reading. His publications include *Inspirations for Grammar* (1994, Scholastic) and *Curriculum Bank: Reading at Key Stage 2* (1995, Scholastic). He is a regular contributor to the *Books for Keeps* magazine.

Gillian Lathey was a primary teacher in north London for 15 years and an advisory teacher before becoming Senior Lecturer in Language in Education and Children's Literature at Roehampton Institute, London. She administrates the Marsh Award for Children's Literature in Translation. She has just completed a comparative study of German and English language autobiographical children's literature on the Third Reich and the Second World War.

Liz Laycock is Principal Lecturer in Education and was Coordinator of Language Teaching studies for six years. She is Programme Convener of the primary Post Graduate Certificate of Education programme with particular interests in early literacy, narrative, the teaching of children with English as an additional language, and assessment of language and literacy.

Maureen Lewis was a primary teacher for many years before becoming a research assistant on several literacy projects at The University, Exeter, and then the Research Fellow for the influential Exeter Extending Literacy (EXEL) Project funded by the Nuffield Foundation. She is currently codirector of the second stage of the EXEL Project. She has written many books and articles relating to these projects. Her most recent book (with co-author David Wray and published by Routledge) *Extending Literacy; Children Reading and Writing Non-fiction* was awarded the 1997 Donald Moyle Award for making a significant contribution to literacy.

Michael Lockwood taught in schools for eight years before becoming a Lecturer in English and Education in the School of Education, The University of Reading. Recent publications include *Opportunities for English in the Primary School* (Trentham, 1996) and *Practical Ways to Teach Standard English and Language Study* (1998, Reading and Language Information Centre, The University of Reading).

Tony Martin is the Head of Education Development at the University College of St Martin. He spends his time running projects, courses and consultancy for teachers in primary and cross-phase English. He has published *The Strugglers* (1989, Open University). He was the president of the United Kingdom Reading Association in 1997.

Catriona Nicholson was a teacher in primary and special schools before becoming a Lecturer in English and Primary Education at The University of Reading. She has taught at Westminster College, Oxford, contributes to the MA course in Children's Literature at Reading and is an associate director of the Centre for International Research in Childhood: Literature, Culture, Media.

Chris Powling was in education for 30 years as a class teacher, a head and a lecturer in English at King Alfred's University College. He is the author of many books for young readers and was editor of the magazine *Books for Keeps* for seven years. He is an enthusiastic participant in the Writers-in-schools initiative and regularly undertakes INSET with primary teachers.

Anne Rowe was a primary class teacher and head teacher, specialising in supporting children to become confident writers and readers. She has lectured on literacy development at The University of Reading and has published articles and books on literacy development and children's literature.

Liz Slater has a wide experience as a teacher in all key stages, particularly Key Stages 1 and 2, and was deputy head in a primary school. She became an English adviser for Essex where she directed projects on reading and children as researchers. Her current post is in Thurrock as a general primary adviser with special responsibility for literacy.

David Wray is Professor of Education at The University of Warwick. He was previously Reader in Literacy at The University of Exeter and co-director of the Exeter Extending Literacy Project (EXEL) funded by the Nuffield Foundation. He has a wide experience of working in primary schools and has published many books and articles related to literacy.

The literate classroom: an introduction

Prue Goodwin

This book is about teaching reading and writing in primary classrooms. The authors are all experienced classroom practitioners, accomplished at literacy teaching and committed to supporting colleagues through the sharing of good practice. The book aims to give practical guidance on teaching methods whilst highlighting issues about literacy teaching which are currently under debate. Contributors cover between them all the primary years, dealing with topics from the introduction of the alphabet at Key Stage 1 to an investigation of historical fiction by Key Stage 2 pupils in year 6. With 17 contributors to the book there is bound to be diversity of opinion as well as agreement about the best ways to support children's developing literacy. In fact, the different points of view and the overlap of advice creates a healthy debate between concerned colleagues – a model for discussion in any primary school staffroom.

What is a literate classroom?

If asked, 'What is a literate classroom?' I would have to say it is a place where there is a lot of talking. Get any group of adult readers or writers together and animated discussion is inevitable. A classroom that reflects that mix of celebration and opinion offers a productive environment where embryo readers and writers can grow. However, surely, some people may be thinking, children are not capable of 'animated discussion' of that sort? Only when children have been taught to read and write, when they have read the particular books deemed by society to 'make' them literate, then they may be entitled to offer opinions or share literary enthusiasms. In this view, school should be about instruction, analysis and being shown how to read and write 'correctly'.

Unfortunately, such a rigidly pedantic approach has been tried and has failed large numbers of pupils. But problems have also arisen when schools have taken an alternative approach, providing lots of lovely books in the hope that somehow the 'quality' of the literature would inspire children to learn to read and write. One approach concentrated on method, and the other on resources. Neither took into account the importance of being in the company of other readers and writers engaged in purposeful discussion.

A literate classroom is one where children experience how literate people behave. Yes, there must be well-understood teaching methods; yes, there must be a range of high-quality children's books. However, there must also be the creation of a community of readers and writers who – through purposeful discussion – spark ideas, support each other's initiatives and celebrate successes. So how can this model of the literate classroom fit with the current prescriptive trends in literacy education?

The National Literacy Strategy

Schools in England are engaged in the National Literacy Strategy (NLS), an initiative to improve literacy standards which is offering advice to primary teachers about how best to teach reading and writing. However, in *The National Literacy Strategy Framework for Teaching* (DfEE 1998) there are actually very few new ideas about literacy teaching. If we look at the suggested teaching methods we find references to the 1970s when James Britton (1970), Vera Southgate (1972), Don Holdaway (1979) and many others were explaining techniques such as modelling, scaffolding and supporting young readers and writers. All these approaches involve creating a learning environment based on interaction and collaboration – the quality of the talk being the most important feature. *The Framework* (p.8) states that the most successful teaching is 'discursive – characterised by high quality oral work: interactive – pupils' contributions are encouraged, expected and extended'. To put it more bluntly, successful literacy learning takes place where there is purposeful talk about reading and writing. The teacher's role in providing this, through teaching methods founded on research and experience, is the focus of this book.

A literate environment

Every primary classroom is a special place with its own values; how children feel about reading and writing will be reflections of those values. Children's first impressions of the status given to literacy will be based on the physical environment. Books should be at the heart of the resources collection and other texts (journals, comics, letters, calendars, etc.), although posters, labels and instructions will all contribute to an authentically literate environment. There should be displays of children's work celebrating success, demonstrating progress and emphasising the central role which reading and writing play in the general organisation of the classroom. Although all teachers would like to have more and newer resources, even the least promising materials can be used to give positive messages, e.g. a label saying 'This book has been read so often that it is falling apart!'. Of course, if it is falling apart because it has been thrown around during a wet playtime, something important is missing – a respect for books.

Respect for books

It is sometimes difficult to get the balance right when it comes to respect for books. On the one hand we want books to be valued, on the other hand we want children to pick them up and devour them. In a classroom, as in reality, not all texts will have the same importance. Beautifully produced books with crisp new pages and that special smell may be valued objects but, so often, the truly precious text is valued because of the ideas that it contains or the associations that it has with uplifting experience (my childhood copy of *The Secret Garden* is literally falling apart, but I would not swap it for a new copy – no matter how beautiful). By discussing what makes anything precious it is possible to explore the special feelings that readers have for books. Children's own precious texts must also be valued; the programme from the weekend's football match may be just as important to them as *The Secret Garden* is to me. There will be really special books which must be treated reverently, but most of the time a book should be valued for its content and treated well so that as many readers as possible can read it before it disintegrates.

Becoming a reader

There is more to being a reader than being able to read. Readers know about reading, are confident about their preferred literary choices and know how their literacy influences every-day situations. Teachers, anxious to create readers, are only too familiar with complex interweaving of skills and experiences in learning to read and write. Getting the balance right, however, is essential because what happens at primary school can determine whether a child who is able to read becomes an avid or reluctant reader.

Years of advice about which approach to employ or which books to use as resources have made it obvious that no single teaching method nor set of books will cater for the needs of all pupils. Both the National Curriculum (SCAA 1995) and the NLS have acknowledged this by avoiding the trap of suggesting that certain materials teach reading. One of the principles of the NLS is that most literacy teaching should be based on real texts, and not decontextualised exercises or the rote learning of lists. Literature as the focus for literacy development has been advocated for years (see, for example, Holdaway (1979), Chambers (1985) and Meek (1988)). All the contributors to this volume assume that teachers will have access to a good collection of children's books, whether their pupils are in the very early years or nearing the end of Key Stage 2. There is also an expectation that children will have ample opportunity to respond to what they have read. Lesley Clark points out how in the very early years, when tackling the early stages of phonemic awareness, good books that engage children's attention will support learning (Chapter 2). Tony Martin (Chapter 5) shows how comprehension and response are totally intertwined. This is evident from the depth of understanding shown by children discussing *Rose Blanche* (McEwan and Innocenti 1985) as described by Catriona Nicholson in Chapter 8.

It is pleasing to see children's literature given the status that it deserves by the NLS but it is essential that teachers continue to share books for their own sake and not only because they are useful for teaching specific skills. Judith Graham (Chapter 9) considers why we must not lose sight of the essential experience of reading aloud to children and Geoff Fenwick (Chapter 6) reminds us that getting lost in a book needs time. We must guard against using books in ways that detract from their intrinsic value. As Judith Graham points out, there are some books which must be kept safe from becoming mere teaching resources. There will still be no shortage of books that supply children with the range of experiences recommended by the NLS. The 'best' books will be for reading aloud in ways which engage imaginations and inspire youngsters to pick up texts for themselves. What better way to teach the purposes of literacy than to demonstrate how it provides us with enlightenment, comfort and delight.

Planning for the teaching of reading involves a lot more than choosing materials and monitoring progress:

- Teachers must provide experiences that demonstrate and develop the processes of reading and the meaning-making strategies for all the different sorts of reading,
- they should read aloud to the class as often as possible from a range of books, including non-fiction, and demonstrate an enthusiasm for books as a source of pleasure and enlightenment and
- they must plan opportunities for children to explore literature through imaginative response (for example through creative activities such as drama).

Children should have regular opportunities and time for the following:

- sharing reading experiences with an adult;
- reading alone;

- discussing books in group reading sessions;
- sharing reading experiences with others;
- responding to books in a variety of ways;
- choosing from a range of texts and taking time to develop literary preferences.

Both the NLS and the National Curriculum require children to develop preferences in their reading and yet there is very little advice as to how teachers should facilitate this in classrooms. If children are to discover their personal tastes in reading they must have time to read independently. Two pleas come from the heart, from Chris Powling and Geoff Fenwick, for children to be given access to a wide and varied diet of reading. In Chapter 16 Chris Powling considers the poetry offered to children (the same points could be made about any other literary form), while Geoff Fenwick stresses the time needed for personal reading. Free choice and variety do not exclude the possibility of directed reading when appropriate. Gillian Lathey shows that there is an important place for supporting the wider curriculum through books in which complex and sometimes disturbing ideas are dealt with in an accessible way for youngsters.

Children making meaning

Liz Laycock (Chapter 1) points out the fundamental relationship between reading and writing and this is reiterated in all the chapters on writing. Learning to write involves everything necessary to express ideas in written form, e.g. having something to say, being able to use a writing tool (be it a pencil or a word processor), or knowledge of the conventions of written language (such as spelling). By far the most important reason for being able to write is 'having something to say'. Unfortunately, many teaching approaches have led children to believe that they learn to write in order to be able to spell correctly and to produce neat handwriting. As Liz Slater points out in Chapter 4, it is important to ensure that the learning of handwriting and spelling fits with the growing confidence of being an author. Nigel Hall explains some of the research currently taking place into how children learn to punctuate with a description of a study of two Year 1 pupils. So far, findings indicate that children experienced and confident as writers will learn to use punctuation conventionally when they see that it has a real function in their writing.

From the start, the development of reading and writing will go hand in hand. Chris Powling, Anne Rowe and Prue Goodwin, Maureen Lewis and David Wray all see the texts that they read with children as complementary to any writing that follows. A child steeped in poetry will have a confident stab at writing in this genre, a young researcher observing an adult making notes will attempt note making too. However, even with excellent models to emulate, writing can be a difficult task. Selecting appropriate vocabulary for different writing purposes is challenging and expressing ideas in conventional written standard English can be taxing, even for the average adult. George Hunt highlights the value of engaging children in activities that develop vocabularies and enhance children's knowledge about language. Michael Lockwood finds that explicit discussion about dialect gives junior children an opportunity to learn the relevance of different registers. As they become more familiar with the conventions of standard English, children gain confidence in its use when writing. Urmi Chana, Viv Edwards and Sue Walker also explore the implications of linguistic diversity, although in this case, they are looking not at standard English but at the impact of a word-processing program in Urdu on the writing of Pakistani children in a multi-ethnic primary school. Working together with bilingual teachers and parents, children discover a range of real reasons for reading and writing. Drama is another excellent way of providing a context for purposeful literacy use. As Suzi Clipson-Boyles demonstrates in Chapter 17, drama motivates children and, as imagined experience reflects reality, 'genuine' contexts for writing can be created in role play areas and through improvisation.

The structure of this book

This book is organised into four parts. Part I, Starting points for literacy, covers the early years including both reading and writing. Liz Laycock considers the value of shared reading and writing in introducing children to literacy. Chapters by Lesley Clark, by Nigel Hall and by Liz Slater look at how young children acquire a knowledge of letter–sound relationships, punctuation, spelling and handwriting whilst preserving their belief in themselves becoming independent readers and writers.

Part II, Becoming readers, looks at reading as it develops through the primary years. It includes content relevant to both Key Stage 1 and Key Stage 2, e.g. in Tony Martin's exploration of how comprehension follows response. With group and class teaching taking the foreground in recent initiatives, Geoff Fenwick looks at the place of silent reading. Judith Graham brings together many elements of classroom practice as she seeks to safeguard children's literature from becoming over analysed. Gillian Lathey and Catriona Nicholson complement each other in their considerations of how older primary pupils apply their skills confidently when tackling more complex texts.

Part III, Becoming writers, concentrates on children's experience of the process of writing, especially how teachers can support their growing independence as writers. The chapter by Anne Rowe and Prue Goodwin on organising writers' workshops provides the context within which children may write in different genres. Maureen Lewis considers using stories as support for writing fiction and she joins with David Wray to look at writing frames for writing non-fiction. Urmi Chana, Viv Edwards and Sue Walker consider the place of word-processing in promoting children's confidence and skill as writers.

Part IV, The world of literacy, introduces wider issues which are relevant to all the primary years. It includes Suzi Clipson-Boyles' description of the place of drama in supporting literacy learning. George Hunt looks at working at word level with the aim of encouraging vocabulary development. Michael Lockwood considers the importance of explicit discussion about dialect and standard English. Chris Powling, using the first-hand experience of teacher Sean O'Flynn, explores the need for teachers to introduce children to a wide range of poetry.

Into the classroom

Literacy is an integral part of all learning. It influences success in every other subject on the school curriculum and, when formal schooling ends, in society as a whole. It also provides a framework for thinking that allows children to consider the 'possible worlds' (Bruner 1986) beyond their immediate environment. A literate classroom is one which provides children with the experience of being literate in the company of fellow readers and writers, where – no matter what children's ability or the quality of resources – literacy and literature are perceived by all as central to their everyday lives. In an ideal world we would have classrooms fully stocked with all the resources for reading and writing that we could possibly want. In reality we can only be certain to provide the most important factor that creates a literate classroom – a literate teacher.

References

Britton, J. (1970) *Language and Learning*. London: Allen Lane.

Bruner, J. S. (1986) *Actual Minds, Possible Worlds*. Cambridge, Massachusetts: Harvard University Press.

Chambers, A. (1985) *Booktalk*. London: The Bodley Head.

DfEE (1998) *The National Literacy Strategy Framework for Teaching*. London: DfEE.

Holdaway, D. (1979) *The Foundations of Literacy*. Sydney: Ashton Scholastic.

McEwan, I. and Innocenti, R. (1985) *Rose Blanche*. London: Jonathan Cape.

Meek, M. (1988) *How Texts Teach What Readers Learn*. Stroud, Gloucestershire: The Thimble Press.

SCAA (1995) *Key Stages 1 and 2 of the National Curriculum*. London: HMSO.

Southgate, V. (1972) *Beginning Reading*. London: The University of London Press.

Part I

Starting points for literacy

Chapter 1

Shared reading and shared writing at Key Stage 1

Liz Laycock

It is now 20 years since Don Holdaway published *The Foundations of Literacy* (1979) which introduced the idea of shared reading to thousands of teachers. Drawing on what was then new research about literacy learning before school, especially Clay (1972) and Clark (1976), Holdaway proposed a pedagogy which attempted to replicate some of the factors which seemed to promote literacy development in the home environment, in the 'bedtime story routine'. One of the reasons for the success of this reading was the books which were used; texts were chosen, not for their suitability for 'teaching' reading, but because they were enjoyable. As Holdaway says, 'The language of the books used by parents, even with infants below the age of two, is remarkably rich in comparison with the caption books and early readers used in the first year at school.' Parents read to their children and the children engage in this activity, for the sheer pleasure and satisfaction of sharing the books.

Holdaway also recognised the collaborative nature of adult–child reading experiences in pre-school settings, as well as the 'visual intimacy with the print'. If these were factors in the successful learning about reading that children had engaged in at home, he suggested, we should attempt to recreate a similar non-competitive, collaborative learning context in school. His proposals for the use of enlarged texts for 'shared book experience' with large numbers of children took account of these insights. The teachers with whom he worked decided that there should be 'lots of books' – 'simple stories that the children will readily understand'. They produced enlarged versions of both the favourite stories and the rhymes, songs and poems used in the classroom. From the beginning it was apparent that the children were fully engaged and that, in subsequent readings, they began to join in with repeated parts of the text.

Before long, this work was supported by publishers who began to produce enlarged versions of books, alongside standard sized versions. The arrival of commercially produced big books, and the publication of Holdaway's book in England, introduced British teachers to these resources for the teaching of reading. Once they had begun to use shared reading as a teaching context, teachers wanted to use the most popular picture books in the large format, but they were not often available; so they continued to produce their own. The class-made versions of stories often involved the children, which made teachers increasingly aware of the potential of this collaborative writing as a teaching context. Thus, many teachers and their classes began to compose, through 'shared writing', new texts which, in turn, became reading material for 'shared reading'. In both activities there was a focus on a meaningful text as a context for teaching the skills of reading and writing. There was also a healthy collaboration in this learning enterprise, between adults and children, and among the children.

Children's participation in both shared reading and shared writing involves them in activities which they could not do alone, but from which they can learn a great deal, with the support of others. Thus, these learning contexts fit with what we understand about effective learning, from developmental psychologists such as Vygotsky (1978) and Brunner in Wood *et al.* (1976). Vygotsky showed that essential elements in learning are social and collaborative, where learners are enabled to attempt things which are beyond their current developmental stage. He believed that activity within this 'zone of proximal development', which the child could not do independently, was when real learning takes place; 'what the child can do in co-operation today, he can do alone tomorrow?'. Bruner (in Wood *et al.* 1976) talks of 'scaffolding' the child's learning, providing support until the child can act independently in a particular area. In shared reading and writing, children are supported as they take on more and more of the tasks for themselves.

Others, (see, for example, Smith (1984, p.150)), have pointed to the importance of 'demonstrations' which teach children about what readers and writers have to do. In learning to be literate, children need to know not just how, but why, particular kinds of reading and writing are done. Smith says that 'each demonstration shows an aspect of the power of written language' and that reading and writing need to be purposeful. There are differences between demonstrations and formal decontextualised instruction; 'demonstrations provide opportunities for learners to engage in the purpose of the activity, to share an intention with the demonstrator, whether to construct a story or to discover what someone else is thinking or planning'. In shared reading and writing activities the teacher can be explicit about the purpose of the writing as well as about the conventions of how meanings are communicated or transferred to the page. These activities thus provide contexts for appropriate demonstration.

Shared reading in practice

With the inclusion of shared reading in the Literacy Hour framework, it is important to understand the potential of this teaching context. It has been stated that the Literacy Strategy is a 'framework for teaching' but we need to use it to create a framework for learning. The first priority must be the selection of texts. Publishers, who had begun to produce fewer enlarged versions of popular books, have responded by going to the other extreme! Because of the Literacy Hour, there are now hundreds of texts to choose from. Some of these are the high-quality children's literature which Holdaway felt should be used, while others are merely 'big' versions of rather uninspiring books. You will need to consider whether the enlarged texts that you use have sufficient depth to be worth sustained study and analysis. You will also need to select a book which is matched to your teaching and learning intentions for a particular session. If, for example, you wish to focus on encouraging readers to use their knowledge of what has gone before to predict what might happen next, the book must be sufficiently predictable to enable readers to use the language and/or story structure to do this; if you wish to focus on an aspect of punctuation, you will need to make sure there are examples of what you intend to teach in the text.

What happens in shared reading?

The book will need to have print large enough to be seen clearly by the children sitting furthest away; this may seem an obvious point, but some commercially published big books have print which is difficult to decipher at a distance. The book will need to go on a stand or easel which will give adequate support for the big pages. As you will want to point to words as you read, it helps to use a pointer so that you do not unintentionally obscure parts of the text.

The first time that you read a new book, it should be read right through so that the children are given a sense of the whole story. If children ask questions or make comments, you should respond to these, but without destroying the flow of the reading. In the transcript below, of an actual shared reading session with a Year 1 class, the teacher makes a few teaching points at the beginning but does not interrupt the reading, in this first session, with too many questions. While reading *Hot Hippo* (Hadithi and Kennaway 1992), the teacher points to the text.

Teacher:	We're going to look at *Hot Hippo* together. (Teacher points to title) It's by the same person as *Lazy Lion* I read yesterday (pointing to author's and illustrator's names, Mwenye Hadithi and Adrienne Kennaway).
Child A:	They're both in hot countries.
Teacher:	What do you notice about 'lazy lion' and 'hot hippo'?
Child L:	They're both the same letters.
Teacher:	That's right, 'lazy' and 'lion' begin with the same letter, 'L' and 'hot' and 'hippo' both begin with 'H'. (In both examples, the teacher uses the letter name, followed by the single phoneme. She turns the page and reads aloud, pointing word by word to the text on pp. 1 and 2.) 'Hippo was hot.' (pp. 3 and 4) 'He sat on the river bank and gazed at the little fishes swimming in the water.' (pp. 5 and 6 points to the hippo in the picture) What's he thinking?
Child B:	He's thinking he'd like a drink!
Teacher:	(points to 'think' bubbles) What are these? What does it mean? (Many hands are up to answer.)
Child C:	He's thinking
Teacher:	(reads) 'If only I could live in the water, he thought, how wonderful life would be.' (Turns to pp. 7 and 8) What are the other animals?
All:	Giraffes.
Teacher:	(reads) 'So he walked and he ran and he strolled and he hopped and he lumbered along until he came to the mountain where Ngai lived.' (Turns to pp. 9 and 10, picture shows god-like form in the rock.)
Child B:	He's got no body.
Teacher:	(reads) 'Ngai was the god of Everything and Everywhere.' (turns to pp. 11 and 12, looking at the big picture) What can we see?

Children: Elephant, lion, giraffe, shark, horse, crocodile, . . .
Teacher: (reads) 'Ngai told the animals to live on the land and the fishes to live
                     in the sea. (Turns to pp. 13 and 14 to a new picture.) 'Ngai told the birds
                     to fly in the air and the ants to live under the ground.' (Turns pp. 15
                     and 16 to a new picture.) 'Ngai had told Hippo he was to live on the
                     land and eat grass.'
Child B: Why's the god got . . . ?
Child D: Why's he made of stone?
Teacher: (reading pp. 17 and 18) "Please, O great Ngai, god of Everything and
                     Everywhere, I would so much like to live in the rivers and streams,"
                     begged Hippo hopefully. "I would still eat grass." (pp. 19 and 20) "I
                     would show you," promised Hippo. "I will let you look in my mouth
                     whenever you like, to see that I am not eating your little fishes."
                     (Children become really involved, concentrating.)
Child E: He ain't eating it . . .
Teacher: (reading pp. 21 and 22) "But you must come out of the water at night
                     and eat grass, so that even in the dark I can tell you are not eating my
                     little fishes. Agreed?" "Agreed!" sang Hippo happily.'
Child B: When it's dark sometimes in Africa you don't get hot.
Teacher: (reading pp. 23 and 24) 'And he ran all the way home until he got to
                     the river, where he jumped in with a mighty SPLASH!' (Turning to next
                     page (pp. 25 and 26)). – Oh, look what happened . . .
Child H: He sank.
Teacher: (reads) 'And he sank like a stone because he couldn't swim.' (pp. 27
                     and 28) 'But he could hold his breath and run along the bottom which
                     he does to this very day. And he stirs up the bottom by wagging his
                     little tail so that Ngai can see he has not hidden any fish-bones.'
Child B: And he's too heavy. Can hippos breathe under water?
Teacher: (reading) '. . . opens his huge mouth ever so wide.'
Several children: (echoing) Opens his mouth wide! (. . . and opening their mouths!)

After a first reading you could initiate a discussion about the story, to allow the children
to share their responses, to ask questions and to talk about the illustration. In the case of
Hot Hippo, the teacher focused the children's attention on the illustration because they
reflect the heat of the Kenyan setting very effectively and create the context for the events.
There were several points where the teacher could have picked up on the children's
comments and questions: why the god, Ngai, has no body; why he is made of stone. Then
there are the comments about the hippo 'not eating it' , the comment about it not being
hot in Africa when it is dark, and the question about whether hippos can breathe under
water. However, as this was a first reading, the teacher opted to keep the flow of the story
going because the children were concentrating and totally involved; the comments that
they made reflect this involvement. Had the comments been picked up on the class could
have been side-tracked into discussion which would have disrupted the flow. When the
text was read again, the teacher was able to focus on the children's comments and
questions and could allow them to explore more fully the issues that had occurred to them
as they listened the first time. The teacher then moved into looking at particular words and
at the punctuation (especially the use of inverted commas for speech). In classes of young
children, the focus of these reading demonstrations will need to be on what a reader has
to do to read the text. The teacher will need to demonstrate all the cues that the reader

needs to use and will talk about the conventions of print (that the print carries the same unvarying message, that the left-hand page is read before the right-hand page, where to start reading, left to right directionality in English, word boundaries, one-to-one correspondence and letter–sound correspondence). It is necessary to show that you can go back and reread if the reading does not make sense, and that a reader can predict what might come next by drawing on knowledge of what has gone before and on knowledge of how words fit together in English. This can be done simply by covering up words or phrases with masking devices (Holdaway 1979, Chapter 4) and asking children what would make sense. The teacher can demonstrate how to check guesses by looking at the letters at the beginnings or endings of words and show children how to make use of their graphophonic knowledge to work out unknown words. The focus of the teaching will vary according to the observed learning needs of the particular group. It is important, however, that there is a clear focus which avoids cramming everything into every shared reading session.

In shared reading, children should be introduced to a wide variety of different kinds of text. As they are revisited, the texts can be used as contexts for more explicit teaching about the structure of the text (e.g. a letter, instructions, a report or a poem), the words that the writer uses, the spelling patterns, the repeated letter strings and the writing conventions such as punctuation and layout; all these are aspects of the sentence level and word level strands of the Literacy Strategy.

Shared writing in practice

Shared writing can be carried out by pairs or groups of children working without an adult or by groups of any number, working with an adult. Each context will be appropriate for different writing purposes but, in this chapter, the focus is on large groups of children (part of the class or the whole class) working with a teacher.

While shared reading provides opportunities to investigate existing texts, shared writing offers the opportunity to construct texts collaboratively and, at the same time, a context for teaching about the writing process. As Smith (1981, p.86) says; 'Especially when writing is being learned, there is often a great need for and advantage in people working together on a letter, a poem or a story. The ability to write alone comes with experience and is not always easy or necessary.'

The texts created in shared writing could often not be achieved by individual children writing alone; the collaborative undertaking creates a 'zone of proximal development' (Vygotsky 1978), as in shared reading, in which more can be achieved with the support of others. The children who perhaps benefit most from this collaborative context are those who are at the earliest stages of becoming literate and those who find reading and writing alone difficult and demanding. Again it was Smith (1982, p.21) who highlighted the challenge presented to writers of balancing the two strands of writing, the compositional aspects (i.e. getting the ideas, deciding what to say and selecting words and the grammar appropriate to the kind of writing), and the transcriptional aspects (i.e. the physical effort of writing, the spelling and the punctuation). He argued that 'composition and transcription can interfere with each other. The more attention you give to one, the more the other is likely to suffer.' In a shared writing context, the teacher can initially take on the transcriptional task, while children focus on what they wish to communicate in the writing. In undertaking the actual writing down of ideas, the teacher can talk about what he or she is doing, focusing on the structure of the text, the spelling or the punctuation, thus teaching about these things in a meaningful way.

Shared writing can be a valuable context for first attempts at a new genre. The actual shared writing session may be the culmination of a series of activities leading into writing. For example, the class may have read and analysed published examples of particular kinds of text – letters, poems or recipes, as well as stories – and the teacher may have talked about their characteristics and demonstrated how authors have structured these texts. An example of this is a collaboratively written recipe which was produced in a Year 1 class. The children had begun by reading a version of the traditional story, *The Gingerbread Man* as an enlarged text in shared reading. After they had become very familiar with the text, which included considerable detail of how the gingerbread boy had been made, the teacher brought in recipes for gingerbread biscuits. The text of these recipes was enlarged and made into recipe cards, which were also used in shared reading. The teacher pointed out the similarities in the written forms of the different recipes and demonstrated the importance of ensuring that the list of ingredients was complete and that instructions were given in the correct order. The children then worked in groups, actually following a recipe and making their own gingerbread men, for class consumption. Two different recipes were used and the children were invited to evaluate which they preferred. It was only after all this preamble and preparation that the whole class came together to write their recipe in a shared writing session.

In another Year 1 class, shared reading and shared writing were used as a vehicle to draw children's attention to rhyming words. The teacher's intention was 'to develop their ability to detect rhymes, to think of their own rhyming pairs of words and to look at common spelling patterns in order to foster the use of analogy'. She began by enlarging for shared reading, a short poem, 'Imagine' by Roland Egan:

Imagine a snail
As big as a whale,
Imagine a lark
As big as a shark,
Imagine a bee
As big as a tree.
Imagine a toad
As long as a road,
Imagine a hare
As big as a chair,
Imagine a goat
As long as a boat,
And a flea the same size as me.

The children read this together and there was much discussion of spelling patterns and words which had the same sounds with different spellings. The class then moved on to write their own rhyming couplets for an 'Imagine' book.

This is the text that they created.

Imagine a hare
As big as a bear,
Imagine a school
As small as a ball,
Imagine eight men
On a hen,
Imagine a goat

Eating a coat,
Imagine a ghost
Eating some toast,
Imagine a snail
As big as a bale,
Imagine a barrel
As long as a tunnel,
Imagine a flower
As big as a tower,
Imagine a snail
As long as a rail,
Imagine a flea
As big as a bee,
Imagine, I said,
That I was a bed,
Imagine a pear
As bright as a flare.

This was made into a book, with each couplet illustrated by one of the children, which was returned to again and again and read by individuals as well as larger groups.

What happens in shared writing?

It is possible to create all but the most personal kinds of text through shared writing. As with all writing, there needs to be a clearly defined and understood purpose for the activity and an understanding of the genre that is being attempted. The children need to know that they are going to write a list (e.g. of questions to ask a visitor), a letter (e.g. to an author or to parents), an account (e.g. of a class visit), instructions (e.g. how to make gingerbread men), a story or a poem.

The teacher will need a flip chart or several large sheets of paper attached to an easel, placed where all members of the group can see the text as it is written down. It is sometimes helpful to use different coloured pens for the writing – one for text, one for redrafting and/or editing, and one for punctuation – but this is not essential. The implementation of the National Literacy Strategy (DfEE 1998) has brought about an increase in the use of overhead projectors and shared writing can be done very effectively on acetates. Equally, in well-resourced schools, a word processor linked to a large screen can be used! The resources used will vary, but the intention, of making the composition and writing down of a text visible to all involved, will remain the same.

The writing session might begin with a discussion about what needs to go into the writing and how it will be structured, or an initial brainstorm of ideas. This initial thinking needs to be written down, to be referred to later, if the group forgets or loses track of the direction of the writing. For teachers and children new to shared writing, a good starting point might be the retelling of a familiar story, perhaps from the viewpoint of one of the characters. Such a retelling allows children to draw on their knowledge of story form, which is an area that those in Key Stage 1 generally feel confident with. When individual children offer suggestions about who the characters are or what will take place, it will often happen that others will not like an idea. This is when there can be useful discussion in which children must articulate their reasons why an event should or should not be incorporated. Sometimes the teacher will feel that a suggestion is not appropriate and will need to prompt children to reconsider an idea, using open questions, relating the idea to what has already been composed, generally thinking aloud. The interventions should not be designed to push children in a particular direction but should always be encouraging them to reflect on the writing process. Moira McKenzie (1985), who was a great advocate of shared writing said; 'Shared writing obviously requires sensitive, skilled teachers, who listen carefully and who, without forcing ideas, can help children bring together their thinking and their language into a unified text.

Once a consensus has been reached and while the text is being written down, the teacher can focus on whatever transcriptional details are relevant and appropriate to the needs of the children in the group. With the youngest children, this might be as basic as where you continue with the writing when you get to the end of a line, or the need for spaces between words. At other times the focus might be on the use of full stops, capital letters or demarcation of speech. Sometimes it will be appropriate to invite children to offer the initial letter at the beginning of a word or even to tell the teacher how a word is spelt; the teaching focus might be a particular pattern of letters or unusual spellings.

As the writing proceeds the text is read and reread and children will often notice for themselves that the meaning is unclear or can be expressed more effectively. This is when the teacher scribe can demonstrate how writers can cross out, change the order of words, add or remove words or whole sentences, or find a better word or phrase. Through taking part in such redrafting, children can see that writers can and do change their minds and that the writing does not have to be 'right' first time. The completed text will need to be proof read and edited so that a further demonstration of this stage in the writing process is given and editing decisions are made explicit .

In the process of composing a text together, the group is being taught about and is involved in reflecting on the structure of the text; the beginning or opening; the sequencing of events; the characterisation, the setting and resolution if it is a story; the conclusion. Some of this terminology can be used purposefully with the children in discussing the writing as it proceeds. Equally, the whole process is an exercise in comprehension in which children actively work at comprehending and certainly strengthen their grasp of the structure of a narrative (or whichever other kind of text is being written).

A shared writing session is an excellent teaching context for every aspect of writing. In making explicit the processes that a writer must go through in constructing a text, the teacher models what writers actually have to do. She is also in a very good position to listen to the children as they compose the text; because they are working together children have, to some extent, to 'think aloud' and this can be very revealing. Misconceptions and misunderstandings become visible and assessments can be made which inform future planning. For example, in a session with a Year 1 class, the teacher noticed that one child was using the terms 'word' and 'letter' interchangeably; that child was, therefore, probably not making a great deal of sense of the teacher's comments about 'letters' and 'letter patterns' in spelling 'words'! This insight enabled the teacher to plan focused group activities for this child and a few others who were suspected to be just as confused. Figure 1.1 attempts to bring together the various strands which make shared writing a productive teaching context.

Shared reading and writing are sometimes criticised because not all children in a large group can or will participate actively. Clearly the teacher will need to be alert to the individual needs of children. The more reticent can often be drawn in by a carefully directed question or an invitation to comment on a suggestion for the text. Teachers will need to be particularly aware of pupils with English as an additional language to ensure they understand what is being said and can make sense of the demonstrations. That said, shared reading and writing are very good contexts for teaching about literacy in English, because so much has to be made explicit. The supportive participation in reading aloud in unison,

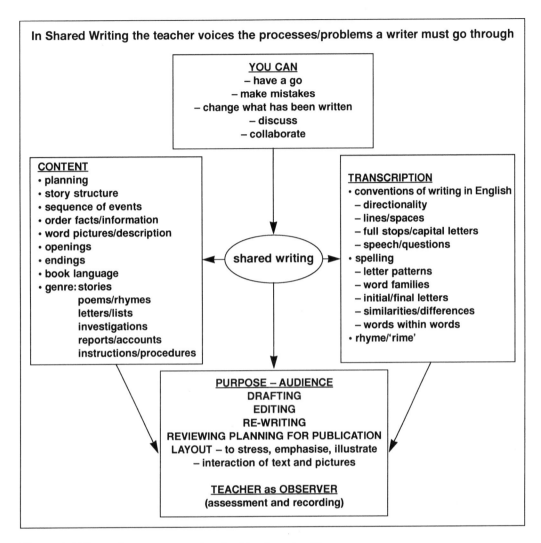

In Shared Writing the teacher voices the processes/problems a writer must go through

YOU CAN
– have a go
– make mistakes
– change what has been written
– discuss
– collaborate

CONTENT
• planning
• story structure
• sequence of events
• order facts/information
• word pictures/description
• openings
• endings
• book language
• genre: stories
　　　　poems/rhymes
　　　　letters/lists
　　　　investigations
　　　　reports/accounts
　　　　instructions/procedures

shared writing

TRANSCRIPTION
• conventions of writing in English
　– directionality
　– lines/spaces
　– full stops/capital letters
　– speech/questions
• spelling
　– letter patterns
　– word families
　– initial/final letters
　– similarities/differences
　– words within words
• rhyme/'rime'

PURPOSE – AUDIENCE
DRAFTING
EDITING
RE-WRITING
REVIEWING PLANNING FOR PUBLICATION
LAYOUT – to stress, emphasise, illustrate
– interaction of text and pictures

TEACHER as OBSERVER
(assessment and recording)

Figure 1.1 The various processes involved in shared writing

which happens often in shared reading, and the memorable repetitive language patterns much used in children's books are immensely supportive to those children new to English. Even when children are not contributing verbally, they can be participating and be fully involved just by listening. Certainly all children are keen to return to the texts that they have read or have composed together to read independently and individually.

Shared reading and writing are important components of a programme for teaching reading and writing. Once children have read texts together or collaborated in writing a text, their confidence in tackling these independently is much increased. The modelling of the reading and writing processes in these contexts offers children strategies for working independently. To conclude where I began in this chapter, I turn again to Don Holdaway:

Our primary responsibility is to provide an enjoyable experience of written language and an emulative model of what successful literacy looks like. Within that framework we actively teach whatever we think appropriate, but if things go wrong – attention flags or children become confused – we get back to our primary role as quickly as possible, we move the story on, show enthusiasm, recapture attention. It doesn't matter whether we are reading to the children or writing for them, the fascinating power of language is what it is all about. Unless we generate this awareness in the children all our instructions will be to little avail. (Holdaway, 1979, p.135)

Acknowledgements

I am grateful to Alison Browning for permission to use the 'Imagine' examples and to Harriet Edwards for allowing me to observe her reading of *Hot Hippo*.

References

Clay, M. M. (1972) *Reading: the Patterning of Complex Behaviour.* Auckland: Heinemann Educational Books.

Clark, M. M. (1976) *Young Fluent Readers: What Can They Teach Us?* London: Heinemann Educational Books.

DfEE (1998) *The National Literacy Strategy Framework for Teaching.* London: DfEE.

Hadithi, M. and Kennaway, A. (1992) *Hot Hippo.* London: Hodder Headline.

Holdaway, D. (1979) *The Foundations of Literacy.* Sydney: Ashton Scholastic.

McKenzie, M. (1985) 'Shared writing', in *Language Matters*, Numbers 1 and 2. London: Centre for Language in Primary Education.

Smith, F. (1981) 'Myths of writing' in *Language Arts* **58**(7). Urbana: National Council of English Teachers. In Smith, F. (1983) *Essays into Literacy.* London: Heinemann, pp.81–88.

Smith, F. (1982) *Writing and the Writer.* London: Heinemann Educational Books.

Smith, F. (1984) 'The creative achievement of literacy', in Goelman, H., Oberg, A. and Smith, F. (eds) *Awakening to Literacy.* London: Heinemann Educational Books, pp.143–53.

Wood, D., Bruner, J. S. and Ross, G. (1976) 'The role of tutoring in problem solving', *Journal of Child Psychology and Psychiatry* **17**, 89–100.

Vygotsky, L. S. (1978) *Mind in Society.* Cambridge, Massachusetts: Harvard University Press.

Chapter 2

Developing phonic skills in the early years
Lesley Clark

Phonics: confusion or confidence?

'Phonics' is a loaded term, steeped in polarised principles and politics. This does nothing to help good practice in the classroom. Teachers seek positive direction and support which acknowledges the complexities and interrelatedness of literacy learning. This chapter celebrates a creative approach to phonics teaching and offers a range of practical strategies founded upon meaningful learning experiences. It invites a wider interpretation of phonics to support both reading and writing and yet provides a developmental perspective and structure based on recent research.

What is phonics?

Phonic knowledge is concerned with the complex nature of how spoken sounds are represented in written form. Our alphabetic system requires an appreciation of phonemes (the smallest units of sound), of morphemes (the smallest units of meaning) and of how combinations of sounds are represented by combinations of graphemes (letters). Our vowel-rich language, together with its colourful evolution, requires knowledge of word origins, derivatives and roots. Before a child can decode or encode using a lexicon of sounds, he or she has to be able to distinguish sound patterns and to have some concept of what 'sound', 'letter' and 'word' mean. To do this implies a level of oral competence, and a background of positive experiences sharing a whole range of texts.

Teaching the relationship between sounds and letters is fundamental to developing literacy. While research evidence has raised concerns over the quality and effectiveness of phonics teaching in the past, there have been few positive models to support classroom practice. Effective literacy teaching must reflect the increasing demands placed upon literacy skills, calling for divergence and flexibility. Phonics can only be part of the picture here, so clearly children need to learn a range of strategies as early as possible. Phonics teaching must support the interrelated complexities and complementary qualities of reading and writing, handwriting and spelling. It must seek to work in harmony with a whole range of cues to promote active literacy learning.

Taken as a whole, the National Literacy Strategy (NLS) adheres to these principles. In fact, it sets out to address a key area of weakness caused by the lack of explicit, contextualised and progressive phonics teaching in the past. However, this concern, together with a political over-emphasis on the value of traditional phonics teaching, is in danger of creating an imbalance in the strategy. The weighty 'word' level requirements should not be read as having a greater priority or value, rather as being an attempt to provide detailed support. A reading of the lists of phonemes also belies the much more balanced holistic approach sketched out in the support materials. The framework should be offered as baseline support for creative phonics teaching which is firmly rooted in purposeful learning experiences with texts. There is no mismatch here with a structured, planned and direct teaching of phonics. The question is one of emphasis and of a professional response to the needs of young learners.

Developing phonological awareness

Children need to be taught to shift from focusing purely on the meaning of spoken language, to the attendant patterns of sounds. Research shows that the ability to identify patterns and similarities in sounds is a key indicator to future success in literacy (Bradley and Bryant 1985, Goswami and Bryant 1990). Before we can teach children sound and letter patterns and segmentation skills, they need to be able to hear and discriminate sounds in speech. This is a conceptual ability which is enhanced through immersion in a rich variety of patterned and rhythmical language. Children in nursery and reception classes therefore, need to experience rhyme and patterned story in the fullest sense. Early-years teachers are adept at exploiting every area of the curriculum and their shared routines with the children, to promote phonological awareness. Greetings at the start of the day, taking registers and lining up for playtimes all offer 5 minutes' speaking and listening opportunities. Speaking in rhyme, clapping names, whispering and making up alliterative phrases, adds spontaneity and purpose. Shared times such as before play, or giving out milk, can be transformed if the role of a 'singer-dancer-rhymer' is added!

Play is a natural vehicle for learning. Role play frees children to speak in different voices, to share rhymes and stories and to rehearse their literacy skills. Puppets are ideal for supporting didactic teaching as 'their' slow or staggered speech, funny mistakes and repetitions can alert children to patterns of sounds and to familiar phonemes. This is not to imply formal decoding, rather to provide an artificial emphasis upon which to practice emergent phonic skills in a secure and entertaining way. More importantly, these play contexts allow children to take on, practice and refine their own learning so that they feel actively involved and in control.

Role play areas provide havens for literacy whatever their focus – a dental surgery, garage, shop, cafe or post office all create 'real' literacy needs. These include repeating messages or menus, remembering songs and rhymes, telling stories, reading letters and names, writing lists and receipts. New names and identities allow the children to explore language, to mimic what they hear around them and to rehearse their oral skills. Early-years teachers can readily justify time planned for sensitive observation and intervention in order to maximise learning potential.

Children will grow as social learners if their play is complemented by the careful teaching of oral skills. This obviously takes time. Techniques such as shared circle times, active listening, paired work and collaborative group work can be used, even with young children. These sessions offer a balance of shared expectation and routine, together with introducing new games and activities. Listening skills may involve the accurate recall of information, or distinguishing different types of sound by responding to a 'trigger' sound, letter, rhyme, word or phrase. Playing plenty of oral matching and 'odd-one-out' games, together with deliberate errors, helps the children to refine their skills.

A daily emphasis on sharing rhymes and patterned stories will offer a stimulus for such games. Movements, body shapes, music and noises can help to reinforce the learning; so let action rhymes and popular songs provide a pulse and momentum for these shared sessions. The children will then readily adapt and extend these ideas in independent and group work. Those with more advanced phonological skills provide support for others. Substituted rhymes, alliterative jingles, clapping games and action songs will flow naturally, given skilful nurturing. Visual supports, such as drawings, pictures, clue cards and objects, should be built up as a resource, together with tapes, computer software and audio visual aids. Teaching opportunities are enhanced by the provision of enlarged texts, anthologies of nursery and number rhymes, word play and poetry. These can then be used as the basis for making bingo, snap, pairs and lotto-type games using visual clues for the sound regularity in focus.

Differentiation and sensitive handling allow teachers to offer appropriate challenges and support so that all enjoy and learn from these sessions. Even children with hearing loss can be imaginatively supported. Non-verbal communication, lip reading, positioning, visual cues and repetition are useful strategies. Auditory memory is complex and difficult to assess, but those having difficulties should be screened as early as possible so that any medical problems can be fully investigated. (Teachers gain enormous insights where specialist peripatetic teachers and speech therapists are given effective liaison time.)

Engaging patterned texts encourage a reflective alertness in young listeners and evoke a spontaneous echo as children respond to the pulse of such material. The younger the child, the more this should be complemented by physical movement, music and sounds. Familiar texts allow active listeners to savour, respond to and anticipate the rhymes and rhythms of the language. Games based on spotting deliberate errors, matching rhymes and alliteration, and creating new nonsense versions, can be played to consolidate the sound pattern.

Alphabetic awareness

Children need to know the name, sound, formation and purpose of letters as soon as possible. Alertness and interest are stimulated through shared reading and emergent writing. It is this immersion in texts that provides an entry into literacy learning. Real reading and writing opportunities, particularly those modelled by a skilled teacher, provide a purpose for the demands of phonics. This may be illustrated by a child's fascination with his or her own name, which provides a natural drive to represent sounds in written form. Regular use of a child's name in messages, written instructions, oral matching games, alliterative play and clapping songs will foster this interest.

Initial curiosity will be excited by an environment which includes the following:

- role play and puppet areas containing texts, print and writing materials;
- plenty of inter-active displays, alphabet charts, mats and games;
- a thriving writing area which is full of print and regularly resourced writing materials;
- plenty of talking tapes, action rhymes and music accompaniments;
- games, sand and different media with which to explore letter formation;
- quiet and welcoming areas with an exciting array of texts;
- a range of carefully selected and progressive texts to support the teaching of reading;
- big books and an accessible library stock;
- an imaginative stock of information technology software, trained staff, peer support and an effective monitoring system.

Nothing in this environment reduces the need to teach alphabetic awareness explicity. Alphabetic knowledge is an important predictor of future progress in literacy, although such skills are likely to be accompanied by broader literary experience, the different competences complementing each other. The pace and methods of teaching vary considerably and this can arouse unnecessary anxiety amongst teachers. There is no one magic solution. Whether letters are introduced at the rate of one a week or one every other day, children must first appreciate their purpose, making connections through shared reading and writing experiences.

Any methodology must reflect the links between spoken and written communication and the conceptual difficulties involved. For example, letter and word recognition requires the 'unlearning' of the concept that orientation and order do not alter an object's identity, both are crucial when distinguishing 'b' from 'd' and 'pin' from 'nip'. To avoid confusion when blending and decoding later, children must be taught 'pure' units of sound from the start. This requires frequent modelling and support, e.g. 'p' and not 'perr' (with the added vowel sound). The rate of learning new letters will depend on several factors, including physical and conceptual development, but should be sufficiently brisk to support wider literacy learning. Links with handwriting, such as teaching common letter strings, should be exploited.

Multisensory learning and the use of mnemonics aids letter learning. Mirrors, tracing letter shapes on the children, in the air, in sand, paint, foam, lentils or dough support kinaesthetic learning. Children respond enthusiastically to whole-class sessions where the alphabet is sung, acted and danced to. They enjoy 'being' the letters, perhaps by dealing out letter or picture clue cards and linking this to a particular initial letter sound. The child in question can then 'blend' with friends to create simple 'cvc' words. This is a useful way to introduce onset and rime (see below). Mnemonics, pictorial aids, alliterative 'jingles' and child-friendly phrases such as 'naughty knicker letter' (to denote the chameleon quality of vowels) give children a foothold into phonics. Teaching the name of each letter provides a constant amidst variables presented by upper- and lower-case formations, alternative pronunciations and vowel sounds. This will impact on a child's invented spelling but should not be interpreted as a backward step. By offering the multisensory approach outlined above and linking this to explicit teaching when reading and writing, a range of learning styles can be supported. Whatever methods are used, frequent revision, modelling and discussion must be planned for, together with time for individual reflection and experimentation. Phonics sessions should have the flexibility to support different levels of learning. Thus a whole-class focus on one sound–symbol correspondence might be followed by some children enjoying patterned repetition and alliterative mnemonics using multisensory lettering equipment. They might then go on to write and say the letter repeatedly, until they can try the entertaining but useful test of doing it with their eyes closed. Cards with the letter shape and a clue picture can be produced for individual memory games. Other children may be able to distinguish initial letter sounds and be making interest-related ABC posters or a list of words sharing the same onset, perhaps using a simple dictionary. These lists could be used as a basis for an 'adjectives alphabet', for making up an alliterative poem to act out or for challenging tongue twisters. Another group might be able to apply this sound to a rime and be writing joined letter strings and using equipment such as magnetic letters to generate new words sharing the same pattern. Raps, poems and songs can be created using this word list as a source.

It is essential (but an organisational challenge) to plan opportunities for individual or small group assessments. Great care should be taken with any objects, pictures or other materials used, particularly in respect to cultural diversity. The information provided can then be cross-referenced with evidence gathered through independent reading and writing. Useful options for this include 'once-a-month' annotated independent writing books, and termly in-depth individual reading conferences with some form of running record. There is a messy and uneven layering of the interrelationship between reading and writing, handwriting and spelling development. Phonic skills may first aid independent writing, where regularities learnt can then be used to aid reading progress.

As phonic skills become refined through a structured teaching programme which is rooted in responding to and creating texts, emphasis shifts from the 'global' to the 'parts'. The supports provided by physical activity and mnemonics can be reduced to avoid the risk that the latter masks the learning purpose. Children who can remember a cue such as 'Annie alligator', but who do not use initial sound to aid their reading or writing, need far greater emphasis to be placed on teaching the purposes of phonics through shared and guided sessions. Children who do demonstrate this appreciation and have a growing sight vocabulary and a confident interest in letters and words (especially as shown in their independent writing) are ready for more focused phonics. This signals the potential for teaching through onset and rime, through analogy and by modelling a mental habit which involves problem solving and looking closely at the order of letters within words.

Why onset and rime?

The 'word' strand of the NLS at Key Stage 1, focuses on two principles: that children should be taught to identify phonemes either before or during a phonics teaching programme, and that letter–sound correspondence should be taught at a rate of at least two to three a week. The latter principle lets the need for a core skill to become embedded as quickly as possible override practical issues regarding individual development and conceptual understanding. The former raises issues about how children learn and apply their phonic skills. Knowledge of phonemes is required for decoding 'c-a-t' into its three constituent parts. However, much phonics teaching implies a necessary deception, because there is no neat one-to-one correspondence in many sound–symbol relations. Indeed, even groups of letters do not necessarily map neatly onto the same groups of sound. Vowel patterns, regional variations in pronunciation and letter combinations which are based on meaning or word origin make these relationships highly complex.

Not only does an emphasis on phonemes produce a confusing array of rules and irregularities, but it also jars with how children predominantly segment sounds in spoken language. Recent studies by Goswami and Bryant (1990) and Goswami (1992) highlight onset and rime as being far easier for children to identify. Any word can be divided before the first vowel to provide the onset, with the remaining segment producing the rime. Earlier work to foster children's phonological awareness and alphabetic knowledge supports this approach. Through sharing patterned texts, children readily start to distinguish and play with rhymes. They develop an interest in sounds and a firmer grasp of what is meant by 'letter' and 'word'. Onset and rime also offer greater regularity for units of pronunciation and spelling than a phonemic approach, thus reducing the potential for early confusion and frustration.

Clapping games and music also allow children to demonstrate the ability to segment words into syllables. Onset and rime provide a further refinement, without sinking to the potential confusion of a purely phonemic approach at too early a stage. Later, children start to match visual and sound patterns and to make connections with already familiar words. Independent writing provides a purpose for learning the mechanics of word building which later fuels a more analytical approach to reading. Phonemes can be taught through a refining use of onset and rime. This builds up to focusing on vowel digraphs, spelling patterns and word study (such as considering homonyms and homophones) when children demonstrate sufficient orthographic knowledge to make such teaching relevant, successful and enjoyable.

Teaching onset

A focus on onsets evolves naturally from teaching alphabet awareness. Initial sounds can be emphasised in big book readings, during book making and when producing labels, messages and notices around the classroom. In order to recognise an onset, children must first appreciate what is meant by a vowel. They need to be taught the metalanguage so that they can discuss their approach, while not masking a lack of understanding. Plenty of alphabet work should precede this stage, so that letter order and concepts are clear, and the contrary nature of vowels can be demonstrated. Colour highlights, together with graphic evidence of how vowels can change their tune in different contexts, should accompany rote learning of 'a, e, i, o, u'. Text analysis will show our vowel-rich language, and how every syllable has a magnetic vowel to sustain it. Oral and then actual breakdown of simple words helps to teach the process of finding the onset.

Consonant onsets can be introduced quite quickly, starting with letters which are clearly visually different, which can be mouthed and which have a strong sound match. Daily investigations should then be made, hunting for particular initial sounds and compiling class lists, displays and word banks. This will all be supported by carefully selected shared reading texts and by collaborative writing. A teacher can model the use of alphabet mats, personal dictionaries and word banks and, preferably, independent spelling, through knowing an initial sound, and can then scaffold the children's learning during group writing sessions. Class books can be made which focus on one letter, using onset to cover letter formation, adjective-rich alliteration and challenging tongue-twisters.

Circle time sessions are useful for introducing games, such as 'picnic basket'. This promotes auditory sequential memory by requiring children to add to a growing list of nouns or adjectives which share an initial sound such as 'six sequinned sunglasses' and 'seven sizzling sausage sandwiches'. A 'bag of words' can be created using objects with the same initial sound, before introducing deliberate errors and mismatches for the children to identify. Children also enjoy creating their own versions of pairs, snap, bingo, lotto or pelmanism, based on initial letter sound knowledge. Dice games and those based on a 'snakes and ladders' format have the added bonus of a chance element which reduces pressure for less confident children. Magnetic and plastic letters provide a useful link with more direct teaching, particularly when wanting to emphasise the visual patterns in words. Strategies for reading, such as 'getting your mouth ready to make the first sound' and looking carefully to detect, name and make the first sound in new words, will be enhanced by working on onsets.

Rime and analogy

Goswami (1992) showed that even children as young as four, in an early alphabetic phase, could spontaneously identify new words by analogy with known words. Children's innate desire to find significance, to make connections and to identify what is similar can be shown in play and early number activities. Rhyming and non-rhyming sounds will have been a feature of developing phonological awareness and, once the skill of analogy has been learnt, it 'becomes a powerful process of self-teaching' (Goswami and Bryant 1990). As with other aspects of phonics teaching, time must be set aside for plenty of oral work. Through enjoying poetry and rhyming stories, children will start to make connections so that rhyming words can be grouped and recorded.

Class-made books along the lines of *Mig the Pig* (Hawkins and Hawkins 1986) demonstrate the 'sameness' of the rime and how new words can be generated by changing the onset. A wide variety of activities and resources should be provided to allow children to demonstrate and feel confident in their learning. Dice games, one dice with onsets and the other with one or two rimes, help children to build up words from patterns of sounds. Card games, bingo, dominoes and jigsaw-type activities will reinforce this idea. Word wheels, walls and windows are all different ways of presenting the same concept. Making, explaining and playing these games reinforces regularities and helps to fine-tune a more analytical approach to word level skills.

These activities must derive meaning from, and return to, pleasurable experiences of shared reading and writing. It is only in this context that the need to employ a variety of strategies to hear and see connections in words can be fully appreciated. Analytic decoding, in tandem with other reading strategies, will aid fluency and confidence in tackling new words. The teaching focus will shift to an emphasis on refining visual sensitivity and memory, and this will be linked to developing a range of effective spelling strategies. Peer support, such as having regular spelling partners, can be useful as part of the editing process and also to provide regular spelling checks for identified words. Techniques such as 'look and say, cover, write and say, check', together with using 'have-a-go' paper during drafting, encourage 'looking with intent' (Peters and Smith 1993). For whether phonic skills are being employed to aid reading or writing, the visual messages and patterns must be processed together with auditory clues. Creative phonics stimulates an holistic enthusiasm for applying word level skills within a range of viable strategies open to mature literacy learners. This sentiment is implicit in the NLS; so do not be swayed by a surface level reading of word level requirements for Key Stage 1.

This approach to phonics emphasises purpose and pleasure above decontextualised skills. It requires rigour, planned progression and skilful teaching to balance the dynamic needs of young literacy learners. Through starting from the whole picture, a balanced perspective that acknowledges the vital contributions made by both 'top-down' and 'bottom-up' approaches, can be achieved. Children need this multistrand approach if they are to cope with the demands of literacy learning with optimism, confidence and independence. Only by doing this are they likely to become successful active learners in today's complex literacy climate.

References

Bradley, L. and Bryant, P. (1985) *Rhyme and Reason in Reading and Spelling*. Ann Arbor, Michigan: University of Michigan Press.

Bryant, P. and Bradley, L. (1985) *Children's Reading Problems*. Oxford: Basil Blackwell.

Goswami, U. (1992) *Analogical Reasoning in Children*. Hove: Lawrence Erlbaum Associates.

Goswami, U. and Bryant, P. (1990) *Phonological Skills and Learning to Read*. Norwood, New Jersey: Lawrence Erlbaum Associates.

Hawkins, C. and Hawkins, J. (1986) *Mig the Pig*. London: Penguin Children's Books.

Peters, M. L. and Smith, B. (1993). *Spelling in Context*. Windsor: NFER–Nelson.

Chapter 3

The struggle to punctuate: a case study of two children learning

Nigel Hall

In this chapter, I want to explore the experience of two children as they learned to punctuate in Year 1 and Year 2. The children responded in very different ways to the challenge and reached quite different points in their development. Part of the function of this chapter is to describe their pathways and to explore the factors that might account for the differences. The study from which the material is drawn was completed before the inception of the National Literacy Strategy and, at the end of this chapter, I will be considering the extent to which the methodology and content of the Literacy Hour might or might not make a difference to the progress of such children in the future.

In Key Stage 1 punctuation is, on the whole, a late arrival in literacy education. For most of this century, and particularly in the second half, teachers of the youngest children concentrated on encouraging children to write meaningfully rather than to worry too much about punctuation. It was usually junior school teachers who were faced with introducing children to the nature and function of punctuation. The catalyst for change was a series of reports from various government agencies, starting with *Language Matters* (Department of Education and Science 1984). For the first time in almost a hundred years a proposal was made about expectations for achievement of all children in English. History does not yet record how these decisions were made, but amongst them was the claim that by the age of 7 years children should be able to 'use full stops and capital letters appropriately' (Department of Education and Science 1984, p.6).

What is certain is that there did not exist any research evidence for the appropriateness of this claim. Indeed, retrospectively one of the most remarkable things about learning to punctuate was its invisibility in the research literature. So where did these expectations come from? It is my guess that it happened by default. The conventional age at which children moved from infant to junior education was 7; full stops are pretty basic and probably seemed to be the first things that should be learned about punctuation. Whatever the reason, the decision, once made, stuck.

The Kingman Report ((Department of Education and Science 1988) appeared to mellow in their requirements. On p. 34 of that report, alongside an example of writing from a 7-year-old, they comment: 'Her spelling errors show that she has begun to comprehend the patterns of English spelling. But this is the work of a 7-year old. As Anne progresses she will learn about the placing of full stops.' Nevertheless, later on p. 55 they demand that, by the age of 7 children should be able to achieve the following: 'Use simple sentences, using full stops, capital letters and commas, word spacing and appropriate word forms. Understand sentence boundaries, i.e. what a full stop and a capital letter are for.' A year later, the Cox committee suggested ((Department of Education and Science 1989) that, by the age of 7 children should be able to 'produce, independently, pieces of writing using complete sentences, some of them demarcated with capital letters and full stops or question marks' – a prescription which became a quasilegal requirement when it was enshrined in the first version of the National Curriculum English document ((Department of Education and Science 1989).

This stipulation was uncomfortable for many teachers of young children. When Robinson (1996) interviewed a range of teachers, she found some common concerns:

- 'I don't think that they actually have a lot of experience of reading and writing actually to see the point to punctuation.'
- 'They are just on the edge of development in their writing and to teach them punctuation would stop that for some children...put them off, you know. I think they expect too much.'
- 'I think that they are having to learn it before they are ready to understand it.'

While criticising the national curriculum expectations, the teachers were not dismissing punctuation as unimportant, in either the long term or the short term, but their concern was for a possible contradiction between encouraging children to write with fluency and comfort, and the demand for accurate punctuation. Allied to this was the problem experienced by all the teachers that at no time in their pre-service or in-service education had they ever been shown how to teach punctuation. To make matters even worse, as has already been stated, there was nowhere for them to turn for guidance. The evidence which would even begin to answer their questions did not exist (Hall 1996).

The study

It was in relation to the uncertainties outlined above that a research project was set up to examine how children came to make sense of punctuation in the classroom. The study was designed to take a very intensive look at how children learned within the classroom setting. As a consequence it focused upon a relatively small number of children but followed their experiences in great detail. The aim was not to reach firm conclusions about how to teach punctuation but to identify a range of issues that might help to set future research agendas. In other words, the study was designed to provoke thinking and to open up an area for discussion, and not to provide quick and easy answers.

The school in which the study took place was situated in an urban area of north-west England and had achieved national recognition for its work on parental and community relationships. It served a multicultural and socially diverse population and was staffed mostly by young but experienced teachers. There was a large range of social problems experienced by the children and every year, as a result of government housing regulations, a large number of children moved into or on from the school. Thus a major concern was with providing a stable and warm environment in which children worked at an appropriate pace.

At the time that the study was carried out the national curriculum was in progress, but government ministers had repeatedly claimed that they were setting targets and not making stipulations about the methodologies to be used by teachers. Thus schools still made their own choices about how to develop literacy knowledge and skills. The dominant choice in this school was common at the time and was essentially child centred. The teacher operated the classroom in a way which Bernstein (1997) termed a 'competence model'. In this model there are relatively few defined pedagogic spaces; the emphasis is on the learner's product and their intellectual construction of it. Criteria are more implicit and diffuse, learners have a relatively high degree of autonomy, and explicit formal instruction is less common. This did not mean that things to be learned were not featured significantly in the classroom. For instance, during the first term in Year 1 the children were introduced to punctuation in many different ways. It was talked about, it featured on the concept keyboard and in *Breakthrough to Literacy* folders, it was displayed in many kinds of ways and the children were encouraged to look for it in the world of print around them in the classroom.

Punctuation was a presence in this room. The children saw it then, and they did 2 years later, as something curious, interesting and to be explored. The approach of both the Year 1 and the Year 2 teachers was to provide opportunities, experience, evidence and feedback rather than formal direct instruction. The consequence was that, although children's interest in and exploration of punctuation was actively encouraged, the teaching and learning of punctuation were not formally defined pedagogic activities as they are now in the Literacy Hour structure.

The two children

The two girls examined in this case study had both been in the school since the beginning of reception class. Both were quiet children and enjoyed writing. Fatima was aged 5.10 years at the start of the study. She was from a Bangladeshi background and had a number of elder brothers and sisters; although her parents spoke only limited English, her father insisted that at home the children spoke as much English as possible. She was effectively bilingual and even at the age of 6, had sometimes been used as a translator by her parents. Lian was 5.7 years at the start of the study, was the oldest child in the family and had two younger sisters, one of whom was a baby.

In this relatively short chapter it is possible to illustrate only a few aspects of the development of the children. However these are drawn from a continuously gathered collection of written work, observations and discussions. The first piece of independent writing that we have for either child was a short piece written on 7 October 1994. Figure 3.1 shows what Lian wrote. She reported that it said, 'I was a potato in our harvest.' The word harvest was copied. Lian was extremely anxious about writing independently, and hence the reversion to copying for the final word. Figure 3.2 shows what Fatima wrote. At first she read this as 'I O T L O T...l' using the letter names, and it was only after hearing other children read their pieces as meaningful texts that she claimed it said, 'I was an old lady in our harvest.'

Figure 3.1 Lian's first piece of independent writing (7 October 1994)

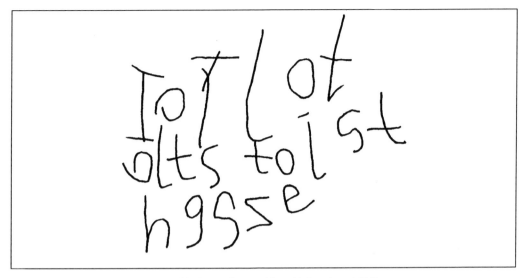

Figure 3.2 Fatima's first piece of independent writing (7 October 1994)

At this point both children seem confused and uncertain about the act of writing. It did not seem to make much sense to either of them and was seen as an activity which involved putting letters down in any order, and then making a claim that it said something. To all intents and purposes the children appeared to be level at this point. However, this similarity did not last very long.

Fatima

While the general classroom experiences of the children were very similar, Fatima soon began to reveal a much greater awareness of punctuation. In January of Year 1, in the guise of a handwriting task, all the children in the class were asked to copy a piece of text. '"Hello!" said the old man. "Where are you going?" The boy just looked at him. "I don't know." The boy was lost. He didn't know where to go.' If capital letters are included, then there are 21 independent punctuation marks. In her copy, Lian included nine, six of which were capital letters, two were exclamation marks and one was the terminal full stop. Fatima successfully copied all 21 and was able to discuss what they were. She was, however, unclear about their functions.

Teacher: What are full stops for?
Fatima: To make a space.
Teacher: When do you use them?
Fatima: At the end of words.

This copying exercise proved to be quite a subtle way of revealing differences in awareness of punctuation (and in an earlier version Fatima had managed to omit all the full stops). That the influence of attention to punctuation was having an effect in this classroom is revealed by a comparison with a class, a year older, who took the test at the same time. The younger class outscored the older class, something which illustrates the amount of attention that was being paid to punctuation in the Year 1 class.

A few days later Fatima was independently writing a letter to the character 'Martin' in the book *Dear Martin*. Figure 3.3 shows what she wrote. A 'translation' of this is as follows.

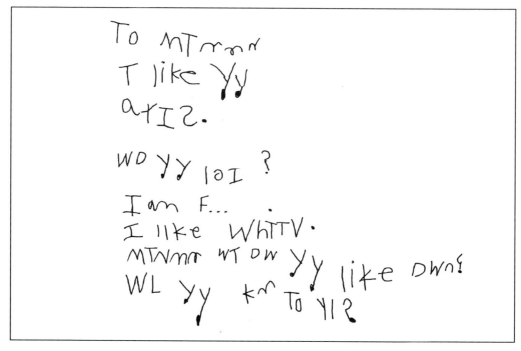

Figure 3.3 Fatima's letter to Martin (23 January 1995)

To Martin
  I like you
  (indecipherable).
  Would you (??)?
  I am Fatima.
  I like watching TV.
  Martin what do you like doing?
  Will you come to Year 1?

Fatima had become curious about punctuation, was noticing it in her reading, contributing to class discussions about it and talking about it to other children. Her movement towards conventional spelling was enabling her to write more frequently, for a wider range of purposes, and at greater length. An example of this enthusiasm for punctuation occurred when the class had been reading a poem laid out graphically without commas, e.g.

Miss Mary Mack
           Mack
           Mack

Another teacher bought in a copy laid out using commas:

Miss Mary Mack, Mack, Mack,

The whole class became fascinated by these differences. Within a few days Fatima had produced a six-page poem based upon *Red Riding Hood* but using the structure of 'Miss Mary Mack' (Figure 3.4). The 'translation' is as follows.

Figure 3.4 Fatima's poem based upon *Red Riding Hood* (30 March 1995)

Red Riding Hood, Hood, Hood,

Perhaps the most significant evidence of a conceptual move forward came in April that year. She was with two other children who dictated a description to a researcher who scribed it on a large sheet of paper. During a discussion afterwards there was a heated debate about the position of a full stop (for a full discussion of this see Hall and Holden-Sim (1996)). Part of the text was as follows:

and she shouts a lot and
she tells us to do our work

One child wanted to put a full stop after 'lot' because full stops 'could go in the middle', while another instantly said that they had to go at the end of lines. Neither child was using a linguistic principle for their choice; middle and end of line are graphic principles. It was Fatima who said the full stop could go after 'lot' as the 'and' belonged to 'she tells us'. The significance of this is for the first time in the classroom a child was explaining the use of a full stop using a linguistic principle.

One month later Fatima used mid-line full stops in her independent writing as shown in Figure 3.5, the 'translation' of which is as follows:

Once upon a time there was a girl
called Sophie she lived in her own home
She had no friends she is lonely.
She has a dog. One day she died
the dog cried. The dog stayed in
the hen's house all by itself.
There was no food and he died.

Thus, towards the end of Year 1, Fatima was satisfying the general criteria of the English national curriculum document and demarcating some of her sentences using full stops, although frequently without using capital letters. In Year 2 this move towards linguistic punctuation continued. In a very long story written in February 1996 she at first put in only

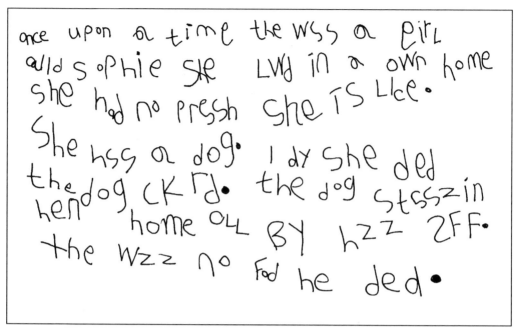

Figure 3.5 A later story by Fatima (3 May 1995)

two full stops. When asked if there was anything she wanted to add, she put in several more full stops. While each one correctly marked the end of a linguistic unit (always the end of a sentence), some of these units included more than one conventional sentence. According to Kress (1982), this was a typical move towards conventional linguistic punctuation. She was grouping by topic (rather than by sentence), although in many cases these units were conventional sentences (for an illustration of this see Hall (1998a)). On 9 July of Year 2 she was writing

> I like you very very very much! You
> are very kind. You hardly shout.
> Do you remember the eid party
> and we played and ate lots of
> food and remember the Christmas party
> and I got a pencil case.
> Remember when we first came
> in Year 2 i was so scared and
> when you read a story i
> wasn't scared then. You
> shouted because some of us didnt
> colour neatly. You shouted at
> some of us because we did'nt
> write neatly.

It is clear that Fatima had succeeded in meeting the criteria without losing interest in writing. She would be able to move on to Key Stage 2 with a fairly good notion of how to punctuate a text conventionally.

Lian

Lian, while appearing to start at the same point as Fatima, took much longer to feel truly comfortable with writing and never did solve the problem of punctuation. She remained dominated, even at the end of Year 2, by non-linguistic beliefs about punctuation.

On the same day that Fatima was writing to Martin (Figure 3.3) Lian was writing the words shown in Figure 3.6, the 'translation' of which is as follows.

Figure 3.6 Lian's early attempt at writing (23 January 1995)

> To Mrs S
> Can we have a fair.

In the three intervening months, Lian, despite following an additional special programme which provided specialist teaching with phonics and reading, was able to convey meaning in writing only through the initial letter sounds of words. Despite what seemed a difficulty, Lian enjoyed writing and was proud of what she achieved. Four months later she was writing at greater length but almost always failing to put in any punctuation. Occasionally after a reminder from the teacher, a full stop might be added right at the end. The failure to use punctuation was not because Lian was unaware of it. If asked, she could name several marks and draw them and even repeat formulae about 'rests'.

In June of Year 1 Lian wrote an extended piece which appeared to use punctuation in an interesting way (Figure 3.7). Its 'translation' is as follows:

> Mum was making cooking. Dad said, 'Is it ready?' and mum said, 'No, it is not.' So (he) went out in the garden.

However, it is likely that, if it had not been for an accident, the punctuation would have been missing. As she was sitting down to write, another child sat down, picked up his pencil and said, 'I'm going to do a full stop.' He then simply put a full stop on his blank piece of paper. Lian, having written 'Mum', watched him do this and promptly put a full stop after Mum. As she wrote her piece, she then added more full stops. At the end, thinking that she had finished, the researcher looked away. As he did so, Lian got her pencils and sprinkled some more full stops through the piece. Lian was unable to offer any explanation for her use of full stops; they appeared randomly distributed.

Lian continued into Year 2, becoming more confident in her ability to write meaningfully, to spell conventionally and to write at greater length. However, punctuation

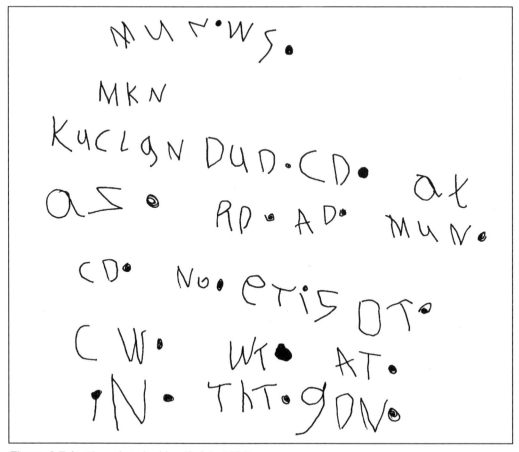

Figure 3.7 Another piece by Lian (9 July 1996)

was largely ignored except when working with the teacher and receiving constant reminders. On 9 July (the same date as Fatima's last piece) Lian wrote an interesting text with only one full stop. She was asked if there was anything she wanted to add; she thought and said, 'Those rest things'. She then added some full stops to the piece (Figure 3.8), the 'translation' of which is as follows:

> I like you. You have nice shoes. I really like Ginn maths. I wish I could do some every day because it is good. It is my favourite. I like playing. I (??) think I am good at them. Do you like the trip the best? It was the best. I kept on going on the slide and I never got off it because it's good. I call it a twirly whirly because it looks like a twirly. Does it to you? It does to me. you have nice clothes. I like the trips what you take us on. I like the name what you have got.

This time, perhaps more confident, Lian was able to offer explanations for the placement of the full stops as follows:

- because it's a bit long;
- 'cos I didn't put one in that line, so I did it there;
- 'cos it's a bit long, from there, there's a lot of words to there;
- 'cos it's long as well.

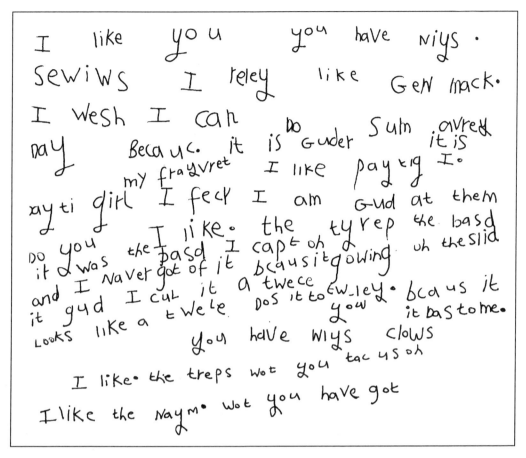

Figure 3.8 A later piece by Lian (9 July 1996)

The explanations have nothing to do with linguistic principles but invoke 'long', 'from there to there' and 'not putting one in the line above'. This is placement and explanation based upon graphic principles. The distribution is according to graphic balance; there needs to be so many; they must not be too close together nor must they be too far apart. Thus, at the end of Key Stage 1 Lian is using underlying principles to punctuate that have nothing to do with the linguistic structure of the texts but have everything to do with what a text looks like as a graphic object. Although this particular example is uncommon, this reasoning is shared by all those children (and for a while in their development this means almost everyone) who put full stops at the ends of lines, at ends of stories and at the end of pages regardless of whether they are sentences (Hall 1998a).

Comparisons

The first point that must be made is that while Lian and Fatima appeared to start at the same point, it is probably an illusion generated by their previous school experience. If the children were not able, or had not been given the opportunity, to develop independent writing skills, then differences are likely to be obscured. Secondly, while it was not the function of this project to test the children psychologically, it was quickly clear that in general Fatima was much more able than Lian. She progressed more quickly in all subjects, was always curious about the world and was a reflective child. There may also have been some less obvious advantages. Fatima was clearly influenced by her elder brothers and sisters, and the appearance of ditto marks and apostrophes in her texts she explained in terms of having seen them in her sister's writing. Fatima had asked about them and been told. It is also possible that her bilingualism made her more aware of the linguistic properties of text. A child who can switch between languages may well be more metalinguistically aware than one who cannot.

To say that children have different abilities and therefore progress at different rates may seem to be obvious, and the achievements between these two children may not be difficult to explain. However, the point of this small case study is to illustrate the qualitatively different ways in which these children understand the object of punctuation. For Fatima it is becoming an intrinsic part of the meaning-making process. For Lian it is an object that is linked to writing solely by the teacher's demand for it to be included. It serves no function in her writing and shares no relationship with meaning making; it is an object which has separate roots from those of written language. Alongside the effort of getting readable words onto the page, the tiny marks of punctuation seem insignificant and irrelevant to the task of authorship.

Will the Literacy Hour make a difference?

The honest answer to this question, of course, is that it is impossible to tell. The Literacy Hour is a recent innovation. At the time of writing the final document has only just been published and training materials have only just arrived in schools. Relatively few teachers have participated in the pilot studies, and most schools face the prospect of starting a complete shift in literacy teaching with only minimal staff training.

Perhaps the better question is: could the Literacy Hour have made a difference to the performance of these two children? It seems doubtful, given the present state of our knowledge. With the exception of a small number of studies completed or under way (see, for instance, Hall and Robinson (1996)), our knowledge of punctuation has advanced very little over the last 10 years and we have yet to address seriously the question of how to teach punctuation. Thus whether the quality of teaching punctuation, and the understanding that underpins it, will improve seems questionable, especially as some of the advice offered in government agency documents is itself problematic. What is certain is that standing in front of a class and talking about punctuation does not necessarily lead to changes in the children's understanding (Arthur 1996).

My own research suggests that there certainly is a role for some explicit instruction and explanation in the teaching of punctuation although, if explanations are too complicated, children may well revert to the most common practice of all and simply omitting punctuation from their texts (Hall 1998b). What also seems clear is that punctuation has to be seen by children as having a real function in their writing rather than being perceived as an imposed rule-bound system, and it does seem rather strange that the structure of the Literacy Hour mitigates against extended and continuous writing. To say that it can be done elsewhere is either naive or deliberately misleading; there is not an elastic space beyond the Literacy Hour into which an ever growing list of missing 'essentials' can be inserted.

Perhaps one of the biggest questions is whether whole class sessions can be relevant to children with very different levels of conceptual understanding? Would formal explanation and instruction of punctuation which addresses the needs of Fatima have had any major effect upon Lian, and would Fatima have been bored while listening to teaching best suited to Lian? The danger of whole-class instruction is that it functions rather like a scatter gun; you spray enough of it around in the hope that some sticks. If it does not then differences are likely to become exacerbated. The sheer quantity of whole class instruction in the Literacy Hour inevitably means limitations in the time spent with children like Lian, children who find it so easy to stick to theories that make sense to them rather than to strive to make more difficult conceptual moves forward. The need now is for serious systematic in-depth studies which examine all aspects of the classroom experience of children and teachers going through the literacy hour process, something which has been conspicuously absent in the pilot work.

Acknowledgements

The material in this chapter derives from research funded by the Economic and Social Research Council. They funded Project R000221796, 'Learning to punctuate: an ecological and conceptual investigation', and Project R000221380, 'Learning to punctuate between the ages of 6 and 7: an ecological and conceptual investigation'.

References

Arthur, C. (1996) 'Learning about punctuation: a look at one lesson', in Hall, N. and Robinson, A. (eds) *Learning about Punctuation*, pp.92–108. Clevedon: Multilingual Matters.

Bernstein, B. (1997) *Pedagogy, Symbolic Control and Identity: Theory, Research, Critique*. London: Taylor & Francis.

Department of Education and Science (1984) *English from 5 to 16: Curriculum Matters 1*. London: HMSO.

Department of Education and Science (1988) *Report of the Committee of Enquiry into the Teaching of the English Language (The Kingman Report)*. London: HMSO.

Department of Education and Science (1989) *National Curriculum English for Ages 5–16 (The Cox Report)*. London: HMSO.

Hall, N. (1996) 'Learning about punctuation', in Hall, N. and Robinson, A. (eds) *Learning about Punctuation*, pp.5–36. Clevedon: Multilingual Matters.

Hall, N. (1998a) *Punctuation in the Primary School*. Reading: Reading and Language Information Centre, The University of Reading.

Hall, N. (1998b) 'Young children and resistance to punctuation', in *Research in Education* **60**, 29–40.

Hall, N. and Holden-Sim, K. (1996) 'Debating punctuation: six-year-olds figure it out', in Hall, N. and Martello, J. (eds) *Listening to Children Think: Exploring Talk in the Early Years, pp.*86–99. London: Hodder & Stoughton.

Hall, N. and Robinson, A. (eds) (1996) *Learning about Punctuation*. Clevedon: Multilingual Matters.

Kress, G. (1982) *Learning to Write*. London: Routledge & Kegan Paul.

Robinson, A. (1996) 'Conversations with teachers about punctuation', in Hall, N. and Robinson, A. (eds) *Learning about Punctuation*, pp.92–108. Clevedon: Multilingual Matters.

Chapter 4

'This is my reading writing and this is my writing writing'
Liz Slater

There are two issues which are often neglected when considering how children develop as writers: first how teaching handwriting and spelling fits into a context based on developmental stages of writing; secondly the organisation of purposeful activities within which handwriting and spelling can be successfully learned and practised. All too often, the handwriting style or the allocation of spelling lists separated from the writing process has dominated discussions on these topics whereas, without well-thought-out approaches, any style or choice of words can cause difficulties for teachers and for children. If, on the other hand, the letters, strings and whole words that are practised in handwriting are related to those needed for spelling, other oral phonological work and decoding, and all are related to the children's actual writing, the links between these literacy skills are mutually supportive.

Another aspect of this area of learning is a public perception that phonics is not taught any longer, which has led to a renewed emphasis on phonic teaching as the most important aspect of the teaching of reading. There is also an assumption that there is one particular order in which to teach the sound system of the English language. The Initial Teacher Training guidance gives a particular sequence for teaching phonemes and in *The National Literacy Strategy: Framework for teaching* (DfEE 1998) this sequence seems to be encapsulated in the term-by-term progression of teaching objectives. However, children come across consonant blends unpredictably – in their names, in songs, poems and literature. Introducing a joined handwriting style linked with spelling very early can exploit those experiences. The focus of this chapter is an exploration of an approach which combines the teaching of handwriting with that of spelling with an emphasis on seeing and hearing onset and rime. This approach also supports decoding skills in reading and independence in writing.

Evidence of children's spelling strategies from QCA

There are indications in the annual analyses on the National Curriculum Assessments that phonics teaching already has a significant place in current practice, particularly at Key Stage 1. There was evidence of aural phonic dependence and a need for visual strategies to be developed at Key Stage 1 in 1996 and 1997 (SCAA 1996a, b, QCA 1997a): 'The difficulty is less in *knowing the patterns than knowing which pattern to use* in each individual word. Some children…spelled almost entirely by reference to sounds, with little reference to visual memory.' At Key Stage 2 'spelling errors tended not to be phonologically plausible' although there was 'some phonetic relationship to the correct spelling' and 'initial letters were mostly correct but final letters less so' (QCA 1997b, p.9). According to QCA (1997a, b, c), 'at all Key Stages, children who are uncertain about spellings tend to rely too heavily on simple sound–symbol correspondence. They need to develop a stronger visual memory for words and letter strings, to extend their strategies for spelling words.' With reading, the picture becomes complex as the assessments and analyses are based on correctness in the running records rather than on the nature of any errors. What is missing from these comments is evidence of the strategies that children employed when making miscues. It is unclear what support there is in classrooms for the development of contextual cueing, which is essential to self-correct wrongly read words which have been arrived at phonemically. It is, however, clear from all these findings that there is a need to develop the related visual and phonemic strategies in spelling which can come about through well-considered approaches to teaching handwriting. Work on onset and rime and analogy will support the knowledge and understanding of final letters and patterns in words and syllables, an important part of the *National Literacy Strategy: Framework for Teachers*.

Personal starting points and classroom experience.

My own involvement with these issues started in the early 1980s when I introduced Sally, a reluctant writer but avid reader in year 2, to a joined handwriting style. I was so impressed by the effect on her confidence with writing that we introduced a joined style to all pupils in Year 2. My colleagues and I introduced letter strings and words with the same visual patterns to practise handwriting, relying less and less on handwriting cards and, without realising it, we had developed work that was essentially based on onset and rime. I then introduced joined handwriting in a reception class. I was concerned about possible confusion for much younger children using both book-print and a cursive script (this is a commonly expressed concern). This fear of causing confusion, however, proved to be unfounded. The comment from a 5-year-old, 'This is my reading writing and this is my writing writing', was the explanation of her distinction between print on a label and her own joined writing. Far from being confused, we found that the children were supported in their word and letter pattern recognition by joining their handwriting very early. Simple sound–symbol correspondence of consonants and consonant blends were being reinforced through the practising of visually similar words, by changing the onset in order to practise the rime in different words. This onset and rime approach to spelling and handwriting meant that letters were linked into blends and then words as soon as possible, once children had learned them. A word such as *and* (which is a rime without an onset) would be practised and then was associated as soon as possible with other words such as *sand, stand* and *hand*. Children learnt initial sounds, including blends, in this context quite quickly. They also played games which relied on continually changing the onset, aurally and visually.

We concentrated on rimes, which usually have a final consonant or consonant blend, and found that children became more confident with these final sounds earlier than expected. Practice did not simply involve writing but also talking about sounds, letter patterns and words. The visual pattern was associated with a word, whether these were onsets of phonemes and blends, or rime strings, or words. We would introduce words with a different vowel phoneme in the rime when the vowel grapheme was the same as the pattern being practised, e.g. *wand* fits with the *and* rime list.

As well as supporting phonological awareness and sight vocabulary, our approach to the early introduction of joined writing had other advantages that we had not expected. We noticed that there were fewer children who reversed letters or transposed letters (as in *wlof* for *wolf*); most children produced consistent letter sizes, were able to write across the page in a straight line and had even begun to develop their own individual handwriting styles. Spellings of high-frequency words were more secure and attempts at spelling unknown words drew on both phonic and visual knowledge. Another unexpected outcome was the children's tremendous enthusiasm for joining accurately – including an effort by one child to join numbers!

Teaching handwriting and spelling

My experience in the classroom led me to consider carefully the principles on which to base a school policy for handwriting which incorporated the development of spelling. There is no doubt that what writing looks like makes an impression on the reader. We know that this happens in public examinations (Maines and Robinson 1990); so we have a responsibility to be realistic about it. At the same time, we do not want to develop practices which result in neat but content-free writing. We must organise the teaching and learning of handwriting so that they are focused and effective, involving plenty of opportunities for children to practise. In addition, we need to preserve and build on what children already know about writing and to separate the handwriting teaching from the opportunities for writing with communicative intent. We want children to realise that handwriting is important, but not so important that it dominates all writing activities. In order to do this, the children must have opportunities to develop such a secure hand–eye–brain motor control ('muscle memories' (Smith 1982)) that, in their writing, they automatically produce the handwriting that they have been taught. Attitudes to writing are set from the beginning, when children are encouraged to see themselves as real authors. This must sit comfortably beside the need to be 'writer–clerks' who can produce conventional spellings and legible presentation.

What children bring with them

When children arrive in school they may already have knowledge of letter shapes. For example, children are likely to know what their names look like and those who have consonant blends at the beginnings of their names (e.g. Tracey and Graham) may begin to make links with words found around the classroom that start with the same phoneme or grapheme clusters (e.g. triangle and group). Many children have developed a knowledge of print from the environment, such as shop names, logos and brand names. Teachers should make opportunities to exploit this knowledge as we should their knowledge and memory of interesting words and sounds in favourite books by drawing it into approaches to spelling and handwriting.

Saying and hearing; reading and writing

A multisensory approach is recommended. Children should be encouraged to say the words as they look at and copy them. Hearing sounds, as well as recognising symbols, reinforces the key decoding skills as well as supporting spelling when seeing, saying and writing are linked. Seeing and saying the words also accommodates different pronunciations whether in received pronunciation (as with *wand* and *hand*), or due to regional variation (vowel sounds often change from region to region). Talking about the tasks that they engage in is also essential.

Phonemes in context

Phonic approaches which emphasise only small phonemic parts rather than onsets and rimes in whole words may contribute to the detailed knowledge of vowel and consonant phonemes but they do not support the children in their knowledge of words in which these patterns occur. Work on rimes, however, provide a more secure knowledge of the end-of-word consonant blends. We found that teaching letters which children recognised first (e.g. the first letters of their names) caused no difficulty and it was possible to introduce joins early because of the normal association of letters in strings, familiar from looking at print.

Fitting with a process model of writing

It is important that children have frequent opportunities to write independently because only with these opportunities do they get the chance to apply what they know about the spelling system. They need a sense that writing is, above all, about communication to different audiences and for different purposes. In the early stages of writing, children's hypotheses about spelling – evident in their attempts at words – will show their increasing understanding of letter–sound correspondences. Children's first draft writing, therefore, provides evidence of spelling development and informs teachers about future intervention. A real test of children's spelling development is the degree to which they do not have to think about spelling and handwriting. With handwriting, a distinction should be made between calligraphic skills, where slow beautiful handwriting is required, particularly for some display, and the fluent legible hand for every-day writing.

Spelling

The initial response to a piece of writing should always be about the content but we must then decide what to do to support spelling. Teachers can respond to the presentation of the writing according to the needs of the child, the stage of development, the audience and purpose for the writing, and the writing context. The time of initial response to children's writing is inappropriate to comment on handwriting but with reference to spelling we might do any of the following:

- do nothing except respond as a reader and keep the writing as evidence of development;
- note any spelling patterns as a basis for practice at another time;
- transcribe for beginning writers and write conventional spellings for more experienced writers;
- talk about spellings with the writer, commenting positively on the spellings or features of spelling known;
- ask writers to indicate words that they suspect are misspelt by circling or underlining in their writing;
- supply reference lists in the classroom, encourage the use of word banks and eventually the use of dictionaries and thesauruses;
- use a personalised, group or topic bank of words for the writer to check, working on her own or with a partner in finding one, two or three words, or more, depending on the child, the time available and the need;
- write the words on a separate piece of paper, on a Post-it®, or in a word book for consideration at another time;
- ask the writer to write drafts leading to a final, conventionally presented version.

Handwriting

There is a variety of writing styles to choose from and some schools develop their own adaptations of these. Whatever style of handwriting is adopted by the school, children should not find themselves in the position of having to unlearn motor movements in order to transfer to a joined style. At the very least, letters should be taught with an exit stroke (except on letters that do not join in the chosen style). Learning experiences must be designed which are appropriate for whole class teaching, e.g. looking at letter shapes together, talking about words, reading onset and rime, and others which are more suited to group work, such as when children require more individual attention. Some teaching is appropriate for the Literacy Hour and some is best at another time, particularly the short sharp observed group practice. Little and often is the best way to develop motor skills. Children need to be sufficiently practised for their letter formation to become automatic. The short time and the frequency are the keys to making progress – ideally daily, but at least three times a week and preferably not more than ten minutes. Children can soon see improvement and are encouraged by their progress. A language-rich classroom will provide plenty of opportunities to talk about the ways in which words and letters are presented on the page.

At the beginning, young children need many opportunities to practise shapes and patterns in a variety of ways. For example, they can trace shapes in sand or paint, use an arm in the air or employ their whole body or a finger on the table. All require large movements which help the memory and support the development of finer motor control. A range of implements will help to establish the control of writing tools. Children should practise strings and words as soon as possible (lines of the same letter do not support spelling or handwriting development). We can contextualise handwriting practice from the start through using the letters, letter strings and words in children's names, labels around the classroom, and high-frequency words linked with letter strings. Many of the books written for young children have strong repeated syntactic patterns that are ideal for handwriting practice. For example, Michael Rosen's *We're Going on a Bear Hunt* offers an opportunity to look more closely at some of the onsets starting with s blends.

Practising spelling and handwriting

Choices about which words to practise can be made for a variety of reasons. As well as words which link visual patterns (e.g. said, maid and paid), you might choose the most frequently used words (the list in the *National Literacy Strategy: Framework for Teaching*), words from the current topic and words from the children's own writing. Many of the most frequently used words are irregular in terms of phonic patterns (e.g. *who* and *could*) and grammatical in function (e.g. *the* and *about*) which are harder to read out of context as they have no easily defined meaning. Seeing and hearing them in as many meaningful contexts as possible will help to establish them in children's minds. Looking for words within words can be valuable and fun. For example, in the words *the, that,* and *then* you can find *he, hat* and *hen*. Links with reading can be made during shared reading, especially with well-loved key texts which children will return to on a regular basis.

You may want to make separate lists for groups or individuals of the words collected in response to children's writing. Opportunities to talk about and practise writing and spelling with young children are most effective when they are using the words to achieve a real purpose. Encourage the children to 'look and say, cover, write and say, and check', as they practise each word. They can also do this with letters and strings. Children can partner each other in this activity so that lists are not only self-reviewed but peer-reviewed. This collaboration supports learning. An area where children display their most recent practice will give status to handwriting. A file of polypockets for 'handwriting that I have enjoyed doing' can be changed and commented on by the children on a weekly basis. This should not be neatly mounted work or best handwriting; it is *practice*, which may not look wonderful but is demonstrating to everyone the progress that they are making. Calligraphic copies have a place in different displays.

Conclusion

We want children to realise that handwriting and spelling are important, but not so important that it dominates all writing activity. Children must have regular opportunities to develop secure hand–eye–brain motor control so that they make use of the handwriting and spelling that they have been taught automatically. This will not happen right away but, from the beginning, provision of frequent opportunities to practise handwriting shapes and movements, and spellings with the same visual patterns, develops confidence with the transcription skills. When this happens alongside opportunities to write purposefully and independently, children develop as writers with something to say rather than clerks only concerned with presentation.

References

DfEE (1998) *The National Literacy Strategy Framework for Teaching.* London: DfEE.

Maines, B. and Robinson, G. (1990) *Joined up writing: a guide to the teaching of writing and spelling.* Bristol: Lame Duck Publishing.

QCA (1997a) *Standards at Key Stage 1, English and Mathematics: Report on the 1997 National Curriculum Tests for 7-year-olds.* London: QCA.

QCA (1997b) *Standards at Year 4, English and Mathematics: Report on the Use of Optional Tests with 9-year-olds.* 1997 National Curriculum tests for 7-year-olds. London: QCA.

QCA (1997c) *Standards at Key Stage 2, English, Mathematics and Science: Report on the 1997 National Curriculum tests for 11-year-olds.* London: QCA.

SCAA (1996a) *Standards at Key Stage 1, English and Mathematics: Report on the 1996 National Curriculum Assessments for 7-year-olds.* London: HMSO.

SCAA (1996b) *Standards at Key Stage 2, English, Mathematics and Science: Report on the 1996 National Curriculum Assessments for 11-year-olds.* London: HMSO.

Smith, F. (1982) *Writing and the Writer.* London: Heinemann Educational Books.

Part II

Becoming readers

Chapter 5

Responding to fiction
Tony Martin

From its title, this chapter may not appear to be high on the agenda of a literacy co-ordinator in a primary school busy implementing the National Literacy Strategy (DfEE 1998). After all 'response' does not appear as one of the key areas at text level (comprehension and composition). In fact, references to it do appear at different points in the 'termly objectives' (e.g. text level work, Year 6, Term 1, 'to articulate personal responses to literature') and in the Literacy Training Pack (e.g. Module 5, teacher's notes, Appendix 1, 'Encourage children to share their responses...'). However, there is no explicit examination of the meaning of response or of the key teaching strategy which enables children to investigate the ways that literary texts work: begin with the reader's response and use that to explore the features of the text.

What is 'reader response'?

> 'The reader can begin to achieve a sound approach to literature only when he reflects upon his response to it, when he attempts to understand what in the work and in himself produced that reaction, and when he thoughtfully goes on to modify, reject or accept it' (Rosenblatt 1976),

The above quotation is over 20 years old. There are now many books, articles and research projects which have been published describing and discussing 'reader response' in terms of adult, adolescent and child readers. There has been work on novels, short stories, poetry and picture books, all of it making the same fundamental point. Response is *not* just about the personal responses of readers to what they read in the sense of likes and dislikes. In the classroom, questions concerning who enjoyed a story or a novel are just the starting point for response work. As the Rosenblatt quotation clearly states, it is the quality of how a reader 'reflects upon his response' which really counts.

Reader response is about reflection – thinking about what has been read. However, its starting point is not just the text (the story, novel, picture book or poem) but the way in which the reader responded to it and found it exciting or sad or funny or frightening. The interesting question then is 'Why did the text provoke the particular response?' and will involve two considerations simply represented by reader – interaction – text. The interaction between reader and text is the response, and both sides of the process will contribute towards it. First readers bring themselves to what they read; their personalities, beliefs, memories, relationships and indeed their whole lives will impact upon the reading. I am 4 years old listening to *Go To Sleep Little Bear* by Martin Waddell and staring wide eyed at Barbara Firth's illustrations. The reason is that I too am frightened of the dark and need a loved adult to reassure me. I am an adult reading a romantic novel and responding in terms of my own relationships–'I've been there' or 'I wish...'. As a private reader that sort of response may well be enough and much of it may not be articulated but in the classroom we can build on it to examine the second aspect of response; the ways in which texts work to produce their effects on readers. 4-year-olds can join in patterned repetitive texts and appreciate how they work. They can focus on particular words, phrases and sentences. Older children can search for words, phrases and sentences which made the text exciting or frightening or funny, mark them and discuss them, use them in their writing. This idea of distinguishing between the part played by the reader and that played by the text is not explored explicitly in the National Literacy training materials. Therefore the major teaching strategy of beginning with the reader and then moving to explore the text is unclear.

Response or comprehension: what's the difference?

Look back at the Rosenblatt quotation in terms of defining 'comprehension' of literature. What we have is a powerful definition of comprehension, which is generally discussed as an active process of readers engaging with what they read. However, there is a danger that it is viewed in the classroom as a passive process with questions focused purely on the text rather than building on how the reader responded. At its worst, it simply becomes a weekly test to answer questions on an extract in a course book. Here there is a confusion between an assessment tool and a teaching strategy. Presenting children with a passage and asking them questions will certainly tell us something about their ability as readers but it is not a teaching strategy. Oral and written response work aimed at children reflecting on what they have read is far more likely to produce 'thinking' readers who 'comprehend' what they read:

> As opposed to worksheets, which encourage "right answer" responses and rarely expand thinking...the student is encouraged to interact with the text and use her own experiences and the book to interpret and construct meaning from what she reads. The student is always encouraged to go back to the text to support her response (Routman 1991).

Examining the text to support and justify response means that we are a world away from simplistic notions of likes and dislikes. Of course, each reader will create their own meanings so that no two readers will read the same text in the same ways but 'to go back to the text to support...response' means the parts played by both the text and the reader are recognised and given status in the classroom. There is no difference between response and comprehension.

Response and the sharing of big books

Arthur Koestler (1964) wrote that 'literature begins with the telling of a tale' and so fiction begins with narrative books in the early years. Big books, around which the children sit so that they can see both pictures and print, will be used in Literacy Hours. The organisation of the Literacy Hour begins with 30 minutes whole class teaching made up of 15 minutes' text level work followed by 15 minutes word level work. So, where does response fit in? I would argue that the real issue is the difference between the first reading of a text and the further readings which will take place. Certainly the use of large-format books to teach children about different aspects of reading at the levels of sentence and word is highly effective but on the first time that children hear a story surely the agenda needs to be different. The danger of rushing on immediately to draw attention to the print itself is just that – a rush. For the first reading the focus for narrative needs to be on book knowledge (titles, authors, illustrators, front covers and back covers) and response. There are five ways in which we can highlight and give status to response at a first reading:

1. We look at the title and the picture on the cover and ask, 'What do you think this is going to be about?' This is answered on the basis of clues in the text (the cover). I like to put children into pairs so that the question is posed to a pair and they whisper their ideas to each other. Then we all hear some of them. This is wonderful in reception! (As an aside, all of the current promotion of 'whole class teaching' seems to be on posing questions which children have to answer alone. Has no one realised the potential of other strategies? Children in pairs or, as they get older, threes with the chance for discussion and an agreed answer?)
2. We read the text aloud with dramatic intonation. The aim is for our voice to bring the text to life and to show children how it ought to be read. We are almost defying them not to engage with the story.
3. We might stop at an opportune moment and ask 'What do you want to happen now?' In my experience this question is rarely asked, the emphasis being on what children 'think' will happen. What I *think* will happen is a text question. What I want to happen is a reader question. (Do not think that this only works for young children. It is exactly what we do as adults when faced with the dilemmas of characters in the novels we read. It is not the coolly rational 'I think that she will marry him' but the highly emotional 'Oh no, don't marry him!').
4. At the end of the story we share our enthusiasms. This can be done simply by getting children to talk about their favourite page (the teacher having discussed her favourite page first of course!). Some can come out and turn the pages of the book until they reach their favourite. This is much more effective for promoting discussion than rushing in immediately with a set of questions about the text which a child knows he or she might get wrong.
5. We end with silent reading. Grown ups read silently, in their heads; so now the pages of the story are turned and each child gazes at them in silence. If they are unable to read the print they can use the pictures to tell the story in their heads.

Of course we need to teach the range of different skills and awareness that children need in order to learn to read, but a first reading should surely be on response and engagement.

How might this develop in Key Stage 1? One way is to use longer texts, the sort of 'novels' that we might read aloud to children, and help them to focus on a part of it in detail. Infant teacher, Margaret Munn, decided to use the opening page of *The Key* by Jan Mark as a focus for discussion with a group of Year 2 children. She wrote:

I read the opening to them and then attempted to keep pace in scribing their response as the ideas came tumbling out of them. The children used the writing and the pictures to weave their own stories about the text. Their ideas sparked off other ideas, they argued, went off at tangents... The scope of their imaginative creations seemed endless.

The children's responses (Figure 5.1) illustrate vividly the parts played by both readers and the text (as well as containing a wonderful response in Jason's first contribution 'I think he's a Catholic 'cos he certainly looks like one'!). In terms of what readers bring we have connections with the children's lives as both Jason and Amy are reminded about family holidays. For Daniel the name Joe makes him 'think of someone's granda'. In terms of picking up clues from the text, Amy thinks 'it will be an adventure story; he's going to lose that key', while Julia and Andrew are also making predictions. Andrew focuses even closer on one sentence which makes him think 'it will be a good story'. In these comments, no doubt triggered by careful questioning by the teacher, we begin to see how far true response work is from simple notions of likes and dislikes, and how closely it links with a view of comprehension as an active engagement with texts.

Fiction at Key Stage 2

At Key Stage 2, fiction will mean novels and short stories. In the classroom, similar approaches can be used to develop appreciation of both what readers bring and how texts work in order to make children better readers in the sense of thinking about what they are reading and how they are reading it. Such work can be considered under five headings: range of reading; the teacher reading aloud; discussion of fiction; investigation of fiction; reading leading to writing.

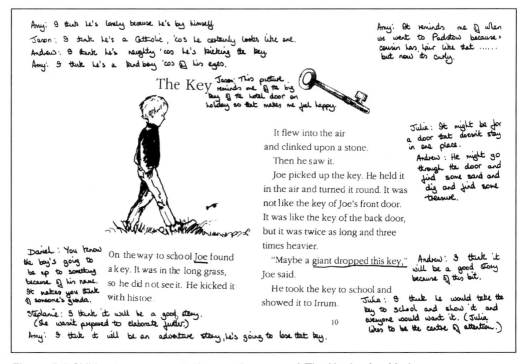

Figure 5.1 Children's responses to the opening page of *The Key* by Jan Mark

A range of reading

Frank Smith (1978) wrote, 'Inexperienced readers must find all texts unconventional.' He was referring here to a key idea in developing children as readers, that of 'literary competence'. This means knowing 'how to read' a particular type of text, knowing how it will go and the conventions which are likely to operate. We develop this competence through reading. For example, if you are given a poem to read, your mind will automatically switch into poem mode. The voice in your head will be your poem voice. You will expect a certain type of text and poetic conventions. However, you can only do this because you have read poetry. Imagine that if you had never seen a poem. How well would you cope then? The same idea of 'literary competence' applies to fiction. As adults we are only faced with how much we know (or what we expect) when we open a novel with an unconventional opening; some of us will not want to read on; we feel lost and not sure what games the author is playing with us!

At Key Stage 2 there is a major distinction between experienced readers and inexperienced readers. The former, by Year 6 will already have read widely. Faced with the next novel, short story or poem they can draw on their experience of all the previous ones. The latter group have not read widely. They have played safe or even been encouraged to do so by teachers who think that reading is only about getting the words right. Faced with a novel of some length the sheer number of pages puts them off. Faced with a subtle short story or poem they cannot 'comprehend' because they have not read enough of them to know how they work. It is interesting to consider how many Year 6 children face the short story in the SAT as inexperienced readers of short stories.

We are able to choose between stories and novels in terms of the following:

- *Subject matter.* Different settings are used, historically, geographically and culturally, some of which children can identify with in terms of their own experience and some which take them into places and times and situations far removed from their own. Likewise the effect on the reader should vary so that children feel the power of fictional narrative – stories which make them laugh, cry and hold their breath, stories which shock and stories which delight. Some ought to have strong story lines so that the plot is the main attraction, but others will have less plot and instead focus on underlying themes as they explore character or situation.
- *Style.* Some stories are written in the first person with a character narrator and others in the third person so that they can explore who is actually doing the telling. Some with a lot of dialogue, and others with the emphasis on description.
- *Structure.* Some stories are based around one major idea. In others there may be a major plot and one or more subplots. Endings can tie up all the loose ends or may be left open so that readers are invited to speculate about what might happen.

Through being encouraged to read a range of fiction, children will develop the 'literary competence' necessary to appreciate the varied ways in which different stories and novels work.

Teacher reads aloud

This is a vital element in developing children as readers for two reasons. First, through reading aloud we model reading for children, demonstrating to them just how such a story ought to be read. We let them hear the 'voice' that they will need when they read themselves. This is vitally important for inexperienced readers, especially those who struggle with reading. In addition they are able to respond to the power of a text without encountering the problems of having to decode it for themselves. Simply listening and responding to a dramatic voice telling a powerful story is a worthwhile experience in itself. While we ought to use texts of all types to focus children on sentence and word level matters, we must not forget the validity of literature for its own sake. It must not always be used for other purposes in the primary classroom. The second reason for reading aloud to children is that we can do so at a level beyond their own reading ability. We can choose challenging texts in terms of the three elements of range described above and through our reading – our use of varied intonation, rhythm and pace – enable them to appreciate a text they could not read for themselves. Teacher reading aloud is a precursor to teaching strategies such as guided reading.

Fiction can be discussed

Before any of us embark on a story or novel we have expectations and these can be explored in the classroom by children working in small groups. So, the story is called 'Who's Afraid?', the author is Philippa Pearce (1977) and it is some six pages long – what are your expectations? There are three main categories of expectation provoked by the following:

- *The title.* 'This is a scary story perhaps, connections with "who's afraid of the big bad wolf?".'
- *The author.* 'I've already read other stories and novels by Philippa Pearce, so I think it will be about modern times and perhaps have lots to think about.'
- *The reader.* 'I think short stories are boring and so I won't enjoy it' or 'I love listening to short stories.'

Expectations can be gathered on a class list and then hidden until the story has been read when they can be a fascinating focus for further discussion.

Some short stories are best read right through to the end in order for their power to affect children. If we constantly interrupt for discussion we can ruin the story. However other stories and certainly novels can be discussed at different points in terms of aspects of response:

- Readers predict their way through narrative, thinking about both what will happen and what they want to happen.
- Readers turn texts into pictures so that they can imagine places, people and events. These pictures are always seen from a particular viewpoint so that we can discuss where children were looking from in a particular scene.
- Readers make connections between themselves and their own lives and those of characters – 'I've felt that' or 'I've been there'. Of course, we must not expect children to share what might be very personal connections, but the teacher should try and make some herself – 'I always feel sad at the end of 'Who's Afraid?' because I remember when my grandmother died.' Then children realise that this is on the reading agenda; this is a powerful reason why adults read. We have engaged in important reading teaching just through modelling our own response.
- Readers are affected by what they read, feeling sad, frightened, shocked or excited.

Each of these aspects of the reading process can be opened up through sensitive questioning and comment so that children are enabled to discuss how they read and what they read.

After reading, as we read the final sentence of a novel or short story, perhaps to the class or in a guided reading group, we have a choice of options:

- Ask some questions. Actually this can kill discussion rather than encourage it (and presumably discussion is what we are trying to encourage). The sort of question aimed at testing memory (what event was Joe attending in 'Who's Afraid?') will involve some children but really miss the point. They immediately begin the process of reducing the reading of literature to memory tests. Indeed I would suggest that any questions involving right and wrong answers are not the best way to proceed at the end of a powerful read.
- It is far better to share our enthusiasm. We must not be afraid to allow a minute's silence at the end to let each reader feel and think. Then I, as the teacher, can say what I felt and thought: 'What an ending!', 'What a story!', 'I really liked the bit where...'. What we provide with such comments is a model of someone who genuinely enjoys reading and who also enjoys discussing it. Such an approach always leads to a much more enthusiastic discussion with children than we get with questions.
- Look back at the expectations that we listed before we began. How far were they met? Who was proved wrong? Who was surprised by any part of the story?

Fiction can be investigated

Earlier I described the range of short stories in terms of subject matter, style and structure. These text features can be investigated by children through careful questioning. The aim is not to introduce some watered-down literary criticism exercise but to enable children to appreciate how stories and novels are crafted and the conventions which operate in them. So, the opening pages of a number of novels can be photocopied and compared. How are they similar? How are they different? Are there any clues in the text, for example, about what this novel might be about and what could happen? What sort of a novel this will be? Will it be a plot with a lot of incidents or more about characters and relationships?

The need for readers to orient themselves to what is going on at the beginning of a story is very important. Experienced readers learn to 'trust the author' and can tolerate a fair amount of uncertainty but we all know children who will not persevere with a novel – 'It's boring', 'Nothing's happened', 'Can I change it?' How many of these children are actually inexperienced readers who do not know 'how to read an opening', children who are unclear about the conventions and who actually lack the 'literary competence' to cope with a sustained read.

Reading can lead to writing

The reading–writing connection can be harnessed powerfully when working on response in the classroom. Children can track their ever-changing and developing responses to a novel through keeping response journals. Instant responses can be captured using 'stickers' attached to each page, just for jotted thoughts and feelings on the aspects described above. These can be summarised at the end and used as the basis for discussion in small groups. Next, the text which has been read can lead to the creation of texts which the children write. In each case the aim is for the writing to reflect the reading and in some cases actually modelled on the reading. So, one or more of the following possibilities could be chosen:

- They could write a sequel – 'Who's Afraid 2', 'The Return of Dicky Hutt'.
- They could not read the ending, write their own ending and then compare.
- They could write an alternative ending.
- They could write an imaginary journal kept by one of the characters through the action of the story.

- They could write a third person story in the first person, in '*Who's Afraid?*', we could write Joe's version or Dicky Hutt's version or Grandma's version.
- They could write letters between the characters after the story has finished.
- They could write poetry which reflects the underlying themes of the story.

In examples such as a sequel or an ending, the modelling can be at the level of the plot, the themes and the style. For some children the plot might be enough but able experienced readers can be helped to consider the way that the story has been written.

Writing is a powerful way for us to make sense of our thoughts and feelings. Through writing, whether it be a response journal or writing based on the text, children can reflect consciously on what they have read, how it affected them and ways in which the text was written to provoke particular responses. Such work can be a precursor to discussion as well as following it. Having written, children are better prepared to discuss what they have read.

We can never capture response in the sense of articulating exactly how we felt at particular moments in the reading of a story, novel or poem. The moment that we try to reflect and put it into words we realise how our language does not really enable us to say what we felt. Nevertheless, as adults we love discussing plays and films that we have seen and books that we have read. To produce children who not only can read but also who do read and enjoy discussing what they have read must surely be a key target of any National Literacy Strategy.

References

Koestler, A. (1964) *The Act of Creation*. London: Hutchinson.

DfEE (1998) *The National Literacy: Strategy Framework for Teaching*. London: DfEE.

Pearce, P. (1977) 'Who's Afraid', in *The Shadow Cage*. London: Kestrel.

Rosenblatt, L. (1976) *Literature and Exploration*, 3rd edn. New York: Noble & Noble.

Routman, R. (1991) *Invitations: Changing as Teachers and Learners K-12*. Portsmouth, New Hampshire: Heinemann Educational Books.

Smith, F. (1978) *Reading*. Cambridge: Cambridge University Press.

Chapter 6

Reading silently

Geoff Fenwick

This chapter intends to justify the use of silent reading in schools, to consider its organisation and to assess its standing at present, particularly in view of the Literacy Hour and subsequent revisions of the National Curriculum.

In classrooms where pupils are developing their literacy, the use of silent reading should be taken for granted. As they grow older, silent reading becomes more frequent and, in most cases, more popular than reading aloud. What, then, is the problem? It rests with what might be termed 'the first s', i.e. the sustained in sustained silent reading (SSR). Attitudes towards reading silently for considerable periods of time have fluctuated over many years. This is something which we need to consider.

The trouble with silent reading

In a developed country almost everyone reads silently. It is, clearly, the form of reading most frequently used. Read a menu out to your friends and, if they have their own copies you will probably be considered condescending or even boring. Read the paper aloud as you travel on public transport and you are likely to be thought an eccentric nuisance. Furthermore, reading silently is quick, convenient and almost impossible to avoid as we pick our way through the mass of environmental print which is such a feature of today's urban society. How could we do this if we were unable to read? It is worth considering, in a perverse way, just how ingenious illiterates must have to be, first to conceal their disability and second to come to terms with it in a society so saturated with the written word.

Yet there are suspicions about reading, especially if we do a lot of it. 'Bookish', 'deskbound', 'Absent minded', 'impractical' and 'bookworm' are expressions which come to mind in this respect. They represent, to some extent, old prejudices and suspicions which contrast the theoretical with the practical, and the manual with the sedentary. They also represent social worries about being too clever. Claims by radicals such as Paulo Freire (1972) that literacy is the key to freedom for oppressed peoples did not go down well with authoritarian regimes. In more light-hearted vein, but not so much removed from opponents to Freire's ideas as they might at first appear, we have the thoughts of Miss Sarah Byng in one of Hilaire Belloc's (1930) celebrated cautionary tales. Sarah, having been tossed into a hedge by a furious bull because she could not read the warning notice associated her plight with the latter and not the former. For Sarah, literature bred distress, as it still does to many people who, for one reason or another, find it unpleasant.

So far, we have considered the problem only generally. Silent reading has not been without difficulties in schools. It was not easy for pupils to be frequent silent readers in schools where books were in short supply. This was a problem even at the turn of the century. The late Laurie Lee (1959), for example, recalled how his early reading owed more to the family gathered around the hearth in the evenings listening to oral readings from single books than it did to school. Later much of his reading depended on the long periods of browsing carried out in the local bookshop.

Book shortages persisted in schools for many years. Primary schools, for example, encountered severe problems in the Second World War. The writer's silent reading at that time depended very much on the books at home, not only on those in the 'show' case in the front room but also on the purchases made by parents at jumble sales and house clearances! By the age of 11, this treasure trove had made it possible to read a number of Zane Gray's western novels, Rider Haggard's *King Solomon's Mines* and H. M. Stanley's *Through Darkest Africa*. It should be added that, although the sources mentioned made up for a dearth of books in schools, many more were lost because of over-enthusiastic waste-paper campaigns. Silent reading in schools, in fact, probably came into its own with the huge growth in paperbacks published in the early 1960s. By then it was possible to build up the stock of books in schools much more cheaply. Just a few years earlier the writer struggled in his first primary school appointment to ensure that the books available would last the year out. To encourage silent reading in such conditions was never easy.

Lack of books has often been a problem but it has been by no means the only one. Another obstacle has been the suspicion with which silent reading has sometimes been treated. It has been regarded as being merely a breathing space for embattled teachers which allows them to check books, to mark the register or simply to have a rest. Jenkinson (1940) was voicing such doubts nearly 60 years ago, as also was Carsley (1957) 17 years later. Is silent reading a form of instruction? Does it involve teaching? Both questions have been asked many times, often by teachers who worry about what visitors to the classroom might think when they find pupils 'only reading'. As we shall see later, such doubts persist even today.

The development of silent reading

A primary teacher on being introduced to SSR some years ago remarked, 'This is just good old fashioned silent reading modernised.' This definition seems to suit the activity nicely. To be sure, whole classes of children have in the past often read silently and for fairly lengthy periods. This at least is better than the arrangement whereby pupils have been asked to read silently after all other work has been completed. Such an arrangement ensures that many children, including some who need it most, will do little, if any, silent reading. Whole-class silent reading, however, needs to be planned.

During the 1970s, reading experts in the USA began to scrutinise silent reading, especially in terms of how it should be conducted. This was important because hitherto the activity had seemed so straightforward that its value and implementation were taken for granted. Even today this assumption creates problems for teachers. Work in the USA in the 1970s established that silent reading could be carried out effectively as follows:

- when it is practised by a whole class;
- for a considerable period of time;
- in either silence or quietness;
- with little or no interruption;
- with no subsequent testing.

These points seem to be eminently sensible although the last might be contentious. Generally, the testing of random periods of silent reading would not be expected. Once it becomes frequent and regular, the temptation becomes greater. Testing, however, implies that when practising silent reading, there must be an immediate end result. This ignores the distinct possibility that the activity is worthwhile in its own right.

In justifying their programmes, US workers in the field made the point that reading, like most skills, requires practice and, to a certain extent, the more that it is practised, the greater the improvement will be. In this respect, reading might be likened to some more physical skills, e.g. swimming, ice skating and marathon running. To become more proficient at these sports, intense practice is required. Once the skills are mastered, however, they cannot be put to one side. The marathon runner, for example, will learn to run economically and with great sensitivity of pace. If he does not continue to practise running prodigious distances his performances will deteriorate rapidly. Similarly, reading needs to be practised to develop what might be termed 'reading stamina', i.e. the ability to read for substantial periods of time. Further justifications involved the conditions under which silent reading could be satisfactorily conducted, the economy of large groups of pupils taking part and the amount of time required. Initially some of the US experiments were perhaps too rigid in terms of the time allowed, 50 minutes being sometimes recommended. Today this would be regarded as too long and duration is now regarded as being age related. In addition, absolute silence and no changing of books were often expected.

As SSR became more frequently practised, its ground rules were not surprisingly adapted to suit individual schools and classes. The amount of time devoted to a session was more likely to be about 20 minutes. In addition, silence was often thought not to be necessary and the changing of books was often permitted during sessions which usually occurred several times a week. By 1980 Moore *et al.* (1980) were able to report that uninterrupted sustained silent reading (USSR) or SSR took place in many schools in USA and that both appeared to be successful in most cases although rigorous evaluation was somewhat sparse. The acronyms USSR and SSR by this time had become well known and were merely alternatives describing the same activity. Since then there have been frequent reports in US journals, notably *The Reading Teacher* and *The Journal of Reading*, of experiments in organisations ranging from the kindergarten to secondary schools. The great majority appear to have been successful although, admittedly, success rather than failure is always more likely to be reported. Two further important points have emerged from these reports. Some schools arranged SSR so that all classes participated at the same time. This has usually been termed 'whole-school reading' and seems particularly applicable to secondary schools where manipulation of the timetable is difficult. In addition, Perez (1986) provided evidence which showed that SSR was more likely to be effective when the teacher took part and read silently, acting as a model of good practice. So far we have examined events on the other side of the Atlantic. How has the activity developed in the UK?

Educationalists visiting USA and Canada in the mid-1980s reported enthusiastically on the merits of SSR. Their comments appeared in the educational press on a number of occasions. One such was Vera Southgate whose later research with colleagues (Southgate *et al.* 1981) claimed that too much time was devoted to hearing children read in British schools and not enough to silent reading. Her research backed up the findings of another study by Lunzer and Gardner (1979) who found that too much reading in secondary schools was of a 'short burst' variety; in other words it was not sustained. These researchers also found that many teachers worried about the consequences of visitors to the classroom observing SSR being practised and regarding it in a negative light.

It is not possible to say exactly when SSR was first adopted by British schools. Clearly, the work mentioned above made some impact. It was followed in the 1980s by descriptions of work which had actually taken place in the UK, (see, for example, Walker (1980) and Maybin (1983)), discussion of the activity (Campbell 1988) and a survey by Fenwick (1988) which included a number of accounts of good practice. Research on how SSR was conducted also provided helpful information. One of the most useful of these was the work of Wheldall and Entwistle (1988) which indicated quite clearly that the teacher as a role model was, as Perez (1986) had claimed earlier, an extremely important factor. Later work by Campbell and Scrivens (1995) showed that although the teacher as a role model was important, help given to individuals and groups of children during SSR could also be useful.

By the early 1990s it appeared as though SSR had become firmly established in British schools, particularly in the primary sector. Wray and Lewis (1993) were able to claim that most primary schools made use of it and, in a survey of 50 primary schools, Fenwick and Reader (1996) found that 95 per cent of them practised SSR. Unfortunately, this situation began to deteriorate during the mid-1990s.

Justifying silent reading today

By 1990, it was widespread in both primary and secondary schools. The length of sessions varied according to age and, in primary schools at least, it occurred on average three times per week. Generally both teachers and pupils were enthusiastic about it, quietness rather than silence was tolerated and pupils were often encouraged to have several books available in order to curb the disruption which was likely to happen when books were changed during sessions. In addition, many teachers read during the sessions and some evaluated their programmes. In short, SSR seemed to be both a popular and a successful part of the reading programme. The following examples have been taken fairly recently from schools where the activity is practised successfully. They show that the way in which SSR is organised depends very much upon the age of the pupils. Furthermore, there are indications that individual schools adapt it to their own needs, a refreshing approach when one considers just how prescriptive the school curriculum has become.

Year 1

SSR was practised by all classes in this school, although not at the same time. Initially the time devoted to it was no more than 5 minutes during daily sessions. This was gradually increased so that by the end of the autumn term it lasted for 10 minutes. By the end of the school year this had been extended to 15 minutes.

During SSR, pupils were required to read quietly and interruptions were discouraged. The reading materials consisted of picture books with a limited number of words and supplementary readers. Initially there had been chaos when the children were permitted to change their books as and when they wished. This ceased when they were allowed to have three different books to work with.

The teacher did not read but instead observed her pupils and anticipated difficulties. At the end of each session she discussed with the whole class what had taken place. In addition, she held regular small-group discussions and kept notes on pupils' individual choices. Enthusiasm for SSR was such that by the end of the autumn term most of the children were bringing in some of their own books to read. The teacher believed that her main function during SSR was to ensure that her young pupils developed the ability to make useful selections.

A particularly novel aspect of this work was the use of an alarm clock to indicate when sessions were coming to an end. During the summer term, when it was warm enough to read outside, some children brought their own alarm clocks and used them for SSR sessions during lunch breaks.

Year 6

A small crowded classroom containing 30 pupils did not appear at first sight to be a propitious venue for SSR. There were, however, a number of old bookcases which contained a treasure trove of reading material, mainly fiction. It was particularly impressive that the books were a delightful mixture of old and new, freshly bought books alongside well-used ones. Such a range presented readers with an excellent variety of choice.

SSR was practised in every class on four occasions a week, Years 3 and 4 reading for 20 minutes per session, and Years 5 and 6 for 25 minutes. The pupils in this group read quietly and when questioned displayed an impressive knowledge of children's literature. Indeed the activity had been so successful that they were allowed to bring in comics for one session each week.

The records which they kept included information about the number of books which they failed to complete. Their teacher vigilantly checked this information, doing his best to break patterns of failure by helping pupils with their selections.

Despite the initial impression of untidiness, it would be difficult to find many classrooms where SSR was working better, although information books and poetry might have been in greater evidence.

Year 8

At times SSR seems to exist despite the most challenging conditions. In this secondary school SSR was practised by all pupils at a set time on 3 days a week, each session lasting for 20 minutes. It was contained within form periods held late in the day. By these means it was removed from the time given to subject teaching and involved all teachers who were responsible for a form, irrespective of their special subject. The reading material available was organised by the English Department.

The group observed, all boys, presented a number of problems. Most of them had reading difficulties and initially they rejected many of the books as being boring or too difficult. Their teacher acted positively by allowing them to use comics, magazines and newspapers. This worked well, except for two occasions when the activity had to be abandoned because of disruption linked with incidents beyond the classroom.

By the end of the autumn term some boys were bringing their own books in and by the end of the school year even more were selecting books from the school library. They were quite willing to maintain records of their reading and their comments on the quality of what they read was uninhibited to say the least, although they became more constructive eventually. SSR can flourish in conditions which might appear to be unpromising provided that the situation is treated with sensitivity. It is important that slow learning pupils should not feel that they are excluded from it.

Recent problems

Yet something went wrong. Now, in the late 1990s, SSR is once again regarded with suspicion. There seems to be two main reasons for this. The first is the increased emphasis on the technical aspects of the teaching of reading and on phonics in particular. SSR, not for the first time creates, the impression that it is not an activity which directly teaches pupils effective skills. Thus, in their survey of the teaching of reading in the primary schools in three inner London boroughs, OFSTED (1996) was highly critical of the activity. It was not guided, it lacked purpose and even the well-tested ploy of the teacher acting as a role model was dismissed.

The second reason is the creation of the new Literacy Hour which might appear, at first glance, to preclude SSR. How might SSR be defended? If this is not done effectively will 'the literate classroom' really be fully literate?

In general, teachers recognise the obvious. Sustained reading assists in learning how to read. This claim was backed up by Smith (1973) when he stated, admittedly rather controversially, that children learned to read by reading. More recently Stainthorp (1997) has stated that the amount of reading which a child does has a direct influence on its progress.

Teachers need to marshal these arguments and show that they are aware of the procedures which are linked to SSR and how they can be adjusted to suit individual situations. They might also need to consider the following.

- SSR is not a separate reading programme; it is part of one. Its links with the other parts needs to be shown.
- SSR is not an inflexible programme. To practice it week in, week out, might create the boredom which sometimes occurs when an activity becomes too routine.
- SSR might involve talking about books with fellow pupils and visitors to the school; by these means pupils can demonstrate their knowledge and enthusiasm.
- Most important of all, evaluative information needs to be compiled. This does not imply testing nor should it involve a laborious round of book reviews. It should involve records of which books pupils have completed, which they have left unfinished and how long it took to do both. With the exception of very young children, pupils can compile records such as this for themselves.

We play into the hands of OFSTED if we take SSR for granted and, it must be admitted, sometimes lose sight of how and why it should be conducted. Teachers who can explain the reasons for their routines and indicate the volume of their pupils' reading in terms of both quantity and quality can, however, argue the case for the retention of SSR very convincingly (Fenwick and Burns 1998).

As for the Literacy Hour, as this is written it is early days, and one inevitably receives mixed messages. A literacy adviser says there is room for it, a teacher who has been on a course says there is not and the Secretary for State is alleged to have said that it is not negotiable. One might counter that, if the language curriculum is not negotiable, then teachers might as well go home. Surely, language is what negotiation is about! Personally, I note a 20 minute chunk of the hour which at both Key Stage 1 and Key Stage 2 is devoted to group and independent work. It is here that SSR might well fit in. In any case, must English simply be confined to the Literary Hour?

It would be a sad irony if, in the Year of Reading soon to commence, the act of reading silently for sustained periods was played down. Ironic because initiatives such as 'Reading is fundamental' are beginning to make an impact, ironic because a recent NFER survey (Brooks *et al.* 1997) has echoed the claims of Southgate *et al.* (1981) that there are still too many children who can read but do not, mostly because they do not like to. The Year of Reading, in fact, offers a golden opportunity to those who wish to reinforce SSR's claims for a substantial part of the school timetable. Already influential voices (Campbell 1998,

Sainsbury 1998) are being raised to point out that, if it cannot be fitted in to the Literacy Hour, then a place must be found for it elsewhere.

We teach children to read so that they can become effective readers. The teacher's task is to try to make as many children as possible enjoy reading and to give them ample time to do so. It sounds so obvious! Should we really have to keep recovering ground which we thought we had won long ago?

References

Belloc, H. (1930) *New Cautionary Tales*. London: Duckworth.

Brooks, G., Schagen, I. and Nastud, P. (1997) *Trends in Reading at 8*. London: NFER.

Campbell, R. (1988) 'Is it time for USSR, SSR, SQUIRT, DEAR or ERIC?', *Education 3–13*, June, 22–25.

Campbell, R. (1998) 'A literacy hour is only part of the story', *Reading* **32**(2), 21–23.

Campbell, R. and Scrivens, J. (1995) 'The teacher's role during sustained, silent reading' *Reading* **29**(2), 52–55.

Carsley, J. D. (1957) 'The interests of children, aged 10–11, in books', *British Journal of Educational Psychology* **XXVII**, 13–23.

Fenwick, G. (1988) *USSR in Theory and Practice*, pp.9–11. Reading: Reading and Language Information Centre, The University of Reading.

Fenwick, G. and Burns, D. (1998) 'Sustained silent reading in the primary school', *Education Today* **48**(2), 9–13.

Fenwick, G. and Reader, P. (1996) 'Sustained, silent reading', an unpublished paper from a primary school survey. Liverpool: John Moores University.

Freire, P. (1972) *Pedagogy of the Oppressed*. Harmondsworth: Penguin Books.

Jenkinson, A. J. (1940) *What do Boys and Girls Read?* London: Methuen.

Lee, L. (1959) *Cider with Rosie*. London: Hogarth Press.

Lunzer, E. and Gardner, K. (1979) *The Effective Use of Reading*. London: Heinemann Educational Books.

Maybin, J. (1983) 'Whole school reading periods' in Hoffman, M., Jeffcoate, R., Maybin, J., Mercer, N. (eds) *Children, Language and Literature*. Milton Keynes: Open University Press.

Moore, J. C., Jones, C. J. and Miller, D. (1980) 'What we know after a decade of sustained, silent reading', *The Reading Teacher* **33**(4), 445–450.

OFSTED (1996) *The Teaching of Reading in 45 Inner-London Schools*. London: OFSTED.

Perez, S. (1986) 'Children see, children do: teachers as reading models', *The Reading Teacher* **40** (May), 8–11..

Sainsbury, M. (1998) *Literacy Hours – A Survey of the National Picture in the Spring Term of 1998*. Slough: NFER.

Smith, F. (1973) *Children's Reading*. London: Holt, Rhinehart and Winston.

Southgate, V., Arnold, H. and Johnson, S. (1981) *Extending Beginning Reading*. London: Heinemann Educational Books.

Stainthorp, R. (1997) 'Reading in the primary classroom', Croll, P. and Hastings, W. (eds) *Effective Primary Teaching – Research Based Strategies*. London: David Fulton Publishers.

Walker, P. (1980) 'Whole school reading', *The English Magazine* Summer, 28–31.

Wheldall, K. and Entwistle J. (1988) 'Back in the USSR', *Educational Psychology* **8**(1–2), 51–56.

Wray, D. and Lewis, M. (1993) 'The reading experiences and interests of junior school children', *Children's Literature in Education* **24**(4), 251–263.

Chapter 7

A sense of time and place: literature in the wider curriculum

Gillian Lathey

A writer's sense of place is unique. Philippa Pearce's (1985) Cambridgeshire, scene of Tom and Hatty's magical race on ice skates across the frozen fens in *Tom's Midnight Garden* or Jill Paton Walsh's (1987) lyrical and sometimes menacing evocation of the same watery landscape in *Gaffer Samson's Luck* are worlds apart. Do we, through reading these books, add to our knowledge of the geography of East Anglia? The answer is both yes and no; statistics and facts may remain as hazy as before, but we gain from each writer an unforgettable vision of the area coloured by the sensations, impressions and mood of her book. In the same way, a writer's sense of an historical period is an imaginative invention that may incidentally inspire and extend historical study. What literature offers us cannot, therefore, be directly harnessed to the service of subjects or topic teaching without courting the danger of damaging the integrity of a writer's intention or a child's response. Stories, novels, plays and poetry must be read primarily for their qualities of language, imagination and thought so that pupils 'respond imaginatively to the plot, characters, ideas, vocabulary and organisation of language in literature' (programmes of study for reading Key Stage 2). Given this starting point, however, there is no reason why a varied reading diet should not positively influence children's understanding of complex ideas across the curriculum. Alun Hicks and Dave Martin (1997) describe a successful cross-curricular project to teach both English and history through historical fiction in a secondary school; making significant links while maintaining the essence of each discipline ought to be more straightforward in the primary sector. By surveying the range of children's literature arising from one historical event – the Second World War – and offering examples of ways to work with specific texts in the upper primary (Years 5 and 6) classroom, I hope to illustrate the kinds of link between literature and history which can enhance both areas of learning without compromising either of them.

Because the Second World War is still – just – within living memory, there is a vast corpus of texts written for children set in the war years. Just as two views of Cambridgeshire may differ so markedly, these books cover a wide spectrum of responses and raise issues about human behaviour which span the whole curriculum. Fiction set in the Second World War may include reference to the war only as a backdrop and catalyst to a child's misunderstandings of the adult world (Bawden 1993) or dramatically portray a turning point in a child's understanding of adult behaviour: the realisation that war is no game but a matter of death and evil (Cooper 1974). Even novels which feature the most memorable effects of the war on British children – evacuation (Magorian 1981, Bawden 1993), or the fear and thrills of air-raids (Westall 1995a, b, Rees 1978) – differ in perspective and purpose. Children's encounters with stray German pilots (the numbers found in children's books bear no relation to reality!) provide an opportunity for an author to attempt a revision of attitudes to the German enemy in Westall's (1997) *The Machine-Gunners* and Michael Morpurgo's (1997) *Friend or Foe*. Indeed, many British writers have looked beyond the British experience to place it in a European or world context; Ian Serraillier's (1960) *The Silver Sword*, first published in 1956, was ground breaking in its treatment of the plight of child refugees in a devastated post-war Europe. Translations take readers further into the world context. Hans Peter Richter's (1987a, b) autobiographical texts, for example, develop insights into the 'enemy's' point-of-view by offering an insider's – and partly confessional – view of a young German boy's growing personal involvement in the persecution of the Jews, while a child's response to the inhumanity of the concentration camps is the subject of the picture book *Rose Blanche* (Innocenti 1985). The allegorical novel *I am David* by the Danish author Anne Holm (1989) addresses the post-war fate of a concentration camp inmate, although the lack of historical context can be problematic. There are also compelling autobiographical accounts for the young by Jewish 'hidden children', namely *The Diary of a Young Girl* by Anne Frank (1997), *The Upstairs Room* by Johanna Reiss (1997), and *Tell No One Who You Are* by Walter Buchignani (1997), and exiles, namely *When Hitler Stole Pink Rabbit* by Judith Kerr (1977). Finally, the war in the far east is represented by Meindert de Jong's *The House of Sixty Fathers* (1966) and a distressingly direct picture book by Toshi Maruki, *The Hiroshima Story* (1983).

Teachers' choices from this varied set of texts will depend on the previous reading experience and current understandings of the children that they teach, as will the question as to when and how books might be linked to the wider curriculum. Selected books can be read, alongside, before or even some time after the study of the history of the war during the final two years of primary school; an opportunity to preview or revisit the theme of war in literary form may prove just as fruitful as an attempt to teach literature and history simultaneously. Whatever the timing, it is the matter of how the teacher engages children's interest in these texts which is, as always, of paramount importance. What I would like to suggest is a comparative approach which addresses the demands of the History National Curriculum in the course of an exploration of literary and aesthetic qualities. The comparison of selected texts and extracts encourages children to reflect on universal themes as well as differences in written style, narrative perspective and – in the case of picture-books – the artist's choice of medium, colour, line and layout. The books can be introduced to children in a number of ways; the teacher reading aloud to children affords access for all children to what are sometimes challenging texts, in addition to private reading both in school and at home. Two short stories can be read, discussed and compared within a week or two, whereas two novels would take a term or longer. Teachers of parallel classes could read aloud two contrasting novels inspired by the same experience – Nina Bawden's *Carrie's War* (1993) and Michelle Magorian's *Goodnight Mister Tom* (1981) for example – so that pairs or groups of children subsequently meet to summarise, reflect on and compare the reactions of the central characters Carrie and Willie to evacuation. Some of the strategies recommended for the Literacy Hour can also be pressed into service. Group reading of short stories or novels can be guided towards the discussion of differences and similarities in texts set in the war years. Additionally, the close comparative analysis of carefully selected extracts from novels and stories, with an emphasis on figurative language and narrative point of view, fulfils the requirement for text level work. Comparison gives textual analysis a purpose, as indicated in the following examples which include whole texts, short stories and extracts.

In choosing texts suitable for comparison, I have the expectation in the history National Curriculum that 'the history of Britain should be set in its European and world context' (programme of study, Key Stage 2) in mind. Reading literature across cultures enables British children to appreciate the repercussions of the war in the lives of children across the world. Although it is painful to take readers beyond stories of evacuation, air raids, stray pilots and spies to confront the inhumanity of the holocaust, I would argue that it is an essential element in any study of the Second World War. A revealing introduction to this subject is to invite pupils to consider the fates of two children, one real and one imagined, in the pages of the prize-winning picture books *War Boy* by Michael Foreman (1989) and *Rose Blanche* by Roberto Innocenti (1985). *War Boy* is a delightful and delicately drawn account of Foreman's own early childhood spent in a village close to the 'front-line' town of Lowestoft. Although touched by sadness at the fate of the young men who went to war and never returned, a mood of innocent nostalgia predominates, expressed in humorous vignettes, luminous watercolour landscapes – yet another vision of East Anglia – and exact technical drawings copied from original sources. The enemy is clearly defined in the separation between the kindly brave British soldiers that the young Foreman meets in his mother's sweetshop, and the propaganda-induced image of the German soldier. The child at the centre of *War Boy* indulges in playful exploits such as 'bombing' school wastebaskets, imitating goose-stepping Nazis and enjoying the carnival-like atmosphere amongst cliff-top spectators as a 'doodlebug' explodes in spectacular fashion over the sea.

To read the whole or sections of *War Boy* to children and then, at a later date when the moment seems right, to read Roberto Innocenti's *Rose Blanche*, is to establish an immediate and evident contrast. Not for Rose Blanche the war-inspired games of an ingenuous child; she knows better and acts against the adult world of the Third Reich by smuggling food to children in a concentration camp. Rose's world is one of bleak contrasts, disturbing glimpses of cruelty and the necessity to act alone and in secrecy. To approach this subject at all requires a great deal of sensitive introduction on the teacher's part, plenty of time to revisit and talk about the text as a whole class, and subsequent opportunities for rereading by individuals or groups. Catriona Nicholson, in Chapter 8, reveals in her account of work with Year 6 pupils just how sophisticated and perceptive children's responses to *Rose Blanche* can be, given the right conditions. Text and images pose questions and tantalise the reader with what is left unsaid; this is a book which demands historical contextualisation as well as reflection on Rose's state of mind. After several readings of *Rose Blanche*, children can be guided to explore the difference between its profoundly troubling implications and the reassuring tone of *War Boy*; comparison highlights the enormity of the crimes and human suffering the book represents. Teachers can ask what each of the central figures witnesses and learns about war and human behaviour. The lightheartedness of Foreman's anecdotes emphasise the burden of responsibility that the young Rose Blanche carries and the terrible unspecified fate of the camp inmates. Children's responses to differing graphic and artistic styles can be linked to the stance of each book towards the war years, with a focus on particular illustrations; the glowing colours of Foreman's celebratory bonfire at the end of the war and the subdued tones of Innocenti's ruined town into which battle-weary troops are advancing convey utterly different moods. The final pages of each book also give rise to a thought-provoking contrast. Both depict landscapes and appear at first glance to offer hope for the future; in *Rose Blanche*, flowers grow again over a devastated landscape, while Foreman's closing words, printed on the delicate wash of a Suffolk scene, set the world to rights with the comforting words of a popular song: 'So it was true, all the things the grown-ups had said during the dark days. Now the war was over everything would be all right, there'll be blue birds over the white cliffs.' However, the flowers in *Rose Blanche* only superficially mask the evidence of the camps, and the final image – of which Catriona Nicholson once again demonstrates children's appreciation – reminds the reader of Rose and her death. In commenting on these two closures, children can be guided to reflect on the contrasting resonances of each book, created in word and image.

If *Rose Blanche* gives children an insight into the fate of the Jews during the Third Reich, the cause of that fate – the pernicious progress of antisemitism in taking hold of hearts and minds – is central to any understanding of the causes of the holocaust. Children are constantly made aware of persecution in their own daily lives and, recently, in the media treatment of conflict in Bosnia and Albania. Racial persecution bridges the curriculum and is of immeasurable significance in human history. After learning that antisemitic persecution resulted in the concentration camps and genocide, children are certain to ask how such crimes could happen, and how individual Germans could develop such an irrational hatred of Jews. An ironic contrast which begins to answer these questions can be made between Hans Peter Richter's account of childhood in the Third Reich, and the subtle treatment of anti-German sentiment in Janni Howker's (1986) short story 'Reicker'.

Two extracts from Richter's (1987a) novel *Friedrich* illustrate the attraction for a young boy of the powerful corporate identity of the Hitler Youth, and the increasing social isolation of a Jewish child. Since the structures of both book are episodic, each section is self-contained and can be read in its own right after a short introduction. The scene 'In the swimming pool' points to the irrationality of a sudden change in behaviour by swimming pool attendants and other children when they discover that the narrator's friend Friedrich is Jewish. Questions can be posed about Richter's written style in relating this event. Sentences and paragraphs are brief; the episode is directly and simply related without comment. Readers are left to make up their own minds about events and to deduce Friedrich's feelings from one description of his behaviour: 'Friedrich blushed, lowered his eyes to the ground.' With guidance, children can appreciate the purpose of this narrative strategy which compels the reader to draw moral conclusions, and which is at its most terse in accounts of the narrator's participation in attacks on Jewish property in the chapter entitled 'The pogrom'. The speed with which one statement follows the next as the action unfolds in this scene is punctuated by glimpses of the narrator's state of mind: 'All this was strangely exhilarating'; 'By now I was enjoying myself' (as he smashes a bookcase in a home for Jewish apprentices), until, finally, he is in tears at the end of the chapter as the flat of Friedrich's family is wrecked. Again, Richter allows the reader to draw conclusions from this emotional roller coaster. The irony and guilt in the narrator's tears are contained – but not explained – in the last two lines of the chapter: 'Mother began to weep loudly. And I wept with her.'

By helping children to question this style and reflect on the reasons why Richter refrains from extensive comment on actions which were a part of his own childhood, teachers can initiate discussion on narrative style in autobiographical writing and the seductive dangers of prejudice.

Richter's novel and his subsequent eye-witness account (*I Was There*) are the work of a writer caught in a web of personal and national guilt. The reverberations of the past in the present are also the theme of Janni Howker's 'Reicker', a compelling story of murder and kidnapping which brings the Second World War into the 1980s, an era closer to children's own lives. The story opens with an unpleasant scene as two young boys shout 'Sieg Heil' and 'Nazi' at an elderly man as they imitate the goose-step and raise their arms in a Nazi salute. Reicker is a former German prisoner of war who worked on a local farm and stayed on after the war. In choosing her title, Janni Howker foregrounds a figure who is marginal to the story's plot but central to its meaning. A conversation about Reicker between one of the boys, Sean, and his father touches on the lingering pain of personal loss – Sean's uncle was killed during the war – and the lasting effects of wartime ideology. Sean's father speaks regretfully of his inability to see Reicker as a person: 'In wars most men fight for what they're told to believe in, I suppose. I don't blame Reicker. I just can't see *him.*' The boys do begin to regard Reicker as a person, however, when he finds a 3-year-old girl who had been taken hostage in a local incident and gently sings her a German lullaby. Howker's artistry lies in the narrative structure of a story which has one final twist. The closing line is Reicker's response to Sean's stumbling apology for calling him a Nazi: 'When I was your age, I was'. No more is said, but the impact of that remark in linking the persecution that Reicker was involved in as a boy to the taunts he is subjected to in old age causes readers to interrogate their opinion of Reicker once again. A parallel reading of 'In the swimming pool' and 'The pogrom' from *Friedrich* will enhance children's appreciation of that last line. Guided group reading of *Reicker*, accompanied by discussion and a close focus on extracts – the discussion between Sean and his father, for example – can highlight both the deft touches of a skilled writer and the aftermath of historical events.

My final example addresses a theme which speaks immediately to all children: the threat and actuality of family separation and the loss of a home. As domestic security is such a primary concern of the young, it is not surprising that so many British children's books address evacuation, or that the fates of hidden, refugee or exiled children should feature in books by British and continental European authors. *Carrie's War* (Bawden 1993) is one of the best known of all evacuation novels. Nina Bawden takes her own childhood wartime experience as the starting point for an exploration of the joys and misunderstandings of growing up; a departure from family roles and routines can lead to new opportunities. Nevertheless, the insecurity suffered by so many children during the war years is caught in the scene where Carrie, her younger brother Nick and their friend Albert Sandwich await selection by a host family on their arrival in Wales. The reader is party to Carrie's fears throughout this passage: 'But she had already begun to feel ill with shame at the fear that no one would choose her, the way she always felt when they picked teams at school.' In discussing this passage and asking who is relating Carrie's thoughts, children's attention can be drawn to the way that a narrator takes us inside a character's mind, revealing as much about Carrie's general lack of self-confidence as about her current situation. This can be contrasted with similar scenes of arrival and family separation endured by Jewish children, where an examination of causes takes the reader into another dimension of history and human suffering. In *The Upstairs Room* (1979) by Johanna Reiss, a book which also records personal experience, Annie and her sister Sini are Jewish girls hidden by a succession of Dutch families during the German occupation of The Netherlands. On arriving at the first of these hiding places, Annie's responses are recorded in a first-person narrative with the jerky immediacy of thought bites. When she and Sini are left alone: 'We looked at the bedspread. It was crocheted. We looked around some more. At the door – it was closed – and at each other.' Annie's anxiety is best conveyed by reading this section aloud, noting her fixation on insignificant details such as the crochet work on the bedspread. Reading passages from both *Carrie's War* and *The Upstairs Room* inspires empathy with both Carrie and Annie while emphasising the difference in their responses. Carrie is passively anxious as she waits to be chosen – she does at least understand the reasons for her evacuation – whereas Annie, who is considerably younger, constantly and frantically questions the antisemitism that she has already experienced and the bewildering consequences of a world which appears to have gone mad.

A third and equally telling perspective on exile from home is that of Anne Frank, whose diary entries record history as it happens and place it in the context of a young girl's journey towards adulthood. The diary entry for the family's first complete day in the 'secret annexe' is remarkably upbeat in tone. While the rest of her family is irritated by the chiming of a clock, Anne comments: 'Not me, I liked it from the start; it sounds so reassuring, especially at night. You no doubt want to hear what I think of being in hiding. Well, all I can say is that I don't really know yet.' (Saturday, 11 July 1942). Here there is no mediating narrator or act of memory involved; the reader has direct access to Anne's moods, hopes and fears as they change and develop. The early reactions of Anne, Annie and Carrie to the confrontation with a new life has a different historical background which requires explanation, just as each writer adopts different strategies in narrating lived history. Differences in the three extracts are sufficiently striking to lead to reflection on the personalities of the three girls portrayed, on the immediacy of Anne Frank's diary entries as opposed to the retrospective narratives of Nina Bawden and Johanna Reiss, and on narrative viewpoint in autobiographical writing.

There are many more potential starting points for comparison to be found in the literature introduced at the beginning of this chapter. Each author's sense of time *and* place – since the physical setting of many of these books plays a key role – animates an interest in individual histories and echoes of the past. At the same time as developing an appreciation of the illustrator's and writer's art, reflection on human history as represented in children's literature both touches and goes beyond the whole curriculum. Indeed, narratives of the human experience of war deepen and extend children's understanding of what history actually *is*. As historical novelist Rosemary Sutcliff (1990) tells us: 'Sometimes there's a gap in known facts that can only be filled by the Truth of the Spirit.'

References

Bawden, N. (1993) *Carrie's War*. London: Puffin Modern Classics.
Buchignani, W. (1997) *Tell No One Who You Are*. London: Puffin Books.
Cooper, S. (1974) *Dawn of Fear*. London: Puffin Books.
De Jong, M. (1966) *The House of Sixty Fathers*. London: Puffin Books.
Foreman, M. (1989) *War Boy*. London: Pavilion Books.
Frank, A. (1997) *The Diary of a Young Girl*, transl. Susan Massotty. London: Penguin Books.
Hicks, A. and Martin, D. (1997) 'Teaching English and history through historical fiction', *Children's Literature in Education* **28**(2), 49–58.
Holm, A. (1989) *I am David*, transl. L.W. Kingsland. London: Mammoth.
Howker, J. (1986) 'Reicker', in: *Badger on the Barge*. London: Harper Collins.
Innocenti, R. (1985) *Rose Blanche*. London: Jonathan Cape.
Kerr, J. (1977) *When Hitler stole Pink Rabbit*. London: Harper Collins.
Magorian, M. (1981) *Goodnight Mister Tom*. London: Puffin Books.
Maruki, T. (1983) *The Hiroshima Story*, text by Elkin. London: A & C. Black.
Marpurgo, M. (1977) *Friend or Foe*. London: Mammoth.
Paton Walsh, J. (1987) *Gaffer Samson's Luck*. London: Puffin Books.
Pearce, P. (1958) *Tom's Midnight Garden*. Oxford: Oxford University Press.
Rees, D. (1978) *Exeter Blitz*. London: Hamish Hamilton.
Reiss, J. (1979) *The Upstairs Room*. London: Puffin Books.
Richter, H. P. (1987a) *Friedrich*, transl. Edite Kroll. London: Puffin Books.
Richter, H. P. (1987b) *I Was There*, transl. Edite Kroll. London: Puffin Books.
Serraillier, I. (1960) *The Silver Sword*. London: Puffin Books.
Sutcliff, R. (1990) 'History and time', in *Travellers in Time*. Cambridge: CLNE.
Westall, R. (1977) *The Machine-Gunners*. London: Puffin Books.
Westall, R. (1995a) *Children of the Blitz*. London: Macmillan.
Westall, R. (1995b) *Blitz*. London: Harper Collins.

Chapter 8

Reading the pictures: children's responses to *Rose Blanche*

Catriona Nicholson

Central to any reading experience is the interaction between reader and text. Encouraging children to talk about their personal reading experiences with other readers has been acknowledged, through the inspiration and crusading zeal of educationalists such as Aidan Chambers (1993), as a prerequisite of good classroom practice. Teachers are now required, within *The National Literacy Strategy (NLS) Framework for Teaching* (DfEE 1998) to provide, during the Literacy Hour, opportunities for pupils at Key Stage 2 to 'contribute constructively to shared discussion about literature, responding to and building on the views of others'. Wolfgang Iser (1974) asserts that the primary function of a fictional text is to tell a story in such a way and by such use of artistic devices or strategies as to stimulate a creative response in readers, i.e. to provoke readers to create for themselves the meaning and the 'reality' offered by the text. This dynamic concurrence between readers and texts characterises effective bookshare sessions within the primary school classroom, when individual reader responses contribute to communal understanding of a text. Having introduced bookshare sessions to groups of children over several years, I am aware of the challenges such a procedure presents in terms of classroom management. However, there is no doubt that the experience of sharing literary responses through group sessions can promote linguistic development and heighten aesthetic and cultural awareness.

In Chapter 8, Gillian Lathey has identified the close relationship that exists between children's literature and history and she exemplifies ways in which these two components of the primary curriculum can be mutually supportive and illuminating. Jill Paton Walsh, to whom she refers, has identified the interface that exists between literature and history (Heins 1977). She suggests that a novel, being 'quintessentially a prose narrative' comments on history through story, character and event rather than through the temporal authenticity of its setting. Paton Walsh's aim as a writer of historical novels is 'to enshrine in the heart of the novel, in the very centre of its being, a truly historical insight'. Her conviction that 'you have to want to write what did happen and what it felt like' perfectly conveys the ideals expressed by Roberto Innocenti in the introduction to his picture book *Rose Blanche* (McEwan and Innocenti 1985) which became the focus for the series of Year 5 and Year 6 bookshare sessions to which I will be referring in this chapter. Not a novel, but undeniably a 'prose narrative', this starkly powerful text explores the nature of suffering, sacrifice and redemption in words by Ian McEwan[1] and pictures by Innocenti. The artist set himself the task of illustrating 'how a child experiences war without really understanding it'. Explaining his theme, he continues, 'I was a little child when the war passed in front of my door...my father did not want to answer my questions but I knew something terrible was happening'. One of my young readers confirmed that the book 'shows how war affects somebody ordinary...it could be you or me'.

The story,[2] set in a drab, nameless village in the winter of 1944–5 near the end of the Second World War, is partly revealed through the eyes of a young German schoolgirl, Rose Blanche. Innocenti hoped the book would 'express a need for peace through images of war' and his title recalls the 'White Rose' movement, a small underground group of German students who were resistant to the war.

Children today are not made aware, unless exposed through book, film or photographic image, of the particular force for evil that generated the rise of Nazism and, by definition, 'sealed the fate of the Jews during the Third Reich' (see Chapter 7 by Gillian Lathey). In Innocenti's picture book, the inhumanity and sadism that prevailed during the Nazi occupation are seen from a child's perspective. The uncompromising poignancy of her vision is starkly relayed to the reader. The compelling full-plate illustrations show what cannot be conveyed in words. Throughout the book McEwan's restrained text locates a narrative for these telling and detailed images. I chose to make this text a focus for bookshares because I believe that children at the right stage of development can, through engagement with stories which offer what Nina Bawden (1980, p.17) refers to as emotional realism', receive a 'faithful account of the human condition' (Bawden 1980, p.32) by glimpsing, from the safe distance of a book, a darker side of life. *Rose Blanche* is a text which compels a reader to respond. The shared experience of reading it enabled the children to explore ways of understanding aspects of human behaviour and to reflect upon the nature of good and evil.

As with all good classroom practice, the concept of book sharing is underpinned by theoretical principles. Iser's (1974) study of the phenomenology of reading and the subsequent work of Aidan Chambers (1977) establish frameworks of reference for examining the responses of the children who shared *Rose Blanche*.

For the purposes of this chapter, I have selected, from several hours of taped bookshare conversations, extracts from the opening and closing discussions for they exemplify his assertion that the act of reading is 'a sense-making activity' (Iser 1978). The group of four Year 5 children were unfamiliar with the picture book but the two Year 6 boys had briefly examined it the previous year. The responses of the two boys support Iser's view that a second reading of a text elicits 'a kind of advance retrospection'. The responses of all six readers show how 'impressions that arise will vary from individual to individual' (Iser 1974). By way of introduction to the book, both groups concentrated on 'reading' the jacket illustration and, as they began to interpret the puzzle of its reflected war images, they began the process of 'establishing connections - filling in the gaps left by the text'. Rose Blanche stares from behind a curtained window onto an unseen outside. Behind her but apparently within her inside world are reflections of injured soldiers. There is compelling engagement between her disquieting gaze and the eye of the reader. Chambers (1977, p.42) reminds us that 'In books where the implied reader is a child, authors...put at the centre of a story, a child through whose being everything is felt...the child...is thus wooed into the book...and led through whatever experience is offered'.

Ian and David, encountering the book for the second time, having offered me remembrances of their initial reading, were clearly 'wooed' into the book:

David: She seems like she's an angel with the innocent blue eyes and yellow hair...she just needs curled hair and a fancy dress and she could live literally in a forest and be another Snow White.

C.N.: Can you describe her gaze?

David: Her eyes are just innocent.

Ian: She's somebody who doesn't seem to belong to any thing because of the war...her eyes have no depth...it's as if she's trying to get out the feeling of all the killing and hatred. The illustration doesn't give her eyes any depth...she's trying to repel something, she's just horrified. This reflection is the other side of war.

C.N.:   Does what you see on this front cover encourage you to open the book?

Ian: It does me. If I was seeing it for the first time I'd think well, what's inside?

Discussing the impact of Rose Blanche's face on the front cover, both boys confirmed once again Chambers' proposal that the implied child reader is led through the book. Ian said:

I can see the war through Rose Blanche's eyes because that's how the words have been written but with the pictures you kind of feel an onlooker at times because all through the book I remember you can see her and you can always see something in there which tells you that's where she was or that's where she is now.

David similarly demonstrates how 'advance retrospection' directs his thoughts as, with the benefit of a previous reading, he recalls the impact of the book:

With the killing and the cruelty to come, if you try and shut it out you can't because of Rose Blanche. If she wasn't there you would shut it out.

The responses of the younger group bore out Iser's theory that a literary text (illustration) is 'something of an arena in which the reader and the author engage in a game of the imagination.' He refers to reading as a 'dynamic act of recreation' and proposes that the process is neither smooth nor continuous but one which:

In its essence relies on interruptions of the flow...we look forward, we look back, we decide, we change our decisions, we form expectations, we are shocked by their non fulfilment, we question, we muse, and accept, we reject...we oscillate between the building and breaking of illusions (Iser 1974, p.288).

The unwritten narrative of the cover promoted animated discussion as the four readers made predictions, modified them and oscillated between the 'building and breaking of illusions'. They began to make sense of the cover illustration by constructing scenarios for the forthcoming narrative:

Sophie: Who is the girl?

James: She's looking out of a window but the men went off to the war but um didn't come back and she's seeing their ghosts...meeting their ghosts.

Rachel: 'Cos if you look at the window you sort of see cobwebby things hanging.... Maybe it's after the war.

Anthony: I think it's the middle of the war.

Rachel: Maybe she's like a Florence Nightingale. She's been helping these people who are ill and um...um...she's been helping those people put bandages round their heads.

James: I think it's a reflection in a mirror...

Anthony: Maybe she's imagining it all. It's a reflection.

James: Yes, it's a reflection.

Rachel: Normally, if there's a reflection, it would be a different way round. I reckon she may be looking out of it.

Sophie: If you have a reflection say, how can you reflect it? Unless there's a pond or something?

Anthony: She looks as if she's been evacuated.

Rachel: Maybe her father's been killed...or her mother.
Sophie: Is she the reflection?

As this group searched for narrative information, located pictorial clues, discarded ideas, hypothesised, hovered between sudden revelation and the conflict of uncertainties, they demonstrated how their expressive and varied conjectures verified Iser's (1974, p.280) view that in reading 'the opportunity is given...to bring into play our own faculty for establishing connections – for filling in 'gaps' which are often so fragmentary that one's attention is...occupied with the search for connections between the fragments'.

Most of the discussion at this point centred around 'fragmentary' details and in particular the illusion created by the window reflection. The discussions reveal how, in group readings of a text, individual responses can be developed and modified by the contributions of others. As the younger group turned the pages, they took turns to read the written story and, in addition, modified their individual ideas, constantly sharing predictions of what the short- and long-term outcomes might be.

The illustrative inset of the title page established a reference for several recurring themes which were identified in the process of turning pages forward and then back: the red bow in Rose Blanche's hair, the tank tracks, the pools of still water which readers took to reflect 'gloom and winter' and 'sadness'. The distant running child was seen as 'running away', 'running to visit the soldiers' or 'running to say goodbye'. Each reader expected the story to be sombre and one reader proposed that the receding figure of the child was 'the only hopeful thing in the picture in her little red ribbon'.

Although the setting for the first full page illustration was unfamiliar to them, the younger readers began to identify and connect familiar pictorial clues: the German helmet and the 'Nazi cross', the foreign signs and architecture. They turned back to the introductory inset illustration and observed that the mud tracks matched the tyres on the lorry or car shown in the left foreground of this full plate. Summing up after heated discussion they referred again to the jacket illustration and, using knowledge of social and historical concepts, tried to make sense of the images:

James: It's the German soldiers going off, waving goodbye. We know it's definitely
            Germans because there's the German cross.
Rachel: I think her father dies because she's wearing different clothes than on the
            cover because on the cover she's wearing black clothes, like Queen Victoria.
            And that's the sort of thing that's going to happen in the story...that person
            dressed in black on this page is getting us ready for it.

The older readers in their discussion of the title page illustration spoke with second reading assurance, informed by what Iser calls 'a repertoire of familiar literary patterns':

Ian: The first small picture is of Rose Blanche running across a muddy track and
            I think that's pretty symbolic because she's there and she's got the bright red
            hairband. Everything else just blends around her. What do you think, David?
David: You can obviously see it's well used by tanks and trucks because of the
            tracks. Rose Blanche...she's the only mark of colour...It's all dismal; grey,
            dark, dark greens mixed with browns. You see her as a glimmer of hope.
Ian: The track looks everlasting doesn't it?
David: Yes, and she's heading into the mist and that's telling us something.

Both groups deliberated over details which might connect their earlier expectations with forthcoming narrative events or experiences. Initially they freely exchanged ideas about how they, as individuals, would feel about being involved in a war but, as the readings proceeded, the discussions began to focus on symbolic images which appeared to convey Rose Blanche's plight; recurring images of barbed wire, fences, barriers and the enclosure were commented upon. At one point David expressed his own concerned involvement as a reader:

> You're an onlooker onto Rose Blanche... You see it all through her eyes. The SS officer looks as though out of the side of his eye he's looking at you... He's trying to see what you're doing. I just hate it... it's awful.

As the regular pattern of the child's visits to the camp become established, the tenor of response within both groups became less animated and the children spoke with feeling and marked compassion:

Rachel: She looks so pale.
Anthony: I feel so sorry for her.
James: We feel like we're Rose Blanche.
Sophie: Because you can't see her (in the double-spread concentration camp depiction) it feels like you're Rose Blanche.
James: I know they are Jewish and they are children like us.
Sophie: Just imagine having to walk away from them.
Rachel: It's the way you're looking at them and the way they're looking at you...

Through sombre ever-darkening shades of colour, Innnocenti uses effective means to convey the sadness and desolation of war and to confront the terrible realms of man's inhumanity. As the ironic tragedy of Rose Blanche's final visit to the site of the concentration camp is revealed, these young readers reached for and found, in the simple eloquence of their words, a language which matched the poignancy of their reading experience. Their response to the mystery and metaphor of the final double page spread is evidence enough that the sharing and interrogating of texts enables readers to 'talk well' about books and thereby to gain insight into the nature of human suffering. Here is an extract from the younger readers' interpretations of that significant page:

James: Those flowers represent the children of the camps and that single flower represents Rose Blanche.
Rachel: Gentleness over the barbed wire, gentleness over cruelty.
Anthony: If the artist hadn't shown that flower bent over the barbed wire, I wouldn't have known Rose Blanche was dead. You've got to read the pictures for a long time to realise the meaning of things like that flower... If you just turned over you wouldn't understand anything because you wouldn't be looking at it properly. You really got to look into the picture to find out the meaning. The pictures are the description.
Sophie: It's like hope is expressed in light and colour...
James: And all these flowers they represent the good of the bad...
Anthony: It's like an invasion of all the Spring and the explosions of colour defeat all the bad things.

The case for promoting reader response activities through group reading rests on the quality and depth of talk that such discussions generate. The Year 6 readers, Ian and David, discussing the final double spread in detail, revealed extraordinary insight. In responding to this text each drew on a language of tenderness, revealing astute powers of discrimination. I offer the transcript of their final discussion as evidence of how their sharing of the text has enabled them to glimpse coherence behind the chaos of war, to make sense of the past and to confirm their faith in the endurance of the human spirit:

David: This [illustration] with the piece that Ian read, the explosions, the uniforms, the parades, the positions of the birds, and the triumph, it's just like the war and now...it looks exactly the same scene as when Rose Blanche was shot, and on the barbed wire you can see the very flower that she was holding. And under it there are flowers of the same variety. The tank tracks are now covered in grass the um barbed wire fence looks as if it was being attacked by creepers. The trees are crowding in and you can hardly see the broken branches – they're all sprouting new. But then when you think how many people have suffered here the beauty is taken away.

Ian: This is where the prison camp used to be.

David: Yeah, and the steel girders have also been attacked by creepers.

Ian: It's really as though it's a war of good against a war of evil and that's what the author Roberto Innocenti is trying to get over to you.

David: (to himself) This picture is just brilliant.

Ian: Yeah...and the flower that Rose Blanche had put there had really, by the looks of things, given up hope and then that seed has spread...it's like Adam and Eve populating the world.

David: Really, if you took away the steel girders and the fence, you'd see a perfect piece of the countryside, you wouldn't really notice it had been the war at one stage...the only signs are the fence the girders and a small section of tank track.

Ian: Yeah...even that pan which was in...(turns back two pages)...which was in that picture where it was all muddy, is still there in the same position. The way that the author has changed scenes from the beginning where everything was desolate, everything was dead, like people's morale, everything was dead, and then suddenly spring comes and morale is lifted but it's the morale of the countryside really. It is just excellent this book. I can see why it's been controversial and I recognise that...this tells how horrible war really is. You can get war books and I'm not saying you shouldn't read them but they just don't tell you what war is really, really like...so many... *Island on Bird Street* does...uh... *Echoes of War* does but this is better than either of them in some ways because (speaks emphatically) the pictures tell the story. (in measured tones) This...is...the advance...of...peace.

David: In the last motif (before the endpaper) there's the flower which Rose Blanche was holding...on the barbed wire and it's covered in rain...

Ian: And it's bedraggled...when you see that, its almost as if there's another war on because there's that dark background and you can see sheet-like rain if you look closely, and the barbed wire. But there's that flower...even though it's dead it's...it's...between two spikes of the wire and it's as though it's separating the two sides in the war – the one on the left is the German spike and the one on the right represents the allies. It's as if the flower is stopping the war from happening any more...with a book like this though you have to let everyone interpret the meaning of the story in their own way.

Roberto Innocenti established the focus for his own partially understood childhood experience in the fictional experiences of the child Rose Blanche. Readers respond to the impact of a relentlessly harrowing narrative which we receive through the filter of her vision. The responses of these six present-day readers became my experience of their experience of Rose Blanche's experience; what was seen but not understood by the young Innocenti has, through a perfect blend of words and pictures, been made visible to the next generation.

Endnotes

1 There are two versions of the picture-book *Rose Blanche*. The illustrations, by Roberto Innocenti, remain the same but the texts differ markedly. One, published by Creative Education (1985) in the USA, has an original text by Christophe Gollaz and Roberto Innocenti. The version discussed in this chapter, with text by Ian McEwan, is 'based on a story by Christophe Gollaz'. McEwan, at the request of Jonathan Cape, translated the Gollaz story and wrote a new text for Innocenti's illustrations. Several interesting and intriguing questions arise from a study of both narratives.

2 The story opens in late autumn with Rose Blanche and her mother waving goodbye to men from the town who are leaving to fight in the war. Apart from queues at food shops, daily life and the routines of home and school remain the same. One day Rose witnesses the violent arrest of a small boy and, furious at the kidnapping, she follows the lorry into which he was bundled, through the streets of the town and out into the countryside. Her trek brings her to the outskirts of a concentration camp where in a clearing 'dozens of silent, motionless children stared at her from behind a barbed wire fence'. This awesome experience marks the turning point in Rose's life. Her humanity and the pity that she feels for the starving prisoners lead her to make daily and nightly visits to the camp where she passes her hoarded offerings of food through the wire fence. Eventually, threatened by invasion the townsfolk leave but Rose Blanche returns to the forest where, in a moment of confusion, the 'sharp and terrible sound of a shot' is heard as a retreating soldier fires instinctively at any movement in the misty gloom of the forest. A desolate wintery landscape, ravaged by the destructive savagery and the ugly barricades of war, frames our last view of Rose, whose tired face, now a death mask, communicates unutterable sadness. A blue flower that she holds rests lightly against broken wire. Poignantly recalling this scene two pages later, Innocenti uses a luminous diffusion of colour and light to convey the symbolic representation of the child and of hope within the 'invasion' of a burgeoning spring. Blue flowers bloom below the strands of barbed wire.

References

Bawden, N. (1980) 'Emotional realism in books for young people', *The Horn Book Magazine* **LVI**(1), 17–33.

Chambers, A. (1977) *Booktalk*. London: The Bodley Head.

Chambers, A. (1993) *Tell Me: Children, Reading and Talk*. Stroud, Gloucestershire: The Thimble Press.

DfEE (1998) *The National Literacy Strategy: Framework for Teaching*. London: DfEE.

Heins, P. (1977) 'Crosscurrents of criticism', *Horn Book Essays 1968–1977*. Boston, Mass: The Horn Book Inc., pp.219–225.

Iser, W. (1974) *The Implied Reader*. Boston: Johns Hopkins University Press.

Iser, W. (1978) *The Act of Reading: A Theory of Aesthetic Response*. Baltimore and London: Johns Hopkins University Press.

McEwan, I. and Innocenti, R. (1985) *Rose Blanche*. London: Jonathan Cape.

Chapter 9

The creation of readers, or Mr Magnolia meets the Literacy Hour. Will he survive?

Judith Graham

I have often wondered whether there is a common denominator in those who write, read, teach, enjoy and promote children's literature. Were we all read to as children? Did we ask for the same story again and again? Did we all read by torch light under the covers? Did we have – early on – one significant book that revealed to us the magic that is in reading? Did we have gifted teachers who 'did the voices', slipped the right books under our noses at the right time and were interested in our responses?

What I think may be true is that, at school, we all survived the model of teaching literature which Lawrie Walker calls the 'dissected corpse' model. This is how it goes:

- Literature is to study rather than to enjoy.
- Literature can be disassembled like a machine, provided that one has a manual and knows where the parts begin and end.
- The response to literature must be ballasted by key terms, such as 'the tragic flaw', 'iambic pentameter' and 'villanelle'.
- The most heinous sin of all is to express a personal opinion or to refer to first-hand experience.
- Literature is for passing exams and gaining favour with authority (Walker, L.).

Devotees of literature, I suggest, survived this model – taught at every level – and perhaps some of us even grew to enjoy the textual analysis at its heart, but we are not typical. Year after year, I meet students who shudder when I ask them their memories of literature teaching at school. For every one who left school with their love of story and of poetry intact, there are scores of people who vow never to read another book or poem again.

There was a reaction to this sort of literature teaching in many British schools in the now discredited 1960s and 1970s when literature was 'allowed to do its own work', taught without vivisection. Story time was timetabled and sacrosanct. 'Story-telling and reading aloud sessions occurred very regularly, and were regarded by teachers as a significant contribution to language development and a prerequisite of successful literacy' (Willes 1983, p.77). Bruner (1984, p.196) confirmed the importance of exposure to stories as far as literacy was concerned: 'What initially attracts children to reading and into mastering all the mechanics of it, is the opportunity that text provides for penetrating possible worlds, worlds beyond the mundanities of here and now'. Beyond initial literacy, total immersion in story and frequent exposure to poetry were believed to effect identification with the character, the teaching of narrative structure, of literary language, of form and theme, that resulted in literate adults who enjoyed reading, enjoyed talking about reading and who wrote with literary tunes in their heads and with little problem.

This time is coming to an end with the National Literacy Strategy (NLS). The authors of the *The National Literacy Strategy Framework for Teaching* (DfEE 1998) may protest and say, 'No, no, not at all, see, there it all is. In Reception: "Understand how book language works and use some formal element when retelling stories" (p.18); in Year 1, Term 1, "describe story settings" (p.20); in Year 2, Term 2: "identify and describe characters" (p.28); in Year 4, Term 1, "explore narrative order" (p.38); in Year 6, Term 2, "recognise how poets manipulate words" (p.52) and so on'. However, we are unmistakably back to the dissected corpse model of teaching literature. Not only is the basic framework predicated on 'pupils must be taught' (an imperative that governs every single one of the 800 instructions to teachers) but, in the introduction to the framework, the insistence on direct instruction is inescapable. Nowhere is there any suggestion that reading aloud to children, frequently and for lengthy uninterrupted periods, could be a source of growing literacy and literary competence. Indeed, it is quite clear that the NLS cannot conceive that reading aloud to children could achieve anything without the teacher's analysis and questioning of children about techniques. At the end of the introduction, we find a cautious 'additional time may be needed for continuing the practice of reading to the class' – not 'will' be needed, only 'may'; no guidance is given, and no suggestion that it is critically important.

One might hope then that reading aloud to children is a central ingredient and taken for granted in the daily 15 minutes allotted to the whole class for 'shared reading and writing', 'text' level work. There, once again, there is no suggestion that giving yourself up to a secondary world created by a book is an essential part of becoming a reader or that having a personal response to what you have heard is part of the process. 'Shared reading' is to be used, at key stage 1 'to read with the class, focusing on comprehension and on specific features e.g. word-building and spelling patterns, punctuation, the layout and purpose, the structure and organisation of sentences' and at Key Stage 2 'for teaching and reinforcing grammar, punctuation and vocabulary work' (p. 11). All this is despite a second period of 15 minutes coming up, ear-marked for 'word' and 'sentence' level work. It is clearly not the intention that this period be used for anything like a traditional story time. The message is clear: reading aloud to children is not direct teaching and therefore it no longer counts.

We need to remind ourselves what it is that goes into the creation of a reader. For this you need to read a story. Enjoy the traditional story which follows, found in a written version in Teresa Grainger's (1997) inspirational book *Traditional Storytelling in the Primary Classroom*. The story comes from Zimbabwe, Africa.

'The children of wax'
It wasn't in my time and it wasn't in your time but it was in someone else's time, that, nestled beneath the Matopos hills in Africa, there lived a family whose children were made entirely of wax. The mother and father were distraught when they realised that their children were not like others, who were made of flesh and blood. They couldn't understand it. Why had they been picked on like this? One wax child was enough, but two, three, four, five children of wax?

Their mother wept and wondered, but she loved them in her heart and came to care for them as all mothers do for their children. Their father loved them too, and built them a dark wooden hut in which they could live. There they stayed, safe inside during the time of sunlight until the twilight hour descended and the heat of the sun's rays could harm them no more. The children therefore slept most of the day and came out to work at night, taking the cattle to the watering holes, tending the crops and cleaning out the compound, much as the flesh children did during the daytime.

Their hut had no windows, so the sun could not penetrate the gloom, although the youngest child, Ngwabi, has scratched and scraped a tiny chink in one wall through which he was able to peer when the sun was at certain positions in the sky. Ngwabi loved to listen to the laughter and voices of the children outside and to catch occasional glimpses of them as they played in the sunlight. His dreams were full of possibilities and imaginings. Unlike his brothers and sisters who accepted that they would never know what the world was like, Ngwabi longed to see the world. At night he would stare into the distance, searching the silhouettes of the hills with his eyes, wondering what lay beyond them. He saw the paths leading this way and that, but could never follow them, for this was far too dangerous at night-time.

He shared his thoughts with his brothers and sisters, speaking to them of his dreams and his desire for freedom.

'We are imprisoned in this hut by day and in a shroud of darkness by night,' he complained. 'We do not know what the world is really like.'

However, his siblings recognised that there were advantages to being wax children, for such children knew no pain and they were duteous sons and daughters who could work twice as hard as a child of flesh for they would never tire. But poor Ngwabi continued to dream. He began to withdraw into himself and his world of silent possibilities. His desire deepened; his frustration increased. He could think of nothing else. One day, unable to restrain his longing any longer, he rushed out of their hut, out into the world, out into the light, out into the glaring temperatures of the midday sun.

Of course, he could not last long out there in the searing heat and, as his body began to melt, he cried out to his family to save him. His brothers and sisters heard his dying cries, but cruelly could do nothing to help him. They were even forced to close the door of the hut against him as the sun's rays scorched in towards them. All strength drained from Ngwabi and soon he was just a pool of melted wax, a liquid mass in the blazing sunshine.

When night fell, the children left their hut and gathered around the now hardening wax which had been their young brother Ngwabi. His eldest sister carefully scooped up the wax and they walked solemnly to their special place, where many a time they had all sat together, talked and told stories. Then, in silence, Ngwabi's sister fashioned a great bird out of the wax. For feathers, they each pressed leaves from the trees into this wax bird. The leaves would protect the wax from the heat of the sun. It was a magnificent creature – its head proud, its eyes inquisitive, its feet firm.

The children took the bird to their parents and told them what had happened. Their mother took the bird in her hands and wept as she kissed Ngwabi good-bye. Their father, too, kissed it tenderly as he held the bird close to his chest. The wax children did not work that night, but placed the great bird on a rock that stood before their hut. Then they joined hands and sat around it together in silent tribute and communion.

As dawn broke, the children returned to their hut and crowded together around the small hole in the wall that Ngwabi had made. Their eyes watched and wondered. As light seeped up over the hills, it seemed as if the bird drew breath and took energy from the sun. Its wing-tips moved, stretched and fluttered. Its head turned as it looked searchingly around. Slowly and gracefully, the great bird which they had created took off up into the air. As it disappeared from their sight overhead, they could hear its wings beating. It circled their hut three times and then took off in the direction of the hills. Ngwabi, their brother, was free at last.

What will happen to a story such as this if teachers try conscientiously to implement the literacy hour? They will have to seek it out in 'big book' form or enlarge it to font size 18 so that all the class can see the print. They will have to parcel it out over the course of a week or more so that no linguistic, rhetorical or structural feature is ignored. They will be obliged to ask their class to identify the figurative language in 'wept and wondered' or 'scratched and scraped' or in 'light seeping up over the hills' or in 'shroud of darkness' and, once they have done that, they will have to ask their class to account for the effect of such language on the reader. They will, I'm afraid, have to ask their class about subordinate clauses and punctuation, and then about vowel digraphs and consonant blends. I am exaggerating only slightly – some would say not at all.

Yet, if this story had been read or told in its entirety, without interruption, by a teacher who liked the story and enjoyed the task (as all teachers should), the class would have entered a secondary world, painted by the original creators of this story, conveyed to them by the teacher's voice with his or her particular emphases and intonation. In fact the class would not just have entered a secondary world – they would have co-created it. Their teacher would have given them the words but they would have lifted the words into images using everything they could – memories of other stories, television, pictures, films, travel writing or news bulletins, their own experience, even if they have never been to Africa. Tolkien (1964) says we use the very first memories of a tree, a valley or a river to flesh out the words on the page. If he is right, the pupils' tactile memory of wax – soft, malleable and warm, and then cooling and hardening – their knowledge of windowless sheds, their experience of day and night, of searing noon-day heat, of love and sorrow, of a restlessness that they bring to Ngwabi's restlessness – all these would have been brought to their engagement in this story. In short, they would have done quite half the labour; they would have been most active without answering a hail of questions rained down on them by their teacher. Their effort would have been, I believe, pleasurable and productive.

In addition, they would have been willing – because of the legacy of their past satisfactions – to believe in this illusion, this fiction that they have heard. They would know at a deep level that, although so much of this story is impossible, that there is truth to be found in it and they would give themselves up to it. They also know – again because of the legacy of past satisfactions (the phrase is James Britton's (1977)) – that all stories have endings. There is, as soon as we start a story, a knowledge that there will be an ending. We are pulled through the story by the sense that after, the disturbance to the status quo that is part of every story, there has to be a resolution. As you accommodate this knowledge, you appreciate and recognise the shape of the story: the complicating action, the development, the crisis, the denouement and the coda. We learn story shape through recognising patterns after long exposure to examples. We learn it through listening to adults telling stories and reading aloud to us. Even when teachers extensively point out features, this cannot compensate for copious amounts of comprehensible input. There is no short-cut to this learning.

We also learn it from other narrative forms such as television dramas, films, mime, opera and dance; children, in this culture, also learn it from picture-books. It greatly saddens me that the NLS so overlooks the part that picture-books play in children's induction into literacy and the role of illustration in children's literary growth. Picture-books are not forbidden but the absence of endorsement is alarming. There appears to be no understanding that picture is text. In so many picture-books nowadays – hold the memory of Eileen Brown's (1994) *Handa's Surprise* or Quentin Blake's (1993) *Simpkin* or Quentin Blake's (1992) *Cockatoos* in your heads for a moment – the pictures tell a story of which the written text seems blissfully unaware. Children read the pictures and in so doing gain great reader of fifty years agopleasure in completing the full story. They rejoice that there are secrets in the book of which the narrator is ignorant. How splendidly superior that makes them feel. They ask for the book again and again because it makes them feel so clever.

However, even where we have a picture-book of a more traditional kind, children are captured by the images. Thousands of children check the detail in the pictures, absorb the atmosphere, link the episodes, build up the sense of character, whether it be Kathleen Hales' inconsequential but delightful details in her Orlando books of fifty years ago or the rich historical detail in Roberto Innocenti's illustrations to *A Christmas Carol* (Dickens 1990) or Sendak's (1963) deliciously differentiated and hugely memorable *Wild Things*. How can we not want to put this sort of bonding text in front of children, this allure? These cobwebs catch flies – of this every primary school teacher is sure – but, if these books are no longer to be shared unconditionally in the Literacy Hour but dissected and raced through (we are to proceed, you will remember, 'with a sense of urgency, driven by the need to make progress and succeed' (p.8)), where is the opportunity to contemplate and behold? The role of picture books in creating readers is too important to be left to chance in any document concerned with reading.

Imaging is just one of the processes that we go through as we listen to a story or read. Typically, after processes have been thought to include the following:

- anticipating;
- reflecting back and revising;
- predicting;
- making connections;
- evaluating.

There are important discussions of these processes in such books as that by Benton and Fox (1985). You may like to check whether you thought that these processes were part of what happened as you read 'The children of wax'. If they were, you might want to ask why they did not inform some of the structuring of the NLS. They have informed some of the best recent ideas for literature teaching.

The next list is also helpful when trying to understand how to keep a text alive. Rather than exploring an attempt to account for what happens *after* reading – what the process is of accommodating the process of reading this list is:

- unrelated talk;
- expression of appreciation or dislike;
- personal anecdote;
- clarification of details, reconstruction of plot;
- discussion of motives and behaviour of characters;
- reflections on wider significance;
- talk about form, structure and/or language;
- discussion of author's intentions;
- discussion and evaluation of piece as a literary artefact or as part of the literary tradition.

(This list arose from a group of teachers who worked on response to literature for several months at the English and Media Centre in London.)

If this order has any truth about it, you will want to note the place in this list of 'talk about form, structure and/or language'. It is pretty near the end. It is there, in that position, for the simple reason that the other stages need to be experienced before fruitful discussion on the building bricks of text can be undertaken. This may be especially true of readers less experienced than ourselves. The nature of the NLS does not allow us to respect this process. It attempts to short-circuit the processes which, as indicated earlier, is a counter-productive move if you want to create readers.

If we are to balance our convictions of how readers are created with the requirement of the NLS, then we need to have a strategy. This is what I propose:

- Ignore what the NLS says about leaving reading aloud – and reading for pleasure and writing in an extended way – to other times of the day. This time will be eroded and anyway the message sent out is all wrong. Read rich texts in their entirety and do not interrupt them with questions.
- Choose texts which are robust and will not lose their impact if you do turn the spotlight on them. In general, I think that this may mean predominantly texts which are either light hearted or are texts where the writer draws attention to his or her language in a deliberate way. Take a linguistically playful text – such as the Kurt Maschler award-winning book of 1997, *Lady Muck*, by William Mayne and Jonathan Heale which tells the tale of the pigs Boarky and Sowky, a loving but uncontrollably greedy and deceiving couple. Here, Mayne and Heale have devised a language that children can analyse, noting his invented endings ('potatio'), dialect use ('I've finded it'), adjectives used as nouns ('What can I do to happy you?'), alliteration ('she twirled and twitched her tail until it went twang') and invented piggy idioms, such as 'from grunt to squeal' or 'the whifflom of the greatest piggly tasties'. In the process, the book will not suffer and the children's admiration for the inventiveness of Mayne and Heale can only increase. If we pick our texts wisely, they will survive and yes, I think Mr Magnolia (Blake 1980) will survive. Those rhymes – boot, rooty-toot, flute, newt, suit, hoot, scoot, chute, fruit, salute and brute, all unleashing Quentin Blake's most inventive images – will bear examining and yield up their phonic irregularities with no loss of delight.
- Do much of the word and sentence work away from the books that children need to come to know and love. I know that we have frequently campaigned for work on the graphophonic and syntactic cue systems to be done in context but, if you ruin the affective pleasure in the book in the process, there is too great a loss. Of course, the NLS expressly forbids decontextualised work ('pupils must be working on texts' (p.13)) but I think that there we can interpret the word 'text' widely. There is no reason why you should not be able to do good word and sentence level work *out* of context. Here is a student who has made a dice (her 'text') with the consonant blends sl, sp, st, sh, sn and sw, one on each of the six faces. With the children in a circle, she rolls the dice to them and they respond to the uppermost face and provide an appropriate word. Not only do they enjoy the game and think of a great selection of words but *they* make the textual links. When they come to share *How Do I Eat It?* (Watanabe and Ohtoma 1980) later in the day they all react to 'spaghetti' by chorusing 'we had "sp" this morning on the dice and Antony said, "spaghetti"!'
- Offer pupils purposeful activities. We need to make most activities take the form of 'real' writing or speaking tasks and not pose exercises or questions which ask for simple factual recall. We have all come a long way in our understanding of how much more readily children write and how much more they achieve when they are writing or talking:
- for *purposes* to which they can relate;
- for *audiences* which they can visualise or imagine;
- in *forms* of which they have seen counterparts in real life.

The *National Writing Project* (1989) has provided much evidence of the truth of this and the original National Curriculum (the 'Cox' curriculum) helped teachers greatly with its 'Approaches to the class novel', to which I refer you for further ideas. In the outside world, there are examples of the hundreds of ways in which this society uses written and spoken language. Children know masses of them. Read The Pied Piper of Hamelin (Browning 1991) to your class and let them, in groups, look at tourist guides to historic towns in this country. Then let them write a tourist guide to Hamelin, directing tourists to the statue of the Pied Piper, to the very spot where the rats were drowned in the River Weser, and to the stained-glass window in the church commemorating the lost children. Inventing this brochure takes your class back into the poem for the detail and the content and out into the real world for the form and the particular register.

Make your activities for whole class and group work relate specifically to the strengths and significant features of your chosen text. A focus on words and grammar is appropriate in a book such as Philip Pullman's (1995) *The Firework-maker's Daughter* where the names of fireworks ('crackle dragons', 'golden sneezes', 'shimmering coins' and 'Krakatoa fountains') or of their component ingredients ('thunder-grains', 'glimmer juice' and 'scorpion oil') invite us to inspect just how the word wizard Philip Pullman has done it. For further ideas along these lines, you could consult *Cracking Good Books* (Graham 1997).

There is some evidence that the NLS is encouraging teachers to read more children's books. If this is true, we must hope that they are appreciating what a treasure trove of literature we have in this country. We must also hope that the benefits that this could undoubtedly bring in creating and sustaining readers are not dissipated in teachers' obedient efforts to implement aspects of the NLS. Texts themselves teach, as Margaret Meek (1988) has often shown. Jill Pirrie (1987), a hugely successful poetry teacher, also claims that 'we do not go into the classroom alone; we take with us the greatest teachers of them all – books'. In the end, children will ignore our irrelevant teaching in their pursuit of what really matters. Here the poet, Miroslav Holub, shows us that children's agenda is always finer and more to the point than ours.

'Napoleon'

'Children, when was
Napoleon Bonaparte born?'
asks teacher.

'A thousand years ago,' the children say.
'A hundred years ago,' the children say.
'Last year,' the children say.
No one knows.

'Children, what did
Napoleon Bonaparte do?'
asks teacher.

'Won a war,' the children say.
'Lost a war,' the children say.
No one knows.

'Our butcher had a dog
called Napoleon,'
says Frantisek.

'The butcher used to beat him and the dog died of hunger,
a year ago.'

And all the children are now sorry for Napoleon.

References

Benton, M. and Fox, G. (1985) *Teaching Literature, Nine to Fourteen.* Oxford: Oxford University Press.

Blake, Q. *Mr Magnolia* (1980) London: Jonathan Cape.

Blake, Q. *Cockatoos* (1992) London: Jonathan Cape.

Blake, Q. *Simpkin* (1993) London: Jonathan Cape.

Britton, J. (1977) in Meek, M., Warlow, A. and Barton, G. *The Cool Web* (see below).

Brown, E. (1994) *Handa's Surprise* London: Walker Books.

Browning, R. (1993) *The Pied Piper of Hamelin* (illustrated by Amstutz, A.). London: Orchard Books.

Bruner, J. S. (1984) in Goelman, H., Oberg, A. and Smith, F. (eds) *Awakening to Literacy.* London: Heinemann Educational Books.

Cox, B. (1991) *Cox on Cox.* London: Hodder & Stoughton.

DfEE (1998) *The National Literacy Strategy Framework for Teaching.* London: DfEE.

Dickens, C. (1990) *A Christmas Carol* (illustrated by Innocenti, R.) London: Jonathan Cape.

Graham, J. (1997) *Cracking Good Books.* Sheffield: National Association for the Teaching of English.

Grainger, T. (1997), *Traditional Storytelling in the Primary Classroom.* Leamington Spa: Scholastic.

Holub, M. (1984) 'Napoleon' in *Speaking to you, A collection of Speaking Voice Poems* ed. Rosen, M. and Jackson, D. Basingstoke: Macmillan Education.

Mayne, W. illustrated by Heale, J. (1997) *Lady Muck.* London: Heinemann.

Meek, M. (1988) *How Texts Teach What Readers Learn.* South Woodchester: The Thimble Press.

Meek, M., Warlow, A. and Barton, G. (1977) *The Cool Web: The Pattern of Children's Reading.* London: The Bodley Head.

Pirrie, J. (1987) *On Common Ground.* London: Hodder & Stoughton.

Pullman, P. (1995) *The Firework-maker's Daughter.* London: Doubleday.

Sendak, M. (1963) *Where the Wild Things Are.* London: The Bodley Head.

The National Writing Project (1989). Walton-on-Thames: Thomas Nelson and Sons.

Tolkien, J.R.R. (1964) *Tree and Leaf.* London: Allen and Unwin.

Watanabe, S. (illustrated by Ohtome, Y.) (1980) *How Do I Eat It?* London: The Bodley Head.

Willes, M. (1983) *Children into Pupils.* London: Routledge & Kegan Paul.

Part III

Becoming writers

Chapter 10

Writers' workshops in action

Anne Rowe and Prue Goodwin

With the introduction of the National Literacy Strategy, the term *composition* has returned to the primary curriculum. There was a time when composition was a slot on the timetable; children found a title on the board and were given, for instance, the session after break to complete a piece of writing in their best handwriting and with as few spelling errors as possible. Composition in the *National Literacy Strategy Framework for Teaching* (DfEE 1998) is very different from that antiquated experience. It is concerned with exploring and developing the craft of writing during the Literacy Hour and is based on shared writing sessions when pupils are taught about the structure and organisation of written texts. The use of guided writing tasks is advised 'to teach children to write independently'. However, while the Literacy Hour facilitates direct teaching about writing, very little guidance has been given about providing opportunities for putting the skills into practice in extended pieces of writing. There is only a brief mention of extended writing in the *Framework* and that is in relation to older pupils, despite the requirement that children in Year 2 produce a sustained piece of writing for Key Stage 1 SATs. It is widely recognised that only by having opportunities to write at length will children become effective writers. Furthermore, to understand the uncertainties that all writers experience, it is necessary for children to learn about being a writer, engaged in a complex process. It could be argued that, even if only by implication, primary pupils need to have sessions when they can write at length, in the knowledge that what matters is the quality of the content of their work, and not its orthographic accuracy. One way of ensuring that all this happens is to make use of the approach known as writers' workshop.

Writers' workshop

Donald Graves (1983) first introduced the writers workshop approach in his book *Writing: Teachers and Children at Work*. Graves suggested that teachers should consider the practices of established writers in shaping classroom experiences. Writers make many choices when writing: choices about the topic, the form that their work will take and the way that they will express their ideas. These choices will be based on the purpose behind the writing and the needs of the audience. Most of their effort concentrates on the *process* of writing, shaping and polishing it until the finished writing, the *product*, is ready for publishing. The workshop approach allows teachers to replicate these choices in the classroom. Many people have argued for the centrality of the writing process to all aspects of the curriculum but time constraints can make this difficult to achieve. Yet time is essential for shaping and polishing: time to write and time to think, to make choices, to change one's mind and to share with other writers, with all the discussion that such activities inevitably involve. Writers' workshop is a very important arena for developing knowledge about the practice of writing, incorporating both the idea gathering and the craft into every-day classroom experience. It has been developed in the hands of enthusiastic teachers who have shaped it to fit the needs of their particular pupils. This matching has been made easier with increased knowledge about how writing skills are acquired and woven together.

Teachers as writers

An important feature of writers' workshop is that teachers engage in writing alongside the children. Most teachers of painting, music, ceramics or drama are experienced practitioners in their fields. They cannot teach without making clear what they expect. The learner has a 'journey' to travel and there is someone alongside, someone who has already made the trip – the teacher (Graves 1983). There is no doubt that writing along with the children provides a powerful model. For example, children watching an adult compose can observe how most writers go through similar stages, how tentative even experienced writers are initially, how they need to rethink and change things, and how a first draft can look really messy. Adults and children have common experiences, often facing the same problems when confronting the complexities of the activity. Sharing these experiences helps to develop a community of writers in the classroom.

The pattern of the workshop

Anyone watching early-years pupils engrossed in their writing will notice their confidence in themselves as writers. They demonstrate their implicit knowledge, gained by the assiduous watching of adult behaviour, of how writing works. They seem to be aware that writing does not begin with the conventions of transcription but grows towards them. They need opportunities to explore a wide range of writing materials and tools, finding out, for example, which mark maker is the most comfortable. They will also begin to make use of other supports, such as word banks and dictionaries. Allowing time for very young writers to demonstrate what they know about writing and its uses is essential. For the emergent writer, the initial response is all that matters. Only later, as they move beyond the egocentric phase can they take the needs of the reader into consideration. This is not to suggest that writers workshops are inappropriate to the infant classroom – far from it – but that the full workshop will probably be most appropriate at Key Stage 2.

Originally writers' workshops were totally child centred providing opportunities for children to make all the choices and to write for their own purposes. However, they have evolved a great deal over time. The topics can be directed, very general (such as a funny experience or a recent happening) or a completely free choice. Children can be asked some days in advance to think and talk about their ideas. For example, they can be asked to note down two topics that they might like to write about and given time to talk about their choices with a partner. Usually this generates ideas which they can jot down before they are forgotten. The teacher should do the same, writing her ideas on a flip chart, talking about those ideas and suggesting why one of them appeals as first choice. The Literacy Hour sessions would be an ideal time to explore the range of ways of getting going with a piece of writing.

The time to write should be as quiet as possible. Children should be encouraged not to worry about spellings at the time of writing but to have a go, to use an initial letter or to leave a space (they will have time to return and find conventional spellings during the proof-reading session). Everyone should write, teacher included, with no interruptions to break the concentration while getting the ideas down. The length of time of this quiet time will depend upon the stamina and experience of the writers. Despite the 'silence', this is usually a very popular part of the workshop.

After writing for a short period, there should be a chance to read some of the first draft to a response partner and to talk about the work in progress. This is a good time for teachers to make use of their own writing and to talk about first drafts, demonstrating that getting the ideas down is all important. There is bound to be evidence of false starts, changes of mind, rejection of specific words or even whole sections. The tentative nature of first drafts and the likelihood of a messy page needs to be modelled again and again.

The routine of time to talk and time to write continues as children become engaged in different aspects of the process towards 'publication'. Writers are often blind to holes in their own work, because they have the whole script in their head, no matter how disjointed the written text might be. Reading the text aloud to themselves can help to identify the gaps. A response partner may point out places where the meanings are unclear, or where readers need more help. This leads to a need to *redraft*.

Very young children rarely look at their writing again; so redrafting is not appropriate. Gradually, as they become more experienced, redrafting takes the form of changing surface details, such as changing a spelling or adding punctuation. However, drafting should eventually be separated from transcription skills and should be seen as the reshaping and clarifyfication of meaning. Children begin to see the purpose of redrafting when they have regularly experienced their teachers modelling this behaviour with their own scripts. For some children, writing is such a laborious task that special help is required for all redrafting.

Conferencing with children about their writing takes place at any point during the drafting stages. It is a time for children to talk and teachers to listen proactively, asking questions and suggesting routes that will take the writing forward. This may involve looking back at plans, talking about impact and structure, discussing a satisfying end, etc. It is very time consuming and it is unrealistic to expect to conference on every piece of work with every pupil. However, it is possible to meet each child on a regular basis to consider their writing, as usually happens with reading. The meeting can be prepared by the teacher by reading and responding to the work under discussion, noting comments and questions on 'Post-it®' notes which are placed appropriately. These can be removed during the talk and stuck on the back of the draft to be actioned or ignored by the writer.

When writers have completed their compositions, they move from being creators to being secretaries. At this proof-reading stage, youngsters need encouragement to read through the script carefully and to consider spelling and punctuation. This is the time to decide on the best means of publishing the work. It is not always necessary to make a fair copy. It can be read to different groups or made into a tape. All writers are delighted to see their work in the hands of appreciative readers.

Organising materials

Workshops should be organised according to the needs of the class and purpose of the session. All necessary materials, for both the creation of the script and its transcription to a fair copy, need to be readily available. Early drafts can be written in a book or on sheets of paper kept in a folder. Each child needs to store notes, brainstorms and first drafts as a record of the whole process of writing and their progress as writers. Books or folders are not just containers. A record of the work 'published' by the young author can be kept on the front cover. The inside cover or flap can have notes about ideas for future pieces of writing to which additions can be made at any time. On the back cover, under a heading such as 'I can now . . .', the child can record what writing conventions have been acquired. If the writing is done in a book, to ease the task of drafting, writers can use one side only of a double spread. The other is then free for amendments, comments from response partners or editors. Because this is somewhat uneconomical, folders are probably more sensible and have the advantage of allowing more flexibility. Using loose paper allows a writer to integrate major amendments by cutting and pasting the text in the same way as on a word processor.

The importance of the talk

As talking is an important part of each session, the workshop is necessarily an interactive experience. The usual pattern involves the following:

- Discussion about getting going with writing. The exchange of ideas will act as a means of 'priming the pump' before settling to write.
- Sharing first ideas with a partner. This works as a reassurance to youngsters that they have made a satisfactory start.
- Response to work in progress. This acts as a support mechanism allowing the writer to hear and gauge the success of a piece.
- Sharing and discussing the final piece of writing.

There are times when discussion will be teacher led and others when children can work in pairs or groups without overt adult intervention. Children learn how to talk about writing, and what to talk about, from listening to adults. A response group provides a way of modelling the skills of editing. A group of writers share their work and the teacher models how to respond, encouraging the children to contribute. Children quickly learn the language of supportive criticism. As they become more experienced they can be paired to create response partnerships. Talking about which comments are useful will make the role of a response partner clear. It is useful to draw up a list of comments that writers find helpful and, obversely, to discuss things that writers do not like to hear about their efforts. The 'helpful comments' list can be duplicated and stuck into each folder. This list might include comments such as: 'It's a terrific beginning. It makes you want to read on.' 'Why would she do that, or say that?' 'I'm not sure about this bit. Tell me what you were trying to say.' 'That bit is magic!' 'I like the ending.'

Writing and the Literacy Hour

Over the past decade our practical knowledge about the craft of writing has grown and teachers have been able to plan to explore the specifics of different genres. Many have combined opportunities to write freely with workshops directed towards a precisely focused learning objective. This can be achieved successfully without compromising the underlying principles of the workshop approach. The teacher still takes her place as role model and chooses the focus. Her most important task is to provide sufficient time, in which children can shape, hone, discuss and share their work. The Literacy Hour provides time to discuss and practise particular elements of the craft of writing: getting going, different ways of planning, rewriting and rejecting, integrating dialogue, developing character or setting, how punctuation supports the reader etc. For example, Key Stage 2 pupils are required to 'write character sketches, focusing on small details to evoke sympathy or dislike'. This could make an exciting session exploring vocabulary and the effective use of syntax to create a character. Another aspect of the Literacy Hour involves the writer as reader. Writers learn from each other and it can be argued that the best teachers of writing in our classrooms are the good writers represented on our book shelves. Reading and writing, for the actively engaged, are but two sides of the same paper and, what we recognise in the art of the one, we can use in the other.

There are many books which will serve our purposes. Books about being a writer (e.g. *The Moon and Me* by Betsy Byars (1991)), about the nature of writing (e.g. *The Better Brown Stories* by Allan Ahlberg (1997)) and examples of outstandingly well told tales (e.g. *Clockwork* by Philip Pullman (1996)). A book shared for the pleasure of reading together can subsequently provide insights into writing. Almost any selection of books will reveal different ways of handling key moments in a story such as the opening or introduction of a main character. Attention can be drawn to aspects such as effective vocabulary, use of dialogue and other techniques for advancing the narrative. It is useful to have examples of different forms. Letters, for example, can be considered when reading *Dear Greenpeace* (James 1991) or the series *Don't Forget to Write* (Selway 1993), *Wish You Were Here* (Selway 1996) and *What Can I Write* (Selway 1998). Picture books can be particularly useful because of their originality and because they can be read and discussed in their entirety in one session. Books can model different story shapes, such as cumulative stories, circular tales or stories within stories (see Chapter 11 by Mauren Lewis). For more experienced young writers, short stories and novels can introduce more intriguing narrative construction or complex descriptive passages, and we must not forget that many children will want to write in non-fiction genres, also required by the *Framework*. Examples of well-written reports, recounts and other non-fiction texts must all feature in the primary classroom. There is plenty of advice forthcoming about the different genres of fiction and non-fiction and about books that, for example, play with format, layout and graphics. There is also a growing number of books that show innovative ways of linking children's writing development with bookmaking skills (for example, Paul Johnson's (1990) *A Book of One's Own*). To have a display of books on one particular theme provides the opportunity to learn from the best.

Conclusion

Gaining confidence as a writer is essential if Literacy Hours on well-structured texts are to be of any value to pupils. Writing can be a risky business. Confidence and security encourage risk taking, something that the youngest writers seem very willing to do but which requires a lot of support as children become older. Many teachers who have used the workshop approach agree that it is of great benefit to children, increasing their independence as writers and influencing their work at times other than during the workshop. So much of the writing diet in school involves producing one-off pieces with little chance to be worked on and improved. Writers' workshop, as a regular part of a child's experience, will provide insights into the nature and craft of writing which, with time to write and talk in the classroom community of writers, will lead to the independence and confidence that we all desire.

References

Ahlberg, A. (1997) *The Better Brown Stories*. London: Puffin Books.

Byars, B. (1991) *The Moon and Me*. London: The Bodley Head.

DfEE (1998) *The National Literacy Strategy: Framework for Teaching*. London: DfEE.

Graves, D. (1983) *Writing: Teachers and Children at Work*. Portsmouth, New Hampshire: Heinemann Educational Books.

James, S. (1991) *Dear Greenpeace*. London: Walker Books.

Johnson, P. (1990) *A Book of One's Own*. London: Hodder & Stoughton.

Pullman, P. (1996) *Clockwork*. London: Transworld Children's Books.

Selway, M. (1993) *Don't Forget to Write*. London: Red Fox.

Selway, M. (1996) *Wish You Were Here*. London: Red Fox.

Selway, M. (1998) *What Can I Write*. London: Red Fox.

Chapter 11

Developing children's narrative writing using story structures

Maureen Lewis

The problem

'They're all right on beginnings. It's the middle where it all gets lost. How can I help them with middles and ends?' This remark, made by a Key Stage 2 teacher attending an in-service course on writing, was greeted with nods and murmurs of agreement from the rest of the Key Stage 1 and Key Stage 2 teachers present. There was general agreement that, although children might write a developed opening with some skill, e.g. writing a detailed and imaginative description of the characters or the setting, the overall shape of the story could still be weak and unclear. Many pupils, these teachers felt, could write a simple sequence of events (an 'and then' story as one teacher described it) but attempts to write more complex stories had often become confused and incoherent.

The problem identified by this group of teachers echoes comments from the reports by the SCAA (1997a, b) evaluating the 1996 SATs. In the writing task, SCAA (1997a) found that a key difference in children's writing (and the levels that they scored) was 'the way the writing was structured' and that some children spent 'all their time and energy in explaining the opening'. They noted that some of the texts 'were based on *well-defined structures* with which children were evidently *familiar*' and that, 'where children did not have this kind of support, they had more difficulty in producing an *appropriately organised* piece of writing. This was particularly the case with stories where unshaped rambling pieces contained undeveloped events following one another in rapid succession and lacking a conclusion.' (my italics throughout).

The problem for teaching and learning appears to be twofold:

- how to help children to recognise that stories have structures beyond a simplistic beginning, middle and end;
- how to help them to use this understanding to support their own story planning and writing.

SCAA (1997a) recommend that teachers should 'provide children with opportunities to work on structuring and concluding their stories'. One effective strategy for this, they suggest, is 'the use of literary models, the organisational features of which can be explicitly discussed with the children.

The strategy of using a book as a literary model is well established. Many teachers for example might use a book such as *Rosie's Walk* (Hutchins 1970) as a model for writing a story of a walk around the playground, or *Funnybones* (Ahlberg and Ahlberg 1990) as a model for a story of the skeleton living in a school and exploring the school at night. However, such work can be taken further and in this chapter I shall discuss how using groups of books which share a common story structure can be used to enhance children's story writing. Working with a class of Year 4 children and their teacher, using picture books as models, we were interested to discover whether the following were true:

* We could identify a range of common story structures.
* Children could identify these structures for themselves.
* The use of graphic story structure frames helped children to record the story structures that they had identified and to plan their own stories.
* The occasional, focused use of writing frames scaffolded some children in writing.
* The children's ability to write stories improved.

The theoretical background

One starting point for the work was based on insights from story grammar. Much of our knowledge about story structure comes from literary critics such as Vladimir Propp (1968) who searched for a universal story structure to be found in popular Russian folk tales, and also from the work on story grammar developed throughout the 1970s and early 1980s. At that time, cognitive psychologists became interested in individuals' mental representations (schema) of story components and how such components fitted together (Mandler and Johnson 1977). Story grammar is characterised as 'a set of rules that will define both a text's structure and an individual's mental representation of story structure' (Whaley 1981). Several researchers developed story grammars (Mandler and Johnson 1977, Rumelhart 1978, Stein and Glenn 1979). Mandler and Johnson, for example, argued that there are six major story elements: setting, beginning, reaction, attempt, outcome and ending. It is argued that, as our experience of stories grows, so does our knowledge about stories and we can draw on this knowledge to help us to predict and understand what is happening when we meet new stories. Others have proposed alternative structures but, whatever the particular structures used, researchers have generally agreed that readers and listeners use story schema in three ways:

* as a set of expectations for the structure of a story;
* to facilitate comprehension of a story;
* to improve memory and recall of a story.

Strategies such as prediction tasks, scrambled stories, cloze tasks and retelling tasks were recommended (Whaley 1981) to help children to draw on and develop their story schema. From this early work on story structures, other classroom practices have been developed to help children explicitly to recognise the story structures that they encountered. Story mapping (Benton and Fox 1985), story shapes (Bentley and Rowe 1990), story comparison charts (Worthy and Bloodgood 1993) and story structure charts (Newman 1989) are now sometimes used to enhance children's understanding of the books and stories that they encounter. Such practices help pupils to recognise key events in a story, can help them to develop insights into characters' motives and can help them to develop character sketches and to appreciate the importance of setting. It is clear from the many accounts of such strategies and their popularity in classrooms that all these activities are viewed as useful in developing children's story schema.

However, many of these activities are based upon helping children to make explicit what they have learnt from reading or listening to a text. More recently, work on textual genres has encouraged teachers to deconstruct written texts with children as a precursor to then constructing further texts using the same structural features (Derewianka 1990, Wing Jan 1991, Lewis and Wray 1995). One strategy which has been developed to help children to make the link between non-fiction textual structures and their own writing is the use of writing frames (Lewis and Wray 1996). The success of this strategy in scaffolding children's writing suggested that frames might also prove useful in narrative writing.

The work in school

Although the account and work samples that follow are all from Year 4 children, the ideas can easily be adapted for older or younger pupils. Each week a selection of picture-books was assembled, all of which shared a similar story structure. The story structures identified were as follows:

- cumulative stories (add-on stories);
- reverse cumulative stories (take away stories);
- journey stories: linear journeys (from A to B), return journeys (from A to B to A) and circular journeys (from A to A);
- turning point stories: character, circumstances or physical characteristics;
- wasted-wishes stories;
- simple problem and resolution stories;
- days-of-the-week stories.

Further details of these, together with examples are given in as an appendix at the end of this chapter.

Picture-books were ideal for our purpose for, not only are they appealing texts in their own right, they also offer a complete text in brief and so allow children to sample several examples in a relatively short space of time (Lewis 1997). They also allow the teacher to differentiate the text for varied reading abilities, e.g. *Rosie's Walk* (Hutchins 1968) and *Hail to the Mail* (Marhak 1992) both provide models of a circular journey text but make very different reading demands during their use in independent activities. Once a selection of books was assembled, a five-step sequence was followed as each set of book were used.

The five-step approach

Immersion in the text type

At the start of the session the children were told that that they were going to hear some stories and that, although all these books and stories were different, there was something the same about them. They were asked to pay particular attention to the 'pattern' of the story. Later this terminology was changed to 'structure' of the story. The children coped well with this metalanguage, having experienced what it meant in context. Two or three of the selected books were read to the whole class (or sometimes this activity was undertaken as oral story telling) and the children encouraged to enjoy and respond to the stories.

Explicit discussion of structure and concrete recording of the structure

The children were then asked about the structure of the story and how it was the same in all the examples that they had enjoyed. The structure was explicitly discussed and this was followed by some kind of whole-class mapping and graphic representation of one of the shared books. This visual representation of the story structure was drawn or scribed by the teacher and the links between the graphic representation and the story were also re-articulated as teacher 'think alouds' as the drawing progressed This move, from recognition into a visual representation of the structure, was important for many of the children and seemed to help them to fix the structure in their minds by moving from an internal abstract concept to an external explicit object.

Independent recording of the structure

The children then worked in pairs to read and map a further example of a story which had a similar structure to that shared in the whole class activity. Here books could be differentiated according to reading ability. Figure 11.1 shows an example of a mapping of an A-to-B journey story structure. This structure is as follows: start of journey, events *en route* (either people or physical landmarks met), reaching destination and concluding act. The events *en route* usually represent problems encountered and overcome.

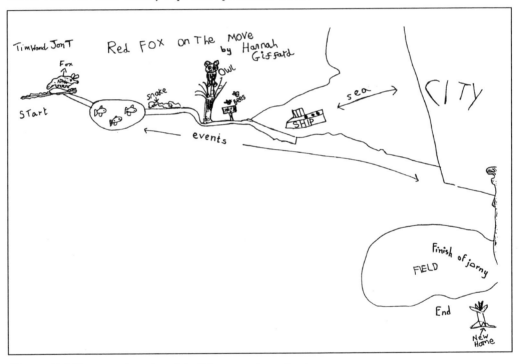

Figure 11.1 The mapping of an A-to-B journey story structure

On some occasions the children were given a mapping frame on which to record the structure of the story that they had read. These mapping frames provided a visual prompt to the story structure. Figure 11.2 shows a completed cumulative story structure mapping frame. The design of this frame helps the child to recognise the elements of the structure opening event or problem, the addition of one new element each time, the explosive climax when overload is reached, and the concluding event to close the story – or to start the sequence again. We also used further graphic mapping frames designed to reflect the story structure for turning point stories, circular stories and 'take-away' stories.

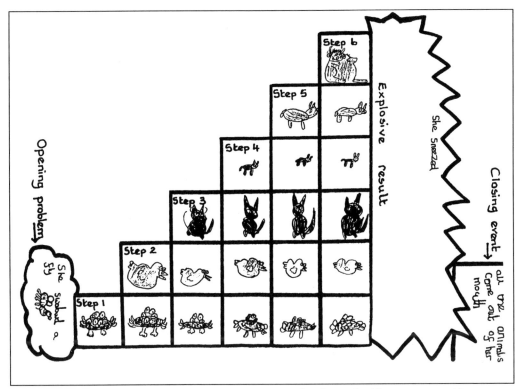

Figure 11.2 Completed cumulative story structure mapping frame for *There was an old woman who swallowed a fly...*

Using the structure to plan their own story

From independent recording of the story structure, the children then moved into planning their own story using the same structure. For some children this involved moving straight into a written story plan but for many children it involved some kind of planning frame to help them. This planning frame was often a further blank version of the mapping frame that they had just used, enabling them to see the links clearly. Figures 11.3 and 11.4 show a child's mapping of *Mrs Armitage on Wheels* (Blake 1987) using a text deconstruction frame, followed by his planning frame for his own story based on the structure.

Drafting the story and sharing the drafts in a plenary

The plans were then used to write a first draft of a story and these drafts were shared in a plenary session when the rest of the class listened and commented on whether the structure was clear, and the story coherent. We never had time within one session to complete the writing process but often the children redrafted and finished their stories during the rest of the week. Figure 11.5 shows the first draft of the cumulative story based on the mapping and planning structures shown in Figures 11.3 and 11.4.

At the first draft stage some children had simple writing frames with sentence starters to help them. Often these were placed on the computer. Figure 11.6 shows the first draft of a cumulative story written by two less able writers using a frame to help them. The given frame is underlined.

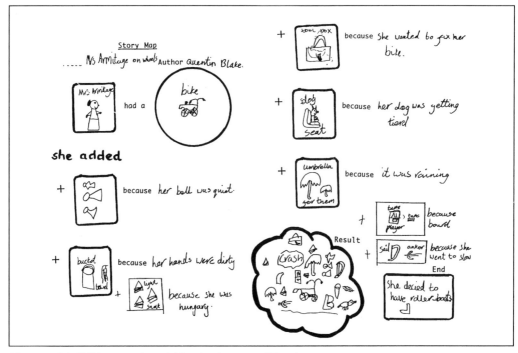

Figure 11.3 Child's mapping of *Mrs Armitage on Wheels*

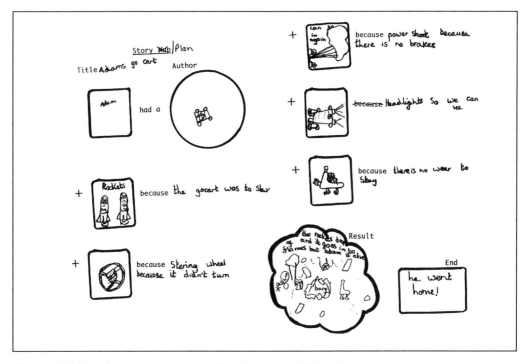

Figure 11.4 Planning frame constructed by the same child for his own story

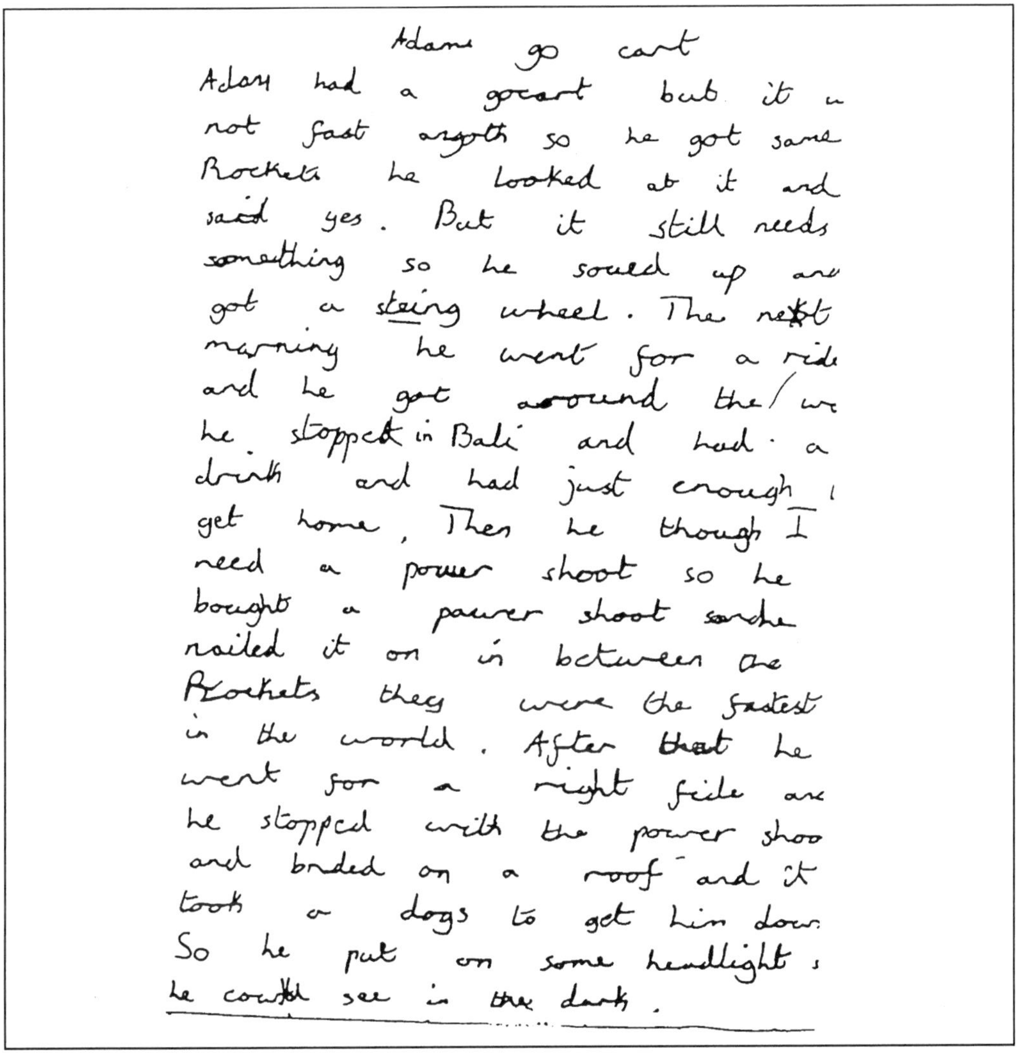
Adams go cart
Adam had a gocart but it w
not fast anogth so he got same
Rockets he looked at it and
said yes. But it still needs
something so he soued up and
got a steing wheel. The next
marning he went for a ride
and he got around the/ wr
he stopped in Bali and had a
drink and had just enough t
get home, Then he though I
need a power shoot so he
bought a pawer shoot sandhe
nailed it on in between the
Rockets they were the fastest
in the world. After that he
went for a night fide and
he stopped with the power shoo
and bnded on a roof and it
took a dogs to get him down
So he put on some headlight s
he couthd see in the dark.

Figure 11.5 First draft of the story based on the mapping in Figure 11.3 and the planning frame in Figure 11.4

Did it make a difference?

In judging whether the work had any impact, we can look at evidence from the children's behaviour during the sessions, the children's work, child interview data, incidents that occurred outside the writing sessions and the class teacher's views.

The class contained the usual mix of children with a variety of attitudes and skills but throughout the term the children appeared fascinated by what they did. Brian Cambourne (1997) argues that two of the criteria for judging successful literacy teaching strategies are 'active engagement' and 'spill-over' (i.e. evidence that the children spontaneously apply what they have learnt on other occasions and make links within other areas of the curriculum). Both of these features appeared to be evident:

One suny morning miss mcintosh was in the stockroom getting books Suddenly the door slammed . "Help! Help! Get me out," shouted miss mcintosh. So mr statton pulled but the door did not open. Then miss lewis came to help. and they both pulled, but the door did not open. Then Jason came to help. Mr statton and miss lewis and Jason pulled, but the door did not open. Then Tracey came to help. Mr statton and miss lewis and Jason and Tracey pulled and pulled.

THE DOOR OPENED and everyone all fell down . miss mcintosh was saved so everyone shouted hurrah. and had a cup of tea.

Figure 11.6 First draft of a cumulative story written by two less able children using a writing frame

Interviewer:	What about 'active engagement'?
Class teacher:	I thought that they were superb because they had all morning and there was very little sign of anybody starting to mess around or whatever. There were large numbers who were always keen to carry on and finish – even after two and a half hours. And it wasn't novelty value . . . it would have easily worn off before the end. They were very well engaged.

Similarly many of the children interviewed talked about their interest in what they had done and how they wanted to continue. Ellie's comments are typical: 'Those story patterns. They were really interesting. It made me want to write a story. I thought my "take-away" story was really good. It was funny.'

'Spill-over' occurred on many occasions with children finding books in their reading sessions which demonstrated structures that they recognised, or elements of a story where they spotted a link. It might have been useful to start a class list or data base to which they could have added their discoveries.

John:	I was hearing my little brother read the end bit of *The Gingerbread Man*. That's kind of a 'take-away' story isn't it? Not all of it. The bit where the fox eats him bit by bit. And it's 'add on' too – all those people who chase him.
Class teacher:	Kylie said that she went home and read, after we'd done our session together. She then went home and looked for the same kind of patterns. So she was clearly up and away.

The class teacher felt that the work had had an effect on the quality of work of many of the children and was particularly pleased with its effect on the quality of the writing of the less able children.

Class teacher:	To start with they did find it a bit difficult – when they were doing that first one some of them found it difficult but last weekend I took all their

books home and went through the last story and most had got a structure – some sort of pattern – and the less able children too.

Many children claimed in their interviews that using a structure frame to help them to plan had been helpful and they were all able to talk, with varying degrees of fluency about story structures that they now knew. The class teacher felt that the children had moved on in their use of story plans because of the explicit teaching.

Class teacher: When we did stories, the plans for stories were character and setting. But I could never get my head around finding some sort of structure to base the story on because I always believed it was up to them actually to think of the structure themselves, whereas now I can see far better how to guide them, and the results are definitely better just reading what they've come up with.

One of the criticisms that can be levelled against such a structured approach to supporting children's writing and the use of frames is that it can stifle individuality and creativity. There was little evidence of this with the work produced. The wide variety of individual stories that the class wrote each week showed that children still used very different characters, settings and ideas within the structures that they were using.

Interviewer: Can it stifle children's creative initiative?
Class teacher: I don't think you do stifle that. Because I remember way back to when I qualified, we weren't allowed to teach them how to paint were we? They had to express themselves. I rarely got anything good in art, whereas now art is quite structured. You do drawings from life or whatever. You do looking at other artist's work – all those sort of things and the quality of art is much better. You see those three-dimensional things, in the class (indicates). I long since realised that you've got to teach them something, because people can only actually be expressive when they can build on some inner knowledge. I think with structures for stories in English we're doing the same thing. They can be as imaginative as they like because they have the tools with which to build. We owe it to them to give them the groundwork. That's what primary education is about. We give them the groundwork and then, when they are able they can take off. They can fly. There are children now who I am sure can write without the mapping or writing frames anymore but can use the knowledge that is now their own.

The Literacy Hour

An explicit approach to teaching children about story structures and the subsequent use of such knowledge to frame children's own writing fits in well with the approach of *The National Literacy Strategy: Framework for Teaching* (DfEE 1998). The five-step approach can also be easily adapted to use in the literacy hour. The sample of books could be read to pupils in story time over two or three days. Then, within the Literacy Hour, the books could be reintroduced, the structure discussed and the whole class mapping of one story undertaken, with the teacher modelling the mapping as a shared writing activity. This would take place during the 15 minutes' whole-class work. An appropriate word level aspect of the text could be developed in the following 15 minutes (e.g. prepositions such as 'over', 'under', 'round', etc., if you were looking at journey stories). In the independent work slot, children could begin their own mapping of another example of the same type of structure and in subsequent days they could plan and draft a story using that structure.

This chapter has described one term's work with one class of children and so any claims that can be drawn from it must be limited. However, these children's increasingly confident use of story structures and the improvements in their ability to produce a coherent story suggests that explicit teaching about story structure and making links between structure mapping and planning is a useful strategy, worthy of further exploration.

Appendix

Cumulative stories

In these step-by-step stories, events or objects or characters are continuously added to preceding events, objects or characters until a climax (often explosive) is reached.

> *The Enormous Turnip* – traditional.
> *Hairy McClarey from Donaldson's Dairy* by Lynley Dodd (1985). London: Penguin Children's Books.
> *Mr Gumpy's Outing* by John Burningham (1978). London: Penguin Children's Books.

Reverse cumulative stories

In these stories, something is progressively diminished until it disappears altogether or something returns to the status quo.

> 'The story of Horace', in *The Faber Story Book* edited by Kathleen Lines (1961). London: Faber and Faber.
> *Five Little Ducks* by Ian Beck (1993). London: Orchard.

Journey stories

In journey stories the participant usually meets people, animals or physical landmarks along the route. These meetings provide a moment where something happens – often a problem and resolution.

Linear journeys (from A to B)
> *Red Fox on the Move* by Hannah Gifford (1995). London: Francis Lincoln.
> *On the Way Home* by Jill Murphy (1984). London: Macmillan.

Return journeys (from A to B to A)
> *The Shopping Basket* by John Burningham (1980). London: Jonathan Cape.
> *We're Going on a Bear Hunt* by Michael Rosen (1993). London: Walker Books.

Circular journeys (from A to A)
> *Rosie's Walk* by Pat Hutchins (1970). London: Penguin Children's Books.
> *The Bad-tempered Ladybird* by Eric Carle (1982). London: Penguin Children's Books.

Circular stories (not journeys)

A series of acts at the end of which the character is back at the beginning. A variant on this is the wasted-wishes circular tale. In these stories, wishes are granted in return for some good deed but these are wasted owing to some flaw (e.g. greed or stupidity) in the character and they end up back where they started

There's a Hole in My Bucket – traditional song.

The Old Woman Who Lived in a Vinegar Bottle – traditional.

Turning-point stories: character, circumstances or physical characteristics

In these stories some distinctive aspect of a character's personality, circumstances or physical appearance is forgrounded. An event takes place because of this characteristic, as a result of which the character is changed by the end of the story. Often a 'bad' characteristic is changed or punished, and a good character is recognised and rewarded.

King Midas and the Golden Touch – traditional.

The Frog Prince – traditional.

The problem and resolution structure

This is a very common structure. It is best first introduced in a simple form of one problem, solved quickly. More complex versions can then be introduced.

Alfie Gets in First by Shirley Hughes (1991). London: Red Fox.

Are You There Bear? by Ron Marris (1986). London: Penguin Children's Books.

The days-of-the-week structure

The days of the weeks are gone through sequentially and on each day a same but different event occurs (e.g. the caterpillar eats each day but different food); on the final day a climax is reached and something new happens.

The Very Hungry Caterpillar by Eric Carle (1974). London: Penguin Children's Books.

References

Ahlberg, A. and Ahlberg, J. (1990) *Funnybones*. London: Mammoth.

Beck, I. (1993) *Five Little Ducks*. London: Orchard.

Bentley. D. and Rowe, A. (1990) *Group Reading in the Primary Classroom*. Reading: Reading and Language Information Centre, The University of Reading.

Benton, M. and Fox, G. (1985) *Teaching Literature 9–14*. Oxford: Oxford University Press.

Blake, Q. (1987) *Mrs Armitage on Wheels*. London: Jonathan Cape.

Burningham, J. (1978) *Mr Grumpy's Outing*. London: Penguin Children's Books.

Burningham, J. (1980) *The Shopping Basket*. London: Jonathan Cape.

Cambourne, B. (1997) 'Key principles of good literacy teaching', Talk and Unpublished Conference Paper. Manchester: United Kingdom Reading Association.

Carle, E. (1974) *The Very Hungry Caterpillar*. London: Penguin Children's Books.

Carle, E. (1982) *The Bad-tempered Ladybird*. London: Penguin Children's Books.

Derewianka, B. (1990) *Exploring How Texts Work*. Newtown, New South Wales: PETA.

DfEE (1988) *The National Literacy Strategy Framework for Teaching*. London: DfEE.

Dodd, L. (1985) *Hairy McClarey from Donaldson's Dairy*. London: Penguin Children's Books.

Gifford, H. (1988) *Red Fox on the Move*. London: Frances Lincoln.

Hughes, S. (1991) *Alfie Gets in First*. London: Red Fox.

Hutchins, P. (1970) *Rosie's Walk*. London: Penguin Children's Books.

Lewis D. H. (1997) 'Working with picture books in the primary classroom'. Talk and Unpublished Conference Paper. Manchester: United Kingdom Reading Association.

Lewis, M. and Wray, D. (1995) *Developing Children's Non-fiction Writing: Working with Writing Frames*. Leamington Spa: Scholastic.

Lewis, M. and Wray, D. (1996) *Writing Frames: Scaffolding Children's Non-fiction Writing*. Reading: Reading and Language Information Centre, The University of Reading.

Lines, K. (ed.) (1961) *The Faber Story Book*. London: Faber and Faber.

Mandler, J. M. and Johnson, N. S. (1977) 'Remembrance of things parsed: story structure and recall', *Cognitive Psychology* **9**, 111–151.

Maris, R. (1986) *Are You There Bear?* London: Penguin Children's Books.

Murphy, J. (1984) *On the Way Home*. London: Macmillan.

Newman, J. M. (1989) 'Online: the flexible page', *Language Arts* **66**(4), 457– 464.

Propp, V. (1968) *The Morphology of the Folktale*, 2nd edn, transl. Law Scott, L. Baltimore: Port City Press.

Rosen, M. (1993) *We're Going on a Bear Hunt*. London: Walker Books.

Rumelhart, D. E. (1978) 'Understanding and summarising brief stories', in *Basic Processes in Reading; Perception and Comprehension*, LaBerge, D. and Samuels, S.J. (eds). Hillsdale, New Jersey: Lawrence Erlbaum Associates.

SCAA (1997a) *Standards at Key Stage 1. English and Mathematics. Report on the 1996 National Curriculum Assessments for 7-year-olds*. London: HMSO.

SCAA (1997b) *Standards at Key Stage 2. English, Mathematics and Science. Report on the 1996 National Curriculum Assessments for 11-year-olds*. London: HMSO.

Stein N. L. and Glenn C. (1979) 'An analysis of story comprehension in elementary school children', in *New Directions in Discourse Proceeding*, Freedie, R.O. (ed.). Norwood, New Jersey: Ablex.

Whaley, J. F. (1981) 'Story grammars and reading instruction', *The Reading Teacher* **34**(8), 762–771.

Wing Jan, L. (1991) *Write Ways. Modelling Writing Forms*. Oxford: Oxford University Press.

Worthy, M. J. and Bloodgood, J. W. (1993) 'Enhancing reading instruction through Cinderella tales', *The Reading Teacher* **6**(4), 290–301.

Chapter 12

The problems and possibilities of non-fiction writing
David Wray and Maureen Lewis

Looking at non-fiction writing

We shall begin by looking at three pieces of non-fiction writing.

Danny is a Year 7 pupil who has been asked to write in a science lesson on how the solar system was made. Here is his explanation:

> How was our solar system made. One day a man called god woke up and fancied a change. He said I will have a red planet a green and blue planet and one with rings round it. And a few glowing spots to make it look pretty and I will play basketball spin shots so some spin. Two hours later a massive energy bang it blew god house down. When he opened his eyes he saw his creation and then he lived for 2 whole years after that he died. Before he died he created two humans called Adam and Eve and if it wasn't for him we would not be here today. Nobody knows if there was life on these planets all we know is people live on earth exsept for god he died. We don't know what it looks like here is a picture of what I think it looks like.

Adam (Year 6) has been asked to write an account of the Spanish Armada. Here is the first half page (of three pages altogether) of what he wrote:

> 'Spainish Armada'
> A long time ago in 1588 King Philip II wanted to invade England. Suddenly a letter came from the Netherlands and it said 'I'm sorry but I'm not going to fight with you because I feel sick.' So the genral said none of them are coming to fight us and so it looks like just us and England this time. But in Spain they were building a very big ship called the armada. When they had builte it they had 130 ship in side the armada had 8,000 sailors and 20,000 soldirs and 180 priests to make people Cathlic again.

Finally Edward (Year 5) has written a discussion paper about life in Tudor times. Here are some extracts from his piece:

> 'Tudor Times'
> The issue we are discussing is whether women and children were treated harshly in Tudor times.
>   Most people living in Tudor times did not think so. They might have argued that children were untamed beasts and when they beat them they would become more tame.
>   Men might also have argued that women should know their place so that beating them was not wrong .

Nowadays, however, most people think that women and children in Tudor times were treated harshly. They claim that men chose their wives and the parents chose a husband for their daughter which is not fair because they might not love them.

Furthermore they argue that poor people in Tudor times had to work hard at a young age.

My own opinion is that women and children were treated harshly in Tudor times. I believe this because women and children were not treated as individuals.

Most teachers would agree that, while each of these three pieces of writing may be interesting and 'creative', the first two are inadequate responses to the task the children were set. They are both written in ways which owe more to imaginative stories than to the structures expected of writing in science and history respectively. A large number of children appear to have similar problems in writing and their difficulty is one of matching the way that you write, the style that you choose and the structure that you use to the particular purposes for writing that you encounter in various curriculum subjects.

Yet, in the third piece of writing, the child has apparently solved this problem. His writing is structured to fit the demands of a discussion paper; it shows evidence of appropriate choice of vocabulary and sentence structure. Because of these features it gives the appearance of a much more mature piece of writing. Yet the author, while clearly a reasonably bright child, was younger than the authors of the first two pieces and, in fact, not noticeably a higher achiever in other aspects of school work. How then has he been enabled to produce such writing? It is central to the argument of this chapter that the answer to this question lies in the nature of the teaching that Edward has received, teaching which has ensured that he is aware of the structural and language demands of particular writing tasks and does not approach them with misguided assumptions about how writing works in this context.

What are the essential characteristics of this teaching? These are twofold. First, it rests upon an analysis of the problems that children face in producing effective non-fiction writing and attempts to help them to overcome these problems. Secondly, it is guided by a model of effective teaching. We shall explore both these aspects.

The problems of non-fiction writing

Writing causes several problems for those not skilled at it (and even for those who are!) From talking to teachers and observing children during the Exeter Extending Literacy (EXEL) Project,[1] funded by the Nuffield Foundation, we have identified four major problem areas:

- the problem of the blank page;
- the difference between writing and talking;
- the 'and then' syndrome;
- the structure of texts.

We shall now discuss these in more detail.

The problem of the blank page

Most writers will agree that the most difficult part of writing anything is the first line or two. Getting started can be so difficult, even for experienced writers, that they invent a number of 'delaying tactics' (sharpening pencils, making coffee and walking around the room) to put off the awful moment. A blank page can be very daunting and for many less experienced writers it can result in abandonment of the writing task. 'Please Miss, I can't think what to write' will be recognisable to many teachers as a familiar response of some children to writing tasks. The blank page has overwhelmed them.

The difference between writing and talking

When talking to another person, the language user receives constant support for his or her language. Talking usually takes the form of a dialogue, i.e. one person says something, this prompts the other person to say something, which in turn prompts the first person to reply, and so on. Talkers thus receive continual prompts for their language production. These prompts also help to model the register in which the language user can join in the ongoing dialogue. We naturally adapt the way that we speak depending upon our relationship with the person that we are speaking with and clues as to an appropriate way to join in a conversation come from the way that the other person speaks.

Writers, on the other hand, do not receive such prompts. They are by themselves, forced to produce language without support from another and to work out for themselves an appropriate register for that language.

Of course, in a classroom, there is potentially support available, from a teacher who may be at a child's shoulder prompting with such suggestions as: 'That's an interesting idea. Tell us more about that.' 'You've described that well. Can you give some more information about why it was there?' 'How exciting! And what will happen next?'

It is difficult, however, in a classroom which may contain up to 35 child writers, for a teacher to be able to provide sufficient of this support to meet the needs of the whole class.

The 'and then' syndrome

Inexperienced writers tend to have a limited range of ways of joining together ideas in writing. Most primary teachers will recognise this by the prevalence of 'and then' in their pupils' writing, as if this were the only way of linking ideas in writing. Mature writing, of course, is characterised by more elaborate ways of joining together ideas, using such connectives as 'furthermore', 'moreover', 'nevertheless', 'on the other hand' and so on. Teachers need to find ways of deliberately introducing these alternative connectives to children and helping them to use them effectively in their writing.

The structure of texts

It does seem to be the case that children often lack experience of different types of text, especially non-fiction texts, and their organisational structures. They need some support in distinguishing between these types in terms of linguistic features such as vocabulary, connectives and structure. A concept which can help to explain and categorise these linguistic differences is that of text genre.

According to genre theory, pieces of writing which share a common purpose will tend to share a common structure. One language purpose might be to provide instructions for someone else to carry out a task, for instance in a recipe. Such instructions, be they spoken or written, will tend to follow the following pattern:

- a statement of the goal (e.g. this is how to make a chocolate cake);
- a list of materials necessary to achieve this. (e.g. you will need...),
- a series of steps to carry out (e.g. first you..., then...).

Language patterns such as this tend to become so routine that we are barely aware of them; yet clearly they have to be learnt. Many children will find such structures difficult because they do not have the right expectations about texts. It is quite common, for example, for children to write instructions in the form of a narrative: 'I got some sugar and put it in a mixing bowl. Then I...'. This suggests that teachers need to teach children to use a range of appropriate language structures for appropriate purposes.

In order to do this teachers need themselves to be aware of various text structures. As we have outlined elsewhere (Lewis and Wray 1995) there appear to be six basic factual genres: recount, report, discussion, persuasion, explanation and instructions. Research suggests that primary children obtain a great deal of experience of writing recounts but rarely experience the other genres. This imbalance is important because in later school life and in adulthood these other genres are very heavily used and are crucial to success. Secondary school examinations, for example, demand the ability to write cogent arguments and discussions and if children have not been taught how to structure these forms of writing they will be disadvantaged.

Non-fiction writing - some possibilities

A model for teaching

The model of teaching upon which we have based the work of the EXEL Project is summarised as follows (the thinking underpinning this model has been fully outlined by Wray and Lewis (1997)):

models and/or demonstration

▼

joint activity

▼

scaffolded activity

▼

independent activity.

The model stems from the ideas of Vygotsky (1978), who put forward the notion that children first experience a particular cognitive activity in collaboration with expert practitioners. The child is firstly a spectator as the majority of the cognitive work is done by the expert (parent or teacher), and then a novice as he or she starts to take over some of the work under the close supervision of the expert. As the child grows in experience and capability of performing the task, the expert passes over greater and greater responsibility but still acts as a guide, assisting the child at problematic points. Eventually, the child assumes full responsibility for the task with the expert still present in the role of a supportive audience. The model seems to make good theoretical sense; yet it can be a little difficult to apply it fully to teaching in a busy over-populated classroom. In particular, it seems that children are too often expected to move into the independent writing phase before they are really ready and often the pressure to do so is based on the practical problem that teachers are unable to find the time to spend with them in individual support. What is needed is something to span the joint activity and independent activity phase.

We have called this the scaffolded phase, a phase where we offer our pupils strategies to aid writing but strategies that they can use without an adult necessarily being alongside them. One such strategy that we have developed which has become popular is the use of writing frames. These can act both as a way of increasing a child's experience of a particular type of non-fiction writing and as a substitute for the teacher's direct interventions which encourage children to extend their writing.

Some example writing frames

We have space here for only a few examples of the writing frames that we have developed. Further, photocopiable examples can be found in the books by Lewis and Wray (1997, 1998) and a more extensive account of the thinking behind writing frames in the book by Lewis and Wray (1995).

Recount genre

Before I read about this topic I thought that...
But when I read about it I learnt that...
I also learnt that...
Furthermore I learnt that...
The final thing I learnt was that...

Explanation genre

I want to explain why...
The are many reasons for this. The chief reason is...
Another reason is...
A further reason is...
So now you can see why...

Persuasion genre

Some people argue that...
But I want to argue that...
I have several reasons for arguing for this point of view. My first reason is...
Another reason is...
Furthermore...
Therefore, although some people argue that...
I think that I have shown that...

Note how writing with the frame overcomes the four writing problems highlighted earlier.

- It no longer presents writers with a blank page. There is comfort in the fact that there is already some writing on this page. We have found that this alone can be enough to encourage weaker writers to write at greater length.
- The frame provides a series of prompts to pupils' writing. Using the frame is rather like having a dialogue with the page and the prompts serve to model the register of that particular piece of writing.
- The frame deliberately includes connectives beyond the simple 'and then'. We have found that extended use of frames such as this can result in pupils spontaneously using these more elaborate connectives in other writing.
- The frame is designed around the typical structure of a particular genre. It thus gives pupils access to this structure and implicitly teaches them a way of writing non-fiction.

How to use writing frames

Use of a frame should always begin with discussion and teacher modelling before moving on to joint construction (teacher and child or children together) and then to the child undertaking writing supported by the frame. This oral 'teacher-modelling' joint construction pattern of teaching is vital, for it not only models the generic form and teaches the words that signal connections and transitions but also provides opportunities for developing children's oral language and their thinking. Some children, especially children with learning difficulties may need many oral sessions and sessions in which their teacher acts as a scribe before they are ready to attempt their own writing.

It would be useful for teachers to make 'big' versions of the frames for use in the teacher-modelling and joint construction phases. These large frames can be used for shared writing. It is important that the child and the teacher understand that the frame is a supportive draft and words may be crossed out or substituted. Extra sentences may be added or surplus starters crossed out. The frame should be treated as a flexible aid and not a rigid form.

We are convinced that writing in a range of genres is most effective if it is located in meaningful experiences. The concept of 'situated learning' (Lave and Wenger 1991) suggests that learning is always context dependent. For this reason, we have tended to use the frames within class topic work rather than in isolated study skills lessons. With the advent of the Literacy Hour we would suggest that this contextualisation is even more important as we try to ensure that children can apply the skills that they learn in literacy to other work across the curriculum.

When the children have a purpose for writing, you may decide to offer them a frame as follows:

- When they first attempt independent writing in an unfamiliar genre and a scaffold might be helpful to them.
- When a child or group of children appear stuck in a particular mode of writing, e.g. constantly using 'and then'... 'and then' when writing an account.
- When they 'wander' between genres in a way that demonstrates a lack of understanding of a particular genre usage, e.g. while writing an instructional text such as a recipe they start in the second person (first you beat the egg) but then shift into a recount (next I stirred in the flour). Mixing genres can of course be a deliberate and creative decision. We must take care to differentiate between those occasions when a child purposely moves between genres and those where different genres are confused.
- When they have written something in one genre (often a personal recount) which would be more appropriate in a different genre, e.g. writing up a science experiment as a personal recount. Although writing accounts from personal experience is a vital part of the process of becoming a writer, we must judge when a child needs help to adopt other genres.

In all these situations we would stress that writing frames are just one of a range of strategies and writing experiences that a teacher would offer to assist the children.

Using frames with a range of writers

We have found writing frames helpful to children of all ages and all abilities (indeed their wide applicability is one of their features). However, teachers have found the frames particularly useful with children of average writing ability and with those who find writing difficult. Teachers have commented on the improved quality (and quantity) of writing that has resulted from using the frames with these children.

It would of course be unnecessary to use the frame with writers already confident and fluent in a particular genre but they can be used to introduce such writers to new genres. Teachers have noted an initial dip in the quality of the writing when comparing the framed 'new genre' writing with the fluent recount writing of an able child. What they have later discovered, however, is that, after only one or two uses of a frame, fluent language users add the genre and its language features to their repertoires and, without using a frame, produce fluent writing of high quality in the genre.

The aim with all children is for them to reach this stage of assimilating the generic structures and language features into their writing repertoires.

Children need to use the frames less and less as their knowledge of a particular form increases. At this later stage, when children begin to show evidence of independent usage, the teacher may need only to have a master copy of the frames available as help cards for those occasions when children need a prompt. A box of such help cards could be a part of the writing area in which children are encouraged to refer to many different aids to their writing. Such a support fits with the general 'procedural facilitation' strategy for children's writing suggested by Bereiter and Scardamalia (1987). It also seems to be a way into encouraging children to begin to make independent decisions about their own learning.

Also, as pupils become familiar with the frame structures, there are a number of alternative support structures which can be used, such as prompt sheets containing lists of possible ways of connecting ideas together. A number of these will be found in the book by Lewis and Wray (1998).

Pupils' responses to the frames

Using a discussion frame Mark (Year 6) wrote about the arguments for and against a new building project. The frame helped to structure the writing and allowed the pupil access to a difficult form:

'Environmental change'
In our group we had a discussion about whether it was a good idea to build a new supermarket in the field beside our school.
   Some people thought it was a good idea because it you needed some think after school. If you needed some milk you only a couple of yards away.
   Other thought it was a really bad idea because the fumes will drift into the playground.
   However, I think the main point is the road will be busy and children will be in danger. After considering all the evidence and points of view I think it is a bad idea.

Marissa (Year 4) used a persuasion writing frame to help her to put forward an argument concerning the number of computers in the class:

'Computers'
Althuogh not evrybody would agree, I want to argue that we need to have more computers in our classrooms. I have several reasons for this point of view. My first reason is that everyone can have their own computer, and they don't have to wait to take turns.
   Furthermore so that the teacher can keep an eye on everyone. Some people might argue they don't want more computers becasue they might fill up the classroom. I think I have shown that comnputers are very intelligent things. If we had own computers we might get intelligent too and we won't have to argue over them.

These two pieces of writing represent only a very small selection of those we have collected so far from children across the country. They suggest that the use of writing frames as a teaching strategy for non-fiction writing can significantly enhance children's writing achievements. Writing frames offer one exciting possibility for developing writing.

References

Bereiter, C. and Scardamalia, M. (1987) *The Psychology of Written Composition*. Hillsdale, New Jersey: Lawrence Erlbaum Associates.

Lave, J. and Wenger, E. (1991) *Situated Learning*. Cambridge: Cambridge University Press.

Lewis, M. and Wray, D. (1995) *Developing Children's Non-fiction Writing*. Leamington Spa: Scholastic.

Lewis, M. and Wray, D. (1997) *Writing Frames*. Reading: Reading and Language Information Centre, The University of Reading.

Lewis, M. and Wray, D. (1998) *Writing Across the Curriculum*. Reading: Reading and Language Information Centre, The University of Reading.

Vygotsky, L. (1978) *Mind in Society: The Development of Higher Psychological Processes*. Cambridge, Massachusetts: Harvard University Press.

Wray, D. and Lewis, M. (1997) *Extending Literacy*. London: Routledge.

Endnote

[1] The EXEL Project, co-directed by David Wray and Maureen Lewis, has, since 1992, been working with teachers at Key Stages 1, 2 and 3 across the country to develop teaching strategies to improve children's reading and writing for information.

Chapter 13

In their own write: word processing in Urdu

Urmi Chana, Viv Edwards and Sue Walker

Discussions of literacy in British schools usually focus on English. Yet large numbers of children have experience of other languages and other scripts. The most competent of these are usually children who have moved to the UK after some initial schooling in the home country. Levels of achievement will depend on many different factors: children from the People's Republic of China, Japan and South Korea, for instance, are likely to be competent readers and writers in their national languages; children whose education has been interrupted by war or who have had only limited access to formal education in the country of origin are likely to be less confident.

The extent of linguistic and cultural diversity in British schools is often underestimated. The language censuses undertaken in the former Inner London Education Authority (ILEA) throughout the 1980s (ILEA 1981, 1983, 1985, 1987) suggested that close to 200 different languages were spoken. Sometimes one main language group predominates in a school, as is the case, for example, with Sylheti speakers in east London or Gujarati speakers in Leicester; on other occasions, as many as 20 or 30 different languages are spoken in one school. The demographics of diversity have also undergone a change. Bilingual pupils have traditionally been associated with inner-city schools. More recently, however, small numbers have begun attending schools in 'outlying districts'. Despite a long history of monolingualism in education – at least in England – very few schools today can claim that all staff and pupils have experience of English only.

Although the priority for children arriving in British schools is the rapid acquisition of English, strong arguments can be made for the school to acknowledge literacy skills in other languages. There is evidence that a good foundation in the first language is extremely helpful in learning to read and write a second language (Cummins 1996, Edwards 1998). Children with experience of the Roman alphabet will find themselves at an initial advantage in learning English. However, fluent readers use similar strategies irrespective of the writing system and children who are already literate in one language will be able to transfer a whole range of skills when they start to read and write a second language. They know, for instance, that print carries meaning, that the stream of speech is broken into words, and that it is possible to skip inessential words and to guess unknown words from context.

By encouraging the use of community languages in writers' workshops (Graves 1983); (see also Chapter 10 by Anne Rowe and Prue Goodwin) or dialogue journals (Peyton and Reed 1990), teachers are helping to promote bilingual children's development as writers. There are also status issues; by being allowed to use the community language, they are able to take part on equal terms in activities which would be beyond their reach in English.

The vast majority of bilingual learners, however, were born and have received all their education in the UK. Their exposure to other languages takes place in the informal setting of the home in the form of calendars, food packaging, newspapers and letters in other languages. By the age of 3 or 4, most will be able to distinguish between numbers, English writing and writing in other scripts and, with the help of parents and siblings, they may practice writing their name, or simple letters and words. Many children also learn to read and write in the more formal setting of a community school or with a private tutor. A study of Bangladeshi families in east London (Gregory 1996) showed that children were spending an average of 11 hours a week outside school in studying Bengali and Arabic.

Although the levels of achievement in community language literacy are very variable, it is important that mainstream schools should take every opportunity to acknowledge and build upon the children's experience. There are opportunities, for instance, in language awareness activities for children to share their knowledge with the class, at the same time enhancing their own status in the class and increasing monolingual children's 'knowledge about language' (Department of Education and Science, 1988).

Multilingual word processing in Redlands

The case study reported in this chapter describes the attempts of teachers in Redlands, a primary school in the south of England, to acknowledge the multiliterate experience of many of their pupils through the introduction of an Urdu word-processing program. The school in question has a long-established policy of positively acknowledging the linguistic experiences that pupils bring with them to school. Children speak a total of some 28 different languages. The largest single minority group within the school consists of Muslims from the Mirpur region of Pakistan who speak a variety of Panjabi at home but consider Urdu as the language of religion and high culture (Edwards 1996).

For some years a lunchtime Urdu club has been run at the school which, although open to all pupils, has tended to attract a small number of Pakistani pupils from Panjabi- and Urdu-speaking families. The school also has a record of maintaining very strong links with parents and there are various regular events, such as 'Mothers' teas', which have been well attended over the years.

The analysis presented in this chapter is based on observation and interviews with teachers, parents and children at the school over a period of 15 months. The research team consisted of a designer and two language educators, including a Panjabi speaker from the British Sikh community. Spoken Panjabi and Urdu are mutually intelligible, although written in different scripts (Khan 1991, Mahendra 1991). Talking to Pakistani parents, non-teaching staff and children in their first language played an important part in data collection.

Termly meetings were arranged throughout the project between the research team and key members of the teaching staff: the head teacher, the deputy headteacher and the two Pakistani teachers. One of the Pakistani teachers had overall responsibility for information technology (IT) in the school; the other was a language support teacher who works in partnership with several class teachers in meeting the needs of children who speak English as an additional language.

The initial meeting allowed us to identify a number of preliminary research questions: what were the potential applications for word processing in Urdu? Which software package would best meet these needs? What were the training needs of teachers? Which were the best ways of introducing the software to children? How might parents be involved in the new developments? Given that there was only enough money to buy one copy of the sotfware, where was the best place to site the designated computer?

This meeting also provided an opportunity to negotiate the most convenient times for access to the staff, children and parents who would be involved in the project. Members of the research team would be present for key events such as staff training and the introduction of the software to children and parents. The Panjabi-speaking researcher would regularly observe the lunchtime Urdu club. She would also be responsible for interviews at the beginning of the project to establish a baseline for comparison, and again at the end.

Data collection with teachers would take the form of open-ended semi-structured individual interviews with members of staff most closely concerned with the project, namely the head teacher and the Pakistani teachers. Three other sets of interviews were scheduled to seek the views of teachers whom we suspected might bring rather different perspectives to the research questions: two language support teachers (both of whom were monolingual English speakers) and class teachers were seen in two separate groups, and a Pakistani teaching assistant on a one-to-one basis. Interviews with parents were also undertaken as a group and individually according to preference. Interviews with children were conducted in school at the end of the Urdu club and at lunchtimes. Teachers, parents and children were given the opportunity to comment on the issues and conclusions which emerged from the initial round of interviews, the termly meetings and the observation in a series of interviews which took place towards the end of the project.

Initial expectations

At the outset of the project, teachers were excited about the possibilities that multilingual word processsing offered for communication with parents, including letters home, parent notices, termly topic webs and Urdu versions of school documents, such as the governors' report (all of which to date had been handwritten in Urdu by one of the support teachers). They were also interested to see how the introduction of the new software might enhance both the IT and the language work in school.

Both staff and children identified a wide range of possible uses for the new Urdu software in the school which mirrored the findings of previous initiatives (Abbott 1996). Because of the shortage of suitable materials in other languages, they looked forward to producing dual-language books in both Urdu and English as well as labels for displays and had ideas such as producing a multilingual school newspaper. These could be produced by various combinations of teachers, parents and children.

The presence of multilingual word processing was seen as acknowledging and supporting literacy development in other languages. Teachers also believed that it would give children an opportunity to show off skills they might be reluctant or shy to admit to in the English-print environment of school. Even in a school as actively encouraging as Redlands, teachers often noted pupils' reluctance to use their literacy skills in languages other than English. One of the language support teachers observed the shyness of her pupils when asked to add the Urdu equivalents for two days of the week on a chart (they had been muddling Thursday and Friday). She felt that, in such a situation, access to Urdu word processing would have given pupils and teacher more confidence to produce writing in another language alongside their English writing.

This feeling was echoed by other members of staff and endorsed by some of the children. As one 9-year-old girl commented: 'I like best the fact that you can type things out and also print them. If you get things wrong, you can change the word.' This facility of being able to edit and correct with ease and produce a piece of writing which looks good has boosted children's levels of confidence and interest in attempting Urdu, whereas previously their reluctance to write may have been affected by their judgements about their handwriting or uncertainty about spelling. The physical aspects of producing a text in a language with a strong calligraphic tradition, such as Urdu, are not to be underestimated.

Getting started

The starting point of the project had been to consider the most appropriate software. Much of the available software is very expensive and often fails to achieve the calligraphic qualities of handwriting. Teachers finally settled on *Page Composer*, a medium-priced program which offers contextual analysis. This means that the correct character variant for its position automatically appears when the word is typed – a much more attractive alternative than searching through levels of shift on the keyboard to find the appropriate form, as is required by a commonly used but less sophisticated program. While it is possible to argue that the more tedious process of searching for the correct variant reinforces children's learning, the general feeling was that ease of use was more important. By the end of the project, teachers' observation was that this facility helped to accelerate pupils' acquisition of literacy skills.

Staff also felt that the project presented an important opportunity for increasing the level of parental involvement, particularly from Pakistani families. There was the possibility of building a partnership with Urdu-literate parents in producing resources for their children to use, and thereby the opportunity for exchange of information and ideas. From the beginning it was envisaged that parents would be offered the chance to be actively involved in the process of developing this new initiative.

The training programme for *Page Composer* involved, in the first instance, two training sessions attended by the Urdu-literate staff, the support teachers and the project team. As one of the Urdu-speaking teachers is also the school's IT coordinator, she was the first to familiarise herself with the program. She worked closely with the other Urdu-speaking teacher and both quickly acquired enough knowledge to be able to introduce the new software to the pupils attending Urdu club.

The new computer and program were then introduced to parents at one of the regular 'Mothers' teas'. This informal gathering provided an ideal opportunity for the staff involved to talk with parents about how they hoped to build upon the school's existing response to children's linguistic heritage. Parents were able to ask questions about the new computer and to 'have a go'. The response of the Pakistani parents on seeing the word 'Welcome' written up in Urdu script on the computer screen was one of amazement. The staff had expected most parents to be reluctant to sit at the computer but, far from being shy of the new technology, they were very enthusiastic to have a turn at writing their names and seeing them printed out. A great deal of talk was generated by simply looking at how the Urdu characters were distributed on the QWERTY keyboard, and delight on noticing that, as a word is typed, initial medial or final variants of each letter automatically appear.

Some staff had expressed concern during the first round of interviews that very few of the Pakistani parents were literate in Urdu and that certainly not many were computer literate. The introduction of Urdu word processing at the 'Mothers' tea', however, made it quite clear that, although they may not have been computer literate, they were often eager to become so. It also emerged during the course of the project that many more parents than teachers had expected were literate in Urdu.

Involving parents

Following the introduction to Urdu word processing at the 'Mothers' tea', parents were invited to attend an afternoon workshop. The aim was twofold: to provide an opportunity for hands-on experience of writing on the computer, and to produce resources which would help their children.

Six parents attended the first workshop. The first hour was spent in semi-informal discussion, setting a context and providing a framework for writing. Teachers reported to parents their particular concerns about pupils' story-writing skills, and emphasised the importance of hearing stories. Attention was particularly drawn towards the role of parents in extending children's vocabulary (both Urdu and English) by talking about every-day events and routines, and by giving more prominence to story telling so that children develop a feel for the style and structure of simple narratives. They were asked to write about recent events reflecting their every-day experiences.

Parents drafted their stories on paper, thus using the computer as a typewriter rather than as an aid to composition. This seemed the most sensible way forward when working with parents who had little or no experience either of writing of this kind or of the new technology. Support was also offered in the drafting process; most of the women chose to write in pairs, seeking feedback from their peers and the Urdu-speaking teachers. By the end of the session, two parents had made a start on transferring their story to the computer. The others made it clear that they had enjoyed the workshop and wanted to know when the next meeting would take place. They were enthusiastic about the new software and wanted the opportunity to learn how to use it.

Teachers had not anticipated such a level of interest and at first felt somewhat overwhelmed, wondering how they were going to find additional time to meet the parents' request. Both teachers had been released for two afternoon workshop sessions, but it was not practicable for the school to maintain this level of support. However, parents were sensitive to this problem: they appreciated the welcoming and accommodating approach of the school and were concerned not to make unreasonable demands on teacher time. They were willing to negotiate support and structure for their own learning. As one mother commented: 'Once you've learnt to set it up and got started, you can get on and learn by yourself.'

In practice, a form of cascade training evolved. Time initially invested by a member of staff in working with one particularly enthusiastic mother has reaped ample rewards as she, in turn, has been able to help other parents to gain confidence. A few mothers have been playing a very valuable role in helping to familiarise children with a second package called Qaida which is designed to teach alphabet skills in Urdu. The program provides pictorial cues and children can progress at their own rate through various levels in this program, from the first stage of typing in initial sounds to that of correcting the spelling of particular words.

In short, teachers have been surprised to find that many more parents than they expected are literate in Urdu, that initial computer phobia can be quickly overcome and that, given a familiar and inspiring context, the level of parental involvement in school can be significantly raised. A small group of parents has worked on producing simple dual-language stories which have then been illustrated by their children at school. Parents have also helped to produce signs in Urdu for display around the school (e.g. a notice about fire drills).

The introduction of Urdu software has also sent very strong messages to parents, reaffirming the school's commitment to cultural and linguistic diversity. Parents have also been empowered to contribute some of their skills to the school's and their children's advantage. The effect on individual parents of being welcomed and invited to participate actively is clear from their enthusiasm to continue to learn and help in school.

New directions

Teachers have been quick to seize upon a number of exciting possibilities raised by the availability of multilingual word processing. One example is the occasion when the Urdu teacher was approached by a pupil asking if she could use the Urdu software to print her name and address on a letter to her grandparents in Pakistan. This request led the teacher to plan the next Urdu club sessions around letter writing. The teacher worked with pupils on collaboratively formulating a letter to grandparents abroad. There was a real excitement in printing out and sending these word-processed letters to their grandparents, and anticipating their replies.

A further example relates to the involvement of parents in book making. As noted earlier, teachers had underestimated parents' levels of literacy and also their willingness to be involved. Existing good communication with parents was built upon by supporting parents in learning to work on the computer with children. Parents were given opportunities, at their own convenience, to observe teacher and pupils at the computer during the Urdu club. They were also given access to the computer to practise during lunchtimes or afternoons and were often assisted by the Pakistani language support teacher. These opportunities, in combination with the discussions about activities that enhance children's language development, have helped to establish a supportive partnership between parents and teachers. A number of different ways of producing books has to date been tried out – children writing with parents on some occasions, and illustrating writing done by parents on others.

This use of Urdu gives both children and parents a feeling of pride and enjoyment as they can share these books with others in the school. Colour copies have been made of some of the dual-language stories and placed in the school library (Walker *et al.* 1998).

Teachers have also felt that they can more clearly observe the progress that individuals make in acquiring Urdu literacy, as the context of typing at the computer provides clues that may have not been so obvious before. Working in pairs at the computer has generated much more talk about the language which has helped to increase pupils' understanding and skills, not just in Urdu but also, of course, in IT.

Breaking boundaries

The examples above give some idea of the enormous potential of multilingual word processing for developing communities of writers (Goodman and Wilde 1992). The response of the children themselves is a testament to the level of success. There has been a significant rise in the level of interest in the lunchtime Urdu club. Previously attended by an average of eight pupils, it now attracts over 20 children from various language backgrounds. The Pakistani children have risen in the estimation of their peers as they are able to demonstrate their skills both in Urdu and on the computer. In discussions with these pupils it is evident that their newly acquired computing and word-processing skills have opened up a whole range of possibilities which they are only too eager to share.

Many other possibilities remain to be explored. The following are just some of the children's ideas on how else the Urdu software could be used at their school: 'I think we should have the same kind of computer with Urdu on it in each class.' 'We could put the computer in the library and every Tuesday, or more often, we could come outside our class and show everybody, and parents could come and watch. Whoever is interested could come along and enjoy it.' 'I'm teaching Rehana and Maryam; others could come and watch also. Me and Sameera know the computer quite well.' 'We've all got different ideas...we could all make our different ideas.'

References

Abbott, C. (1996) 'Young people developing a new language: the implications for teachers and for education of electronic discourse', in *Proceedings of Euro Education*, Vol. 96, Aalborg, Denmark, pp.97–105.

Cummins, J. (1996) *Negotiating Identities: Education for Empowerment in a Diverse Society*. Ontario, California: California Association for Bilingual Education and Stoke-on-Trent: Trentham Books.

Department of Education and Science (1988) *Report of the Committee of Inquiry into the Teaching of the English Language (The Kingman Report)*. London: HMSO.

Edwards, V. (1996) *The Other Languages: a Guide to Multilingual Classrooms*. Reading: Reading and Language Information Centre, The University of Reading.

Edwards, V. (1998) *The Power of Babel: Teaching and Learning in Multilingual Classrooms*. Stoke-on-Trent: Trentham Books.

Goodman, Y. and Wilde, S. (eds) (1992), *Literacy Events in a Community of Young Writers*. New York/London: Teachers College Press.

Graves, D. (1983) *Writing: Teachers and Children at Work*. London: Heinemann Educational.

Gregory, E. (1996) 'Reading between the lines', *Times Educational Supplement* 15 October, 4.

ILEA (1981, 1983, 1985, 1987) *Language Census*. London: ILEA.

Khan, F. (1991) 'The Urdu speech community', in Alladina, S. and Edwards, V. (eds) *Multilingualism in the British Isles*, Vol 2, pp.128–140. Harlow: Longman.

Mahendra, V. (1991) 'The Panjabi speech community', in Alladina, S. and Edwards, V. (eds) *Multilingualism in the British Isles*, Vol. 2, pp.115–127, Harlow: Longman.

Peyton, J. and Reed, L. (1990) *Dialogue Journal Writing with Nonnative English Speakers: A Handbook for Teachers*. Alexandria, Virginia: Teachers of English to Speakers of Other Languages.

Walker, S., Edwards, V. and Leonard, H. (1998) *Write Around the World: Producing Multilingual Materials for Children*. Reading: Reading and Language Information Centre, The University of Reading.

Part IV

The world of literacy

Chapter 14

Working with words: vocabulary development in the primary school

George Hunt

Some issues in vocabulary development

The scale and rapidity of children's acquisition of vocabulary are probably the most impressive aspects of language development. Most children produce their first recognisable word somewhere between their tenth and fourteenth month. Other words follow very rapidly, so that by the age of 18 months the 'average' child can produce about 50 words, and understand five times as many (Crystal 1986). Although estimates of vocabulary size after the child passes the 200-word mark (typically at around 2 years old) are bewilderingly variable, some studies have put the recognition vocabulary of children starting school at roughly 10,000 words (Anglin 1993). Unlike grammatical and phonological development, where the most dramatic achievements occur in early childhood, vocabulary development is a life-long process. Although the rate of vocabulary acquisition is certainly impressive in the pre-school years, there is ample evidence that in some respects it is even more dramatic in the early and middle school years (Anglin 1993).

There are problems when estimating vocabulary size, however, as there are problems in defining both what we mean by a *word*, and what is meant by saying that somebody *knows* a word. Should *schoolchildren*, for example, count as one word or two? Are *swim, swimming, swimmer, swam* and *swum* separate words, or variants of the first term? What about phrases such as *lamb to the slaughter* and *gets on with,* where the seemingly distinct words represent a single concept? The issues surrounding word knowledge are even pricklier as the ability to understand a word does not imply the ability to use it. Consider the word *right*:

My right shoe leaks.
He's my right-hand man.
Drive on the right.
Turn right at the lights.
Turn through a right angle.
Keep on the right path.
Keep right on to the end of the road.
It's right here.
It's miles away; right over there.
Right, let's get going.
Right, I understand you now.
You are in the right.
You have no right.
That's the right answer.
That's the right stuff!
He's right in his belief.
He's very far right in his beliefs.

A complex network of connotations binds these different usages, involving affect, metaphor and shades of meaning. It is the learner's comprehension of this network that would have to be assessed if we were to try to determine whether or not a child knew this word. That is to say, vocabulary size is intimately related to vocabulary depth.

There are important educational implications here. Research is unanimous in identifying close links between the vocabulary size and measures of educational success, including reading and writing ability (McKeown and Curtis 1987). The more words that children have in their vocabularies, the more likely it is that they will be able to process printed words. A large vocabulary also helps a writer to express more precise meanings (Shaughnessy 1978). Conversely, deficits in learners' vocabularies are related to educational failure. At the most obvious level, a shortage of words will result in difficulties in speaking and listening, although the number of children who suffer from this degree of deficit is fewer than is popularly believed (Hughes 1994). At a more subtle level, deficits in particular types of word can have serious effects on learning. Perera (1979) has pointed out how ignorance of sentence adverbs such as *however, hence, therefore* and so on can make an otherwise 'readable' text incomprehensible; she also pointed out problems arising from readers' failure to appreciate unfamiliar meanings for familiar words such as *vacuum* and *liquid*. We cannot, however, deduce from this that efforts to increase vocabulary by rote learning of sets of words will bring about educational improvement. There is no implication that vocabulary size *produces* academic achievement. Both common sense and research suggest that the relationship between vocabulary size and proficient reading, for example, is reciprocal (Adams 1990). Furthermore, there is no reliable evidence that the memorisation of word lists is an effective strategy for expanding a learner's vocabulary. What *would* be effective is an important concern for any teacher attempting to create a literate classroom. Although we cannot prove that knowing words causes academic achievement, there is evidence that not knowing them contributes to 'Matthew effects' (from the Gospel of Matthew 25: 29), whereby the rich get richer and the poor get poorer (Stanovich 1986, p.381):

The very children who are reading well and who have good vocabularies will read more, learn more word meanings and hence read even better. Children with inadequate vocabularies – who read slowly and without enjoyment – read less, and as a result have slower development of vocabulary knowledge, which inhibits further growth in reading ability.

In order to address the question of what teachers can do to help to develop children's vocabulary, it would be useful to look at four procedures which have been held to be effective in this respect: direct instruction of vocabulary, learning words from context, learning words from dictionaries, and morphological problem solving.

Direct instruction of vocabulary

Given the rapid growth in children's vocabulary, it seems likely that only a fraction of the words that children learn in the primary years are acquired through direct instruction or word lists. Most children learn more words than anyone has time to teach them (Miller and Gildea 1987). This is not to say that there is no role for direct instruction; it is often necessary to teach specialist vocabulary for specific purposes. In one of the most thorough attempts to teach vocabulary through direct instruction, Beck *et al.* (1987) taught the meanings of 104 words to Grade 4 children over a 5-month period and achieved an 80 per cent success rate (i.e. an average of 80 per cent of the words were retained 3 weeks later). Although this does not sound impressive compared with the 20 words a day of largely uninstructed learning discovered by Anglin, the following aspects of this programme are worth considering.

- Words were grouped according to meaning.
- Children received multiple exposures to words in a variety of illustrative contexts.
- They received rich and varied information about each word, including how it related to words already known, and to other aspects of current knowledge and experience.
- A strong word play element was included.

Beck *et al.* (1987, p.157) concluded that the active learning approach and the appeal of playful exploration stimulated word awareness and enabled them to seek out words independently: 'We reasoned that because children were being inundated with words and having enjoyable, successful experiences with them, they might become more aware of new words in their environment and more likely to expend effort understanding them.'

Learning words from context

A factor that seems to be more feasible than direct instruction in accounting for the rapid vocabulary growth in children is the capacity to learn words incidentally from context, particularly when reading. Much research has indicated that this is an effective source of vocabulary learning for children (Nagy and Andersen 1984; Shu *et al.* 1995), but *only* when they have become reasonably fluent readers. Unskilled readers cannot learn new words purely from the printed context because until decoding becomes automatic, there is not enough capacity available to make the inferences necessary for the acquisition of new words (Adams 1990). There is also the problem that many of the contexts in which unfamiliar words occur do not provide the novice reader with unambiguous clues about the meanings of such words.

Helping children to learn from context through adult–child discussion of word meanings in texts is a fruitful source of vocabulary acquisition. Collaborative discussion of texts in the classroom is likely to help children to learn specific words from a text and useful strategies of inference which will increase independence with reading.

Learning words from dictionaries

One of the most common vocabulary exercises given to children is to look up words in a dictionary and then to write sentences based on the definitions that they find. One problem with this approach is its dullness and lack of purpose. Another is the quality of some dictionaries. Research by Miller and Gildea (1987) showed that inadequacies in the language of definition caused children to make 'fragment selection errors'. For example, a child looking up the word *erode* wrote the sentence, 'My family erodes a lot' after misinterpreting the familiar phrase *eats out* in the definition. Most teachers will be familiar with gaffes of this nature, and they may well be tempted to despair of using dictionaries as anything other than old-fashioned versions of spell checkers. However, there have been many interesting developments in lexicography in the ten years since Miller and Gildea wrote their paper. Most recent dictionaries for children use 'transparent' definitions rather than the traditional phrases. For example, the definition of *right* in the adult Oxford paperback dictionary begins: '1 (of conduct or actions, etc.) morally good, in accordance with justice'. In the Collins Pocket Primary the definition reads; 'Your right hand is the hand that most people write with'. While this definition reduces one of the most complex and contentious words in the language to its most simple use, its form is more accessible to a youngster than traditional 'definese'. (McKeown 1993). As well as the greater clarity of definese (the style of writing in which definitions are expressed), recent children's dictionaries include example sentences which give further clues to the meanings and grammatical forms of words. Dictionaries are also better illustrated, and their typography is clearer. All these factors should establish the modern dictionary in vocabulary development, but only if children are encouraged to explore them as sources of enjoyment.

Morphological problem solving

Morphemes are units of meaning. Anglin (1993) coined the phrase 'morphological problem solving' to describe how children figure out words which are 'potentially knowable' by relating them to words that they already know. He found that much of the vocabulary growth that occurs in the school years can be explained by children's growing awareness of the structure of words. He also found that children construct meanings by identifying and blending morphemes in unfamiliar words. This study also emphasised that the learners personal vocabulary is highly structured (Miller 1993):

> The mental dictionary is not a homogenous list of concept utterance pairs that have been memorised by rote. Words are related to one another in many ways and it is by taking advantage of those relations that children are able to develop their vocabularies so rapidly.

An emphasis on the learner actively discovering and creatively developing relationships between words and meanings underlies the classroom activities outlined in the rest of this chapter.

Some suggestions for vocabulary investigations in the classroom

The following activities are meant to do three things: to teach children about words, namely their origins, anatomy and usages; to teach children specific sets of words and meanings; to teach children a sensitivity towards words in general. They are compatible with the vocabulary extension objectives laid out in the word level work in the National

Literacy Strategy. Many also can be used to support spelling, phonics, sentence and text level.

Stimulating curiosity about words

Word of the day; word family of the week

Select a word which is relevant to a topical theme and display it in the classroom. Discuss its meaning, spelling and, if appropriate, morphological structure (there is no need to use technical vocabulary when doing this). Ask the children for any words that they know related to the word of the day.

Register games

Ask the children to answer the register by giving a word related to a particular theme. Keep this quick and playful; if a child cannot give a word, supply one yourself and pass on. Themes could include colours, towns, animals, size words, words with specific spelling patterns, and words from other languages.

Words from other languages

Children who speak languages other than English can be asked to contribute mother tongue equivalents for words which the class are currently investigating. For example, children could compare weather terminology in different languages to see how potentially onomatopoeic items such as *thunder* are represented .

Morphemic word webs

This activity is aimed at raising children's awareness of word structure, spelling patterns and relationships between words. Take a root word which is related to a current class topic or story and show the children how you can generate related words by adding morphemes to form a web of words. When you have started the web, ask the children to extend it further with their own suggestions.

Semantic fields

Take any basic concept (such as food or money) and get the children to tell you as many words and phrases that they know for that concept. This might include 'slang' terms, regional and national variants in English, and words used for the concept in other languages. Display the results as a word web, which can then be used as a focus for discussion.

Free sorting of randomly selected words

Take a random collection of between 10 and 20 words, e.g. you might use the answers to a crossword, or open a novel at different pages and select the first word that meets your eye. Put the words on cards. Ask the children, in pairs, to sort the words out in any way that seems sensible. When this has been done, children can explain the rationale for their sorting and compare it with that of other pairs of children. The range of responses to this simple task can be fascinating.

Names

These activities are based on the special role played by names in children's vocabulary development. You need to bear in mind that, for some families, personal names may be inappropriate.

Name origins

Prepare a poster or big book displaying information on the origins of the first names of all the children in your class. Explain to the children that every personal name has a story behind it, and illustrate this with some examples. Children can be encouraged to discuss their own first names and to speculate on their meanings before you turn to the big book to compare their ideas with the 'official' derivation.

Place names

Maps and atlases provide rich opportunities for the study of name origins and name structures. Start with local maps including A–Z-type street atlases and Ordnance Survey material. Ask the children to collect place names and to think of categories into which they might be sorted. These could include names of towns, villages, parks, woods, rivers, farms, streets, housing estates and schools. In covering wider geographic areas, names of counties, countries, mountains, rivers and seas might be included. The listing and sorting activity can be followed by discussion of meanings and origins, regularities in the structures of the names (such as the common English elements -don and -caster, the Welsh Llan and the Celtic Kil-), and investigation into changes of names.

Business names

The *Yellow Pages* or local business directories provide examples of names based on manipulations of spelling sound and meaning. Kwiksave, for example, is a fairly simple spelling manipulation, BlueFlash (a removal firm) borrows its name from a popular metaphor. Children can list examples and sort them into categories before having a go at making up their own.

Investigating and inventing fictional characters' names

Authors often select names for their characters which have a suggestive but immediate impact. A simple starting point for investigating this area would be the *Happy Families* series by Allan Ahlberg. How did Mrs Wishy Washy get her name? Why are alliterative names such as Wishy Washy, Telly Tubby and Tintin so common in fiction for younger children? Can you sort out a set of Dickens' or Dahl's characters into heroes and villains just on the basis of their names? If so, what aspects of language are the authors exploiting here? Compare this with a list of hero and villain names from television, comics and computer games. Children can be encouraged to create their own characters and to give them appropriate names.

Examining and inventing metaphorical compounds

Many folk names for plants and animals take the form of descriptive or metaphorical compounds (e.g. sunflower, foxglove and daisy). Analysing such compounds can help children to coin new descriptive compounds themselves. This can be related to the historical use of such compounds, or kennings, in early English poetry; for example the sea could be referred to as the 'whale path', or the human body as a 'bone house'.

Onomatopoeia

Onomatopoeic words – those that imitate physical sounds such as crash, gobble and screech – are amongst the first that children acquire in their speech.

Collecting and sorting onomatopoeic words

Cartoons, advertising slogans and nursery rhymes are all good sources of onomatopoeic words. They can be collected and sorted into such categories as animal noises, loud and soft noises, human noises, etc. The words can then be regrouped across categories according to patterns of alliteration and rhyme. Children can be asked to extend the categories with their own examples, and to use these words to make up rhymes, songs and slogans.

Investigating sounds

Ask the children to list as many words as they can beginning with sl and to look up their meanings. Is there any significance in the fact that many of these words have negative meanings (slime, sly, sleazy, sloppy, etc.)? What patterns of meaning can be found in words beginning with st-, or ending in -ump?

Inventing words

A good way of helping children to understand how the components of words are organised is to let them make up their own. For example, a child invented *schlerpph* to describe the sound made by a marble dropping into a jelly.

Onset and rime

From a simple table of onsets and rimes, children can construct a set of 'words' that cannot be found in any dictionary (e.g. the onset gl- with the rimes -ont, -ard and -eng). Children can be encouraged to think about possible meanings for such words. This could lead to a discussion of what parts of speech categories the new words belong to, and how they would work in sentences.

Morphoshuffle

A useful teaching tool is a set of cards in which word components are set out in three colours: red for prefixes, blue for roots, and yellow for suffixes, perhaps. By shuffling the cards and setting them out in a fixed red–blue–yellow order, children can generate both real words and new words. (Remember that spelling modifications are sometimes necessary when adding affixes.) Familiarity with the meanings of the word parts will enable children to create meanings and to compose definitions for new words.

From word to text

Although playing with words and word families can be fascinating, it is necessary that children have lots of opportunities to see how words operate in whole texts. Many valuable activities are available for starting with texts and investigating the words within them. For example, children can share lists of favourite words (chosen for their sound as well as their meaning) and arrange them into poetic patterns, they can generate stories from sequences of words which act as prompts for a plot; they can create thematic ABCs with alliterative captions; they can create mini-dictionaries giving definitions for some of the words that they have invented; they can compose concordances around words with multiple meanings.

Words are fascinating objects, and the study of their structure, origins and meanings can be very fruitful for children, but it is only when they start to combine words thoughtfully that they put to use the knowledge they have gained.

References

Adams, M. J. (1990) *Beginning to Read.* Cambridge, Massachusetts: MIT Press.

Anglin, J. (1993) *Vocabulary Development: a Morphological Analysis.* Chicago: University of Chicago Press.

Beck, I., Perfetti, A. and Omanson, R. (1987) 'The effects and uses of diverse vocabulary instructional techniques', in McKeown, M. and Curtis, M. (eds) *The Nature of Vocabulary Acquisition.* Hillsdale, New Jersey: Earlbaum, p.157.

Crystal, D. (1986) *Listen to Your Child.* London: Penguin Books.

Hughes, M. (1994) 'The oral language of young children', in Wray, D. and Medwell, J. (eds) *Teaching Primary English.* London: Routledge, pp.7–21.

McKeown, M. (1993) 'Creating effective definitions for young word learners', *Reading Research Quarterly* **28**, 17–31.

McKeown, M. and Curtis, M. (eds) (1987) *The Nature of Vocabulary Acquisition.* Hillsdale, New Jersey: Lawrence Earlbaum Associates.

Miller, G. (1993) in Anglin, S. (ed.) *Vocabulary Development: A Morphological Analysis.* Chicago: University of Chicago Press.

Miller, G. and Gildea, P. (1987) 'How children learn words', *Scientific American* **257**(3) 94–99.

Nagy, W. E. and Andersen, R. C. (1984) 'How many words are there in printed school English?', *Reading Research Quarterly* **19**, 304–330.

Perera, K. (1979) *The Language Demands of School Learning,* Open University Course PE232, Supplementary Readings 6. Milton Keynes: The Open University.

Shaughnessy, M. (1977) *Errors and Expectations.* New York: Oxford University Press.

Shu, H., Andersen, R. C. and Zhang, H. (1995) 'Incidental learning of word meanings while reading: a Chinese and American cross-cultural study', *Reading Research Quarterly* **30**, 76–95.

Stanovich, K. (1986) 'Matthew effects in reading: some consequences of individual differences in the acquisition of literacy', *Reading Research Quarterly* **21**, 360–406.

Chapter 15

Opening the wardrobe of voices: standard English and language study at Key Stage 2
Michael Lockwood

I can still remember the baffled amusement with which my first Year 6 group heard me call them my 'class', ask them not to go on the 'grass' at break time and tell them that our topic was going to be 'castles'. They were pupils in a middle school in the south of England, I was a new teacher born and educated, a first-generation grammar school boy, in West Yorkshire. University and training in the south had modified my Yorkshire accent, but the tell-tale vowel sounds still resounded in words such as 'mud', 'blood' and 'bath'! Embarrassment and amusement soon turned to fascination with the phenomenon of language variety for all of us. This article is about ways that I have devised of sharing that continuing fascination with the diversity of language with Key Stage 2 children, in the light of national developments in this area of the English curriculum over the past 15 years

Background

The recent revival of interest in what the National Curriculum (NC) calls Language Study probably began with an HMI discussion paper *Curriculum Matters 1* (Department of Education and Science 1984), which proposed objectives for children's 'learning about language' at 11 and 16. The heated debate amongst teachers initiated by this document, expressed in *Responses to Curriculum Matters* (Department of Education and Science 1986), led to an enquiry into the teaching of English language which produced *The Kingman Report* (Department of Education and Science 1988). In this report the phrase 'knowledge about language' (KAL) was first used and a broad model of language proposed to 'inform professional discussion', part of which was concerned with language variety in terms of place, time, social grouping and context.

The Cox Report (Department of Education and Science 1989, pp. 6.16–6.21) incorporated Kingman's recommendations into the NC, defining KAL as including the areas of 'language variation according to situation, purpose, language mode, regional or social group...[and] language variation across time'. Like *The Kingman Report*, it paid particular attention to the subject of standard English and how to teach it. The ill-fated Language in the National Curriculum (LINC) project took as its main concern this 'language variation' strand and produced valuable professional development materials at both local and national level. These materials, however, were never made available to classroom teachers, although some have since been published commercially (see, for example, Bain *et al.* (1992) and Haynes (1992)). My own research at the time suggested that primary teachers remained unsure of what KAL was and urgently needed training and support in its classroom applications (Lockwood 1995).

The change in the political climate that led to the suppression of the LINC materials resulted in a revision of the NC orders in 1995, and the replacement of KAL with 'Standard English and Language Study'. The authors of this 'slimmed down' NC had wanted to use the title 'Language Study and Standard English' for this section of the programmes of study and protested at these and other editorial interventions that gave prominence to standard English (Blackburne 1994). The dispute over wording can be seen as part of a wider debate; should the use and understanding of standard English be set within the critical and reflective context of language study, including the wider study of language variety, or should the purpose of language study be to increase and improve children's use of standard English in speech and writing? The activities described below were designed and taught with the former view strongly in mind: that increasing children's awareness of the phenomenon of language variation, in terms of register, accent, dialect and standard English, was the most effective way of developing their own repertoire of spoken and written varieties.

The project

The NC requires that 'Pupils should be given opportunities to develop' both their 'use' and 'understanding' of standard English (DfEE 1998, p.3). Standard English is defined here as 'distinguished from other forms of English by its vocabulary and by rules and conventions of grammar, spelling and punctuation'. It is accepted that there are differences between the spoken and written forms. It is also recognised that 'spoken standard English is not the same as Received Pronunciation and can be expressed in a variety of accents'. The programmes of study recommend that standard English be seen in the context of wider language variation: 'The richness of dialects and other languages can make an important contribution to pupils' knowledge and understanding of standard English' (DfEE 1998, p.2).

The project described here was designed to meet these requirements and recommendations. The activities were carried out with mixed ability groups of pupils, with an equal number of boys and girls, drawn from two parallel Year 5 classes (9–10-year-olds) in a junior school. The school has an English language programme based on the use of recent commercial schemes, including *Mind Your Language* (Palmer and Brinton 1988) and *Exploring Language* (Lutrario 1993). The school policy document acknowledges that

> . . . recent research indicates that "active processing" is the most effective way of learning
> – opportunities for discussing, investigating and purposefully manipulating language
> should be provided. Using language knowledge in real situations will help to
> consolidate concepts introduced in this (series) progression.

Accent, dialect and standard English

I began by sharing poems with the group that highlighted features of accent and dialect. We read the anonymous poem (Palmer 1994) beginning:

> 'A muvver was barfin' 'er biby one night,
> The youngest of ten and a tiny young mite

and discussed the Cockney pronunciation suggested by the spelling. The discussion widened to include the children's experience of other accents. Working in pairs, the children took a few lines each from the poem and 'translated' them into conventional spelling or 'normal writing'. There were few difficulties with this (apart from the occasional misspelling) and the only non-standard feature not 'translated' was the one element of dialect grammar in the poem which was retained as: 'Your baby has *fell* down the plug-hole'. The group then reread the poem from the conventional spellings in their own accents and we discussed the differences. I followed this with a slightly exaggerated reading of the poem in Received Pronunciation, or 'a posh accent' as the group described it, and we talked about how this affected the humour of the poem. The discussion moved on to consider the concept of standard English as a variety of language used in almost all writing, except where the writer wanted to suggest a particular accent as in the poem.

I made a point of establishing that standard English could actually be spoken in any accent, not just Received Pronunciation but that, when we used it, we normally modified our local accent, made it less 'broad', as with my own original Yorkshire accent.

The second poem read was 'English cousin comes to Scotland' by Jackie Kay (1992):

I got skelped, because I screamed when a skelf
went into my pinky finger: OUCH, loud.
And ma ma dropped her best bit of china.
It wis sore, so it wis, so it wis.

The group initially found the dialect words present this time, in addition to accent features, difficult to grasp. However, investigation of our own experiences of dialect words (e.g. for 'little finger', 'mother', 'splinter' and 'smacked') resolved this and these dialect words became a feature of the work the children recalled frequently (especially 'pinky'!). The use of regional dialect words was related in discussion to the concept of a standard variety, which in speech and writing used only words understood nationally. We talked about the reasons for regional variations and the value that they had. The poems were read aloud in a variety of ways and recorded onto audio tape. Other poems used in a similar way to raise awareness and generate discussion of accent, dialect and standard English were 'Footy Poem' (McGough and Rosen 1979) and 'Wha Me Mudder Do' (Nichols 1988).

Register

From using poetry texts to investigate language variety, I moved on to exploring the children's own linguistic repertoires. We began by considering register, the way that we talk slightly differently to different people at different times about different things. After some initial role playing using a toy mobile phone, when the group had to guess to whom I was speaking, I asked the children as a group to brainstorm onto a large sheet of card all the occasions during a typical week when they were aware of using 'different voices'. With a little prompting, they came up with a spectrum of situations ranging from 'speaking to the head teacher' to 'talking to my friends in the playground'. Some of the situations were briefly role played, as far as time allowed, and we discussed how and why we changed the way that we spoke at different times. The concept of register was related in discussion to the forms of language variation explored earlier, accent, dialect and standard English.

I then introduced the metaphor of 'a wardrobe of voices' to provide the children with an accessible analogy for their experience of linguistic variation. I explained that we all wear different clothes to suit different occasions. Some people have larger wardrobes than others, but we all have a range of clothing from casual to formal. Similarly with language, we all have different varieties which we use at different times and our range changes as we develop, some being added and some lost. There are fashions in words just as in dress!

Next I asked the children to make a plan of their wardrobe, either actual or imaginary. I provided a design of an empty wardrobe with a rail on which, at one end, they could draw old clothes for playing in with friends, then casual clothes for everyday use, then towards the other end, smart outfits for parties and perhaps some 'best clothes' for special occasions. I asked them to decide where school uniform might be fitted in. Any other kinds of clothes that children wanted to include (e.g. football tops) could be fitted somewhere on the rail too. When the wardrobes were completed — in some detail! — the children improvised situations where they might wear the different styles of clothing (I was careful to point out that it was the situations, and not usually the actual clothes themselves, which triggered our selection of language styles).

We moved on next to consider explicitly the idea of each of us having a wardrobe of voices as well as of clothing: casual ways of speaking when we are with close friends, more formal ways on special occasions, and a mixture in between. We related this repertoire to the use of regional accents and dialects and spoken standard English mentioned previously, and discussed the additional linguistic range of bilingual speakers. The children then introduced a range of different voices into their wardrobes, as in this example, and later role played 'wearing' them (Figure 15.1).

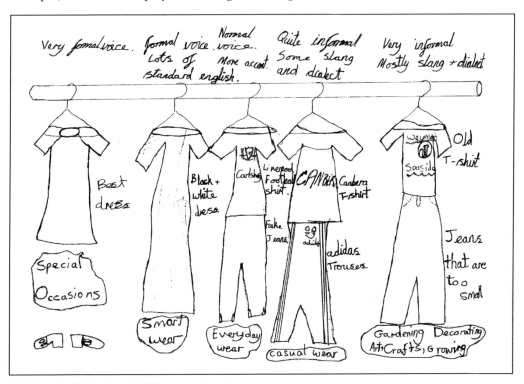

Figure 15.1 The range of different voices for a child's wardrobe

Slang

In the final part of the project, we looked at the informal end of the linguistic wardrobe and explored slang. This was described as a variety of spoken language which uses special words like a dialect but changes quickly over time and is associated less with places than with particular social groups, especially young people. Again we began with poetry, an appropriate choice since slang has been described (by G.K. Chesterton) as: 'The stream of poetry which is continually flowing'. First we shared Michael Rosen's (1994, pp.22–23) poem about a new boy trying to join in with an unfamiliar playground game, beginning:

If one is one
if two is two
I'm Jack Straw
what are you?

We discussed how playground games, chants and dips could all vary significantly between local schools, as well as ones in other parts of the country. Then we read and discussed the playground language in part of Allan Ahlberg's (1989 p.98) *Heard it in the Playground*:

Heard it in the playground
Quality, quality
Heard it in the playground
Skill, skill, skill
Ace, nice, neat.

I asked the children to brainstorm any words, phrases or sayings that they had heard in their playground, either connected with games or not. The children worked in smaller groups of boys and girls, to see whether there were any differences in their choices (the biggest difference was in quantity, the girls' group providing far more examples!). Swear words were explicitly excluded, as being a separate category from playground slang. Working from the amalgamated brainstorm sheets, the children then worked individually to draft dictionary entries for words that they could define, having first looked at classroom dictionaries for a model to follow. Some entries new to me were the following:

* Crocodile (noun) a person who is chasing after people.
* Durbrain (noun) a person who is a bit stupid.
* Fantastico (noun) a person who is nice or brainy; also fantistico (adjective): e.g. 'You're fantistico.'
* Limo (noun) a fast ball game of skill.
* Posthanger (noun) a cheater in the game of 40,40; also posthanger (verb): e.g. 'He's posthanging!'
* Radical (adjective) totally cool (see Cool).
* Well cool (adjective) really, really decent.

The drafts were revised and finally 'published' in the form of a guide for new pupils, using word processing.

Evaluation

As part of the assessment of the children's work during the project, I asked them to write a short description of what they thought that they had learnt. Figure 15.2 shows the description given by one girl.

At the end of the activities, I also gave the groups who had worked with me a diagnostic sheet to complete. I hoped that this would give me some additional insight into both their implicit awareness of standard English and their explicit knowledge of terminology, although it was not intended to measure all the learning outcomes of the activities. The sheet, partly adapted from Palmer (1994), is shown in Figure 15.3.

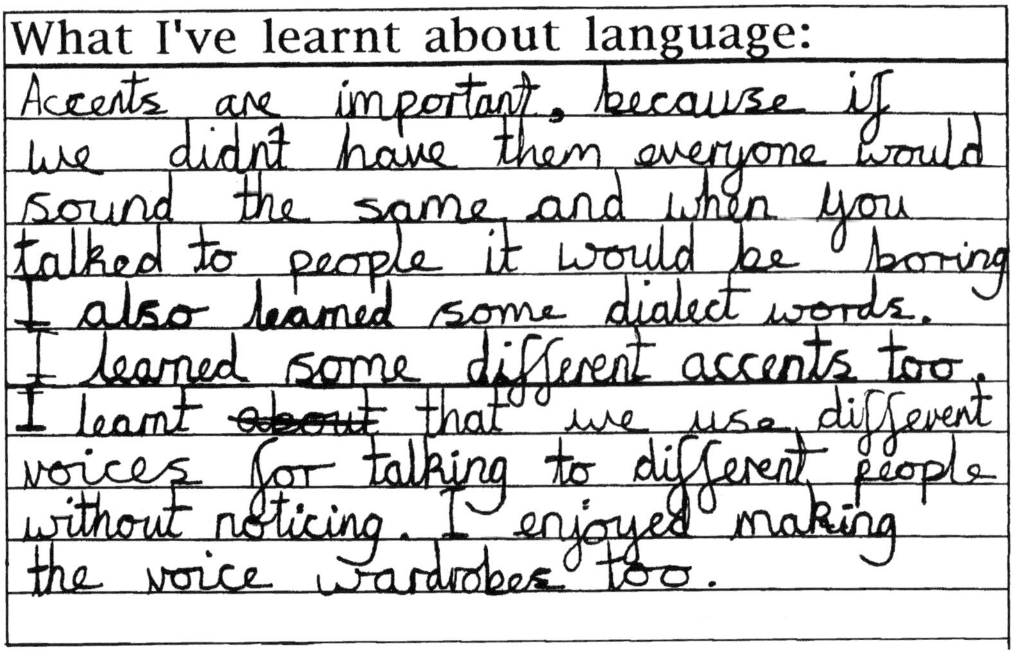

What I've learnt about language:

Accents are important, because if we didnt have them everyone would sound the same and when you talked to people it would be boring. I also learned some dialect words. I learned some different accents too. I learnt about that we use different voices for talking to different people without noticing. I enjoyed making the voice wardrobes too.

Figure 15.2 A short description of what one girl thought that she had learnt

Name: Age:

Are there any words in these sentences which don't sound right to you? If there are, please circle the words and write different ones underneath. If you think a sentence is OK, give it a tick at the side.

1. The stories what the children made up was all good.

2. I were that hungry I could of ate a bowl of cold rice pudding!

3. He were the handsomest of the two men.

4. The girls didn't know nothing about geography.

5. I could of got here no quicker.

6. The boy done all his homework so we were wore out.

7. Me and my brother seen a flying saucer.

Do you know what these words mean? Have a guess if you're not sure.

ACCCENT   DIALECT   STANDARD ENGLISH

Figure 15.3 A diagnostic sheet

I also asked the remainder of the children in the two parallel classes, who had not worked on the project, to complete the diagnostic sheet. Comparison of the two groups of pupils revealed a slightly increased score by the project group in Section A, dealing with implicit awareness of standard English (an average score of 37 per cent recognition of non-standard features, compared with 32 per cent). This, of course, could be accounted for by differences in the ability range in the two groupings. A clearer difference was observable in the responses to Section B, where, as expected, the project group showed much better understanding of the metalanguage. The children who had not taken part in the project, although they were following language schemes which dealt with these areas, were successful only in describing accent (59 per cent were able to define this term at least partly). There were no satisfactory responses to dialect; guesses included 'someone who shoots animals' and 'something to do with a phone'! Similarly, none of the non-project children demonstrated understanding of the term 'standard English'. There was a frequent tendency in the guesses recorded here to equate it with a 'high' standard and with assessment: 'a very good standard of English', 'hard English or original English or the best standard of English' and 'English up to your standard' were some examples.

The NC level descriptions do not mention pupils' knowledge or understanding of language, only their skills in using it in terms of speaking and listening and in writing. However, the project described certainly gave the participants the opportunity to demonstrate an observable development in their awareness of standard English, along the lines of progression outlined in the NC for Key Stage 2:

- Level 2. They are beginning to be aware that in some situations a more formal vocabulary and tone of voice are used.
- Level 3. They are beginning to be aware of standard English and when it is used.
- Level 4. They use appropriately some of the features of standard English vocabulary and grammar.
- Level 5. They begin to use standard English in formal situations.
- Level 6. They are usually fluent in their use of standard English in formal situations.

More detailed profiles of pupils would, of course, be needed to set children's awareness and use of standard English in the context of wider knowledge about language, as revealed during a project such as that described above.

The project could certainly have been expanded and continued to develop language study further in the context of reading and writing, rather than spoken language, which was the focus for most of the activities. Poetry of the kind used here would be an ideal vehicle for investigating and creating written texts which explore language use. (Further practical activities of this sort and suggestions for other rewarding texts and resources to use can be found in *Practical Ways to Teach Standard English and Language Study* (Lockwood 1998).)

Conclusions

Since this project was carried out a further significant political shift has led to the forthcoming introduction of The National Literacy Strategy. *The National Literacy Strategy Framework for Teaching* (DfEE 1998) defines literacy as uniting 'the important skills of reading and writing'. Speaking and listening skills 'are not separately identified in the Framework...[but] are an essential part of it', since 'Good oral work enhances pupils' understanding of language in both oral and written forms and of the way language can be used to communicate' (DfEE p.3).

Looking at the teaching programme proposed for Year 5 in the *Framework for Teaching*, it is encouraging to see that some of the areas covered by the activities described in this chapter are included:

- Year 5, Term 1, Sentence Level 2. To understand the basic conventions of standard English and consider when and why standard English is used.
- Year 5, Term 2, Sentence Level 6. To be aware of the differences between spoken and written language.
- Year 5, Term 3, Word Level 9. To understand how words vary across dialects.
- Year 5, Term 3, Word Level 13. To compile your own class/group dictionary using personally written definitions, e.g of slang, technical terms.

The emphasis here is clearly more on the grammatical features of standard English used in writing, but there is still a very clear requirement to set the standard form in the context of language variation in terms of mode, context, place and social grouping (and also time, in the Year 6 framework). It is interesting to find in the 'Technical vocabulary list' for Year 5 (DfEE 1998, p.71) the terms 'dialect', 'standard English' and 'slang', though 'accent' only appears in the glossary at the end (DfEE 1998, p.73).

It is also heartening to notice the centrality of texts to the *Framework for Teaching*, including poetry. The use of poems to investigate language variety in the ways suggested here would certainly be highly appropriate, not to say essential. For Year 5, for example, there is a requirement to 'read a number of poems by significant poets and identify what is distinctive about the style or content of their poems' (Year 5, Term 1, Text Level 6), 'to perform poems in a variety of ways' (Year 5, Term 2, Text Level 5), to read 'poems from a variety of cultures and traditions' (Year 5, Text Level 3), and to explore older literature through 'discussing differences in language used' (Year 5, Term 3, Text Level 6).

What will undoubtedly be more difficult under the National Literacy Strategy will be to incorporate the activities described here into the constraints of the Literacy Hour and its closely prescribed structure. This will be one of the challenges which lie ahead for primary teachers: how to include extended language investigations, and particularly activities which focus on the development of speaking and listening, into their dedicated literacy time. If the spirit of the Literacy Hour is allowed to prevail, rather than the letter only, then there is no reason why it cannot incorporate the sort of project detailed in this chapter, and ultimately lead to the literate classroom, in the fullest and widest sense of that term.

References

Ahlberg, A. (1989) *Heard It In the Playground*. London: Viking Kestrel.

Bain, R., Fitzgerald, B. and Taylor, M. (1992) *Looking into Language*. London: Hodder & Stoughton.

Blackburne, L. (1994) 'English advisers in revolt', *Times Educational Supplement* 13 May 12.

DfEE (1998) *The National Literacy Strategy: Framework for Teaching*. London: DfEE.

Haynes, J. (1992) *A Sense of Words*. London: Hodder & Stoughton.

Department of Education and Science (1984) *English from 5 to 16: Curriculum Matters 1*. London: HMSO.

Department of Education and Science (1986) *Responses to Curriculum Matters 1*. London: HMSO.

Department of Education and Science (1988) *Report of the Committee of Inquiry into the Teaching of the English Language (The Kingman Report)*. London: HMSO.

Department of Education and Science (1989) *National Curriculum English for ages 5–16*

(The Cox Report). London: HMSO.

Kay, J. (1992) *Two's Company*. London: Blackie.

Lockwood, M. (1995) 'What's happening to knowledge about language in the primary years?' in Raban-Bisby, B. (ed), *Developing Language and Literacy*. Stoke-on-Trent: Trentham Books.

Lockwood, M. (1998) *Practical Ways to Teach Standard English and Language Study*. Reading: Reading and Language Information Centre, The University of Reading.

Lutrario, C. (1993) *Exploring Language*. Aylesbury: Ginn.

McGough, R. and Rosen, M. (1979) *You Tell Me*. London: Kestrel.

Nichols, G. (1988) *Come on into My Tropical Garden*. London: A. & C. Black.

Palmer, S. and Brinton, P. (1988) *Mind Your Language*. Harlow: Oliver and Boyd.

Palmer, S. (1994) *The Longman Book Project: Language Books*. Harlow: Longman.

Rosen, M. (1974) *Mind Your Own Business*. London: Andre Deutsch.

Chapter 16

Who's afraid of the big bad verse?
Chris Powling, with Sean O'Flynn

Let us begin with the perfect endorsement of a teacher's work. It is written inside the front cover of *Poetry Please!* (Causley 1996), a selection of poems from the popular BBC Radio 4 programme (Figure 16.1).

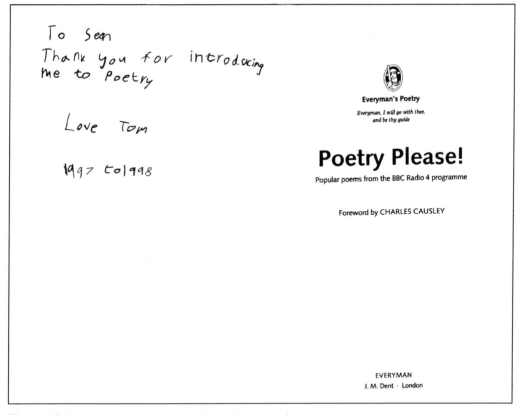

Figure 16.1 A perfect endorsement of a teacher's work

The inscription comes from Tom, aged 7, a pupil in an inner-city primary school. Sean O'Flynn is his teacher. At the end of their school year together, *Poetry Please!* was Tom's farewell present to Sean.

Well, it is not a SAT score. In its own modest way, however, it seems to me to represent something of a bullseye for Sean. No doubt he was not entirely surprised when it arrived. After all, Tom's enthusiasm for poetry must have been evident for some time – not least in his own writing:

'The red thing' by Tom
It looks like a
Hot man with leaves on top.
It is the red world.
It looks like they are green nits.
It is a red fat finger.
It's a soft cloud.
It feels bumpy.
It feels like hairs.
It smells like a sweet apple with angels.
It smells like a new book.
It is sweet like an orange.
It tastes like all the juices in the world.
It tastes like the juice in a orange
It sounds like it is saying 'Hey strawberry'.

For Tom, clearly, a poem is not just a red thing. It is a written thing, too (and with Sean as a teacher I bet he would spot the joke).

From the outset, then, Tom's encounters with poetry embrace both the consuming and the producing of it. His writing will reinforce and extend his reading . . . and his reading will do the same for his writing. To Tom, quite rightly, poets are not superior beings with a gift beyond any that he can lay claim to but simply people like himself who happen to have lived, read and written a little longer than he has. At this stage in his education, should anyone wish it otherwise?

In all that follows, then, the focus on how we can best create readers of verse among children of primary school age must not be taken as a downgrading of our complementary obligation to help them to become writers of verse as well. On the contrary, the two go together with a neat classroom-proof handiness that prose simply cannot match.

Back to reading, however – just how was Tom introduced to poetry as a Year 2 pupil? Here, I shall hand over to Sean himself:

"You find a poem. You like it. But what can you do about it? Adrian Mitchell (1993) has some ideas in 'What to do when you find a poem you like':
    Read it again
    And write it
    Learn it by heart
    Recite it

What appeals to me about this view is its appreciation of poetry as a 'messy' activity. You can be as involved in a poem as in an experiment, a painting or a football match. The poem does not have to stay on the page, pristine and awaiting dissection.

    Instead, it can be learnt by heart; this was at the core of poetry activities in my classroom. Every week the children were introduced to a 'poem of the week' which they would try to learn. The

National Curriculum says that children should 'listen to poetry, learning some by heart'.

The poem would be blown up on the photocopier and displayed in a frame next to the book from which it came. A handful of photocopies would be made onto card, laminated and placed in the reading corner – an increasingly bulky area as the year went on.

I would read the poem once or twice before letting the children see it. If I did not do this, the children were distracted from listening by trying to read the text as fast as they were hearing it. Then we might briefly discuss anything that the children noticed about the poem – rhyme, unusual vocabulary, etc. We read the poem again when we could see it, with children joining in if they could remember it, or read it, or both.

Those who felt confident enough would have a go at reciting the poem there and then; others would wait until they had taken their copy home to learn. As the week went on, more and more of the class would 'have' the poem by heart, the less confident being supported by the variety of recitations from teacher and classmates.

When reciting, all efforts were applauded, but absolute precision was also demanded. We discussed how hard poets had worked to select just those words we saw.

Interspersed between recitals would be readings of many other poems, and lots of talk: Do you like this? Why do you like that part? What can you say about the way that it sounds or looks? None of these questions is earth-shatteringly original. More important is the time allowed for consideration of them and of the children's responses. The more seriously their responses were taken, the more thoughtful they became.

Poetry appreciation and response are difficult to assess in a measurable SAT-type way; it relies on the old-fashioned method of valuing a teacher's perception, and what I perceived was a welling-up of enthusiasm about poetry that never ebbed. Children often asked for copies of poems other than the poem of the week to take home and learn. Snatches of poetry were often heard being shouted out in the playground. 'Yes!' became the response to being told, 'We're going to look at some poems.' The classroom atmosphere, dictated by the poem, was joyous, silly, awestruck and solemn, but always committed.

This willingness to make poems their own by learning them, questioning them, reciting them, writing their own versions and so on grew markedly as the year went on. The children seemed to share Charles Causley's view of poems as 'a living organism ...of which we make something new every day'."

As good a start as any, I would say. What's not so good for young teachers of poetry, especially those such as Sean who feel a little diffident about not being English specialists, is the bated-breath reverence which verse can inspire.

The most recent example of this is an article by the well-known anthologist Anne Harvey (1988) published in the children's book magazine *Carousel*. It is called 'Children's poetry: the real or the rubbish?'. Now let me say at once that I have much sympathy with Anne's main purpose in this piece – to ensure that we encourage youngsters to read as wide a range as possible of the best verse that's available. Who could possibly disagree with that? What bothers me are the terms in which she casts her argument about what counts as the Real (hurrah!) and the Rubbish (boo!). Here is how she sets it up:

Children's poetry has suffered...and I use the term intentionally, a boom. The controversy over what poetry is continues; more people are trying to churn it out than you'd believe, and in the children's literature world plenty of very dubious stuff is published. Much of it does not later stray into the memory, or send shivers down the spine as Houseman wished. It does not 'begin in wisdom and end in delight'... Robert Frost's idea. It fails to 'enrich a child's heritage of words' which Rumer Godden called the real work of a writer.

As the article develops, the 'very dubious stuff' that Anne finds so objectionable seems to have three interrelated characteristics: it is popular in that it requires no mediating adult; it fails to take proper account of poetry's 'transforming' power; it is 'condescending' in the tone of voice that it adopts.

All three aspects raise issues of genuine critical interest. Here, however, they are treated so simplistically that what emerges looks more like a parading of private hobby-horses than a canter through literary options. Anne asserts, for instance, that 'Children will write and discover the rubbish for themselves: lavatory jokes and garish pictures will always sell'. The real, apparently, will not get a look-in unless 'teachers, parents, librarians' and other 'caring, responsible adults' are in close attendance.

Well, that is not my experience (or, as we shall see, Sean O'Flynn's). Certainly, the boom which Anne so regrets has produced a measure of what a poet friend of mine calls 'snot-and-bogey-pie verse'. A little of this goes a very long way with me, too. However, the suggestion that children left free to make their own choices will invariably settle for 'smut' strikes me as little short of libellous – on the children themselves as well as on James Berry, Jackie Kay, Roger McGough, Grace Nicholls, Brian Patten and umpteen other writers who have done so much to make poetry a form that is as accessible and compelling today as any picture book or story. Should we not be rejoicing in their success?

Of course, no one would deny that their achievement has included some adjustment of the familiar poetic repertoire to incorporate new preoccupations, new modes of address and even new ways of 'reading' – on tape, on video or through public performance, for instance. What I do not accept is the proposition that initiatives such as these are undermining the entire poetic enterprise. Yet Anne Harvey offers just such a reaction as if it clinches her case (Hamlyn 1998):

I hate poems.
I hate poems because
They're always about custard
And teachers who are not like my teachers
And putting your fingers up your nose
And monsters in the classroom
And children who are rough and being sick.

I hate poems.
I hate poets who come and shout
Their words batter me with language
I do not use in accents I can't understand.

I hate poems.
Because they shut the windows in my mind
With their custard and their fingers
And their shouting.
When poets come I look
Out of the windows to the gardens opposite
And watch the daffodils dancing.

Er...really?

I find it rather hard to trust Sue Hamlyn's poem. Since we are told, in a footnote, that the poet is also an English teacher who is writing 'in the voice of (her) daughter then aged

11', are we being invited to believe that it is her own child's experience that she is offering us? If so, then it is clear that these custard-toting nose-picking versifiers must have been virtuosos when it came to shouting. It cannot have been easy to obliterate the home influence of such a mother with a couple of author visits.

If, on the other hand, it is some other child who is being ventriloquised – or, more likely, the poet impersonating a child for her own purposes – I am still left very uneasy. What is a child reader, or an adult reader for that matter, supposed to make of these lines? 'Their words batter with language I do not use in accents I can't understand.' Would the language and accent in question be anything like the following, I wonder?

> explain yuself
> wha yu mean
> when you say half-caste
> yu mean when light an shadow
> mix in de sky
> is a half-caste weather
> well in dat case
> england weather
> nearly always half-caste
> in fact some o dem cloud
> half-caste till dem overcast...

There are no daffodils there, I admit. Nevertheless, whoever the implied author of 'I hate poems' is intended to be I would recommend introducing her to the work of John Agard (1997), for example, as a matter of urgency. Faerie casements are not the only windows in the mind that poetry can open.

At this point, both Sue Hamlyn and Anne Harvey may well protest that it is not John Agard that they are objecting to, not inspired vernacular such as his...gracious no. It is those others, for goodness' sake. You know, the custard-toting nose-picking kind who shout.

A firm 'maybe' on that one. I might be more convinced of Anne's case if 'Children's poetry: the real or the rubbish' had given a little more space, and a little more credit, to the verse in recent years that has won readers among children who had little idea that poetry can also include them, their preoccupations and where they happen to be coming from. Yes, we do still need Adlestrop, as Anne recommends, and Omar Khayaam, too. Stopping by woods on a snowy evening will always be a good idea, but we also need to be aware that the transforming power of poetry can operate much closer to home (Dixon 1988):

> She's at the window again!
> Bug-eyed,
> Dressing gowned, and grey.
> 'See her!'
> squeal the Brownie pack returning from St Johns.
> 'See her!'
> chorus the boys returning from nowheremuch.
> And there she stares -
> Tall
> and gaunt
> and hair unpinned... staring
>   staring
>   staring
> staring beyond the silver slates
>   of Stanley Street

of Wilmer Way
and distant Arnos Grove.

This is also shockingly short of daffodils.

Yes, I am teasing now. Nevertheless, amid Anne's blanket condemnation of 'published rubbish on loos, smelly granpas, bristly aunts, amorphous mums and dads whose stomachs gurgle', I would have welcomed a compensating mention of Miss Hubbard, staring at the moon, or Michael Rosen's (1985) 'Babah and Zaida' or Kit Wright's (1981) 'Useful Person'... or, indeed, any hint at all of the entirely successful attempts by recent children's poets to counteract Adrian Mitchell's (1993) famous pronunciation that the reason that most people ignore most poetry is because most poetry ignores most people. Had she acknowledged this, I would not be nearly so anxious to remind her of the popular dross of yesteryear – the poems of Enid Blyton, for instance – which had a tweeness that is far more likely to terminate children's interest than a bit of silly lavatory humour. My chief complaint about Anne's article is the impression that it gives that rubbish is a recent publishing phenomenon... and that 'real poetry', defying the evidence of her own excellent anthologies, peaked at about the same time that the church clock stopped in Grantchester.

Meanwhile, what about Rotherhithe? These days, with so much material to choose from, and so many literacy constituencies to satisfy, it is not easy to devise a regimen of poems for youngsters such as Tom – as Sean O'Flynn explains:

"My choice of poems for the class was guided by the simple principle: would they enjoy them? Of course, enjoyment should be part of all learning. However, I was also motivated by my own experiences of poetry at school where any potential for delight in words had been pushed aside by the pressure to analyse.

In the early part of the year, especially, it was vital for the children to experience success in learning poems by heart. Many of the poems of the week, then, were short, rhyming poems at the beginning. Their first poem was by Michael Rosen:

Down behind the dustbin
I met a dog called Jim
He didn't know me
And I didn't know him

This is memorised almost as soon as it is heard. A very few repetitions and it is securely known. That was the point. The children became aware that they could deliberately and consciously learn a poem. This produced an excited buzz which was exactly the sort of association with poetry that I wanted them to have.

The poem which they memorised had also made them laugh – a very obvious indication of enjoyment. It might have been tempting to limit the range to humorous poetry; at least this would have guaranteed enjoyment, and this would not have been as limiting as it might sound. There is a huge range of 'funny' poems, from the vernacular humour of Michael Rosen (1981), through word play of Ogden Nash, to the whimsicality of Eleanor Farjeon, and so on. All these poems are capable of serious consideration by children.

But, of course, children would be missing much of what poetry can do if they thought it could only be funny. So from the start of the year I occasionally read them more serious poetry that I thought they could enjoy, such as 'The charge of the Light Brigade'. I would often read these without probing for response. One of my concerns about the Literacy Hour is that it does not seem to recognise the value of children meeting literature purely for enjoyment. I am convinced, however, that the expectation of enjoyment that had been built up around poetry in my class helped enormously when I did ask for a response to these more 'weighty' poems. This expectation made it easier for the children to concentrate on the parts that they liked, rather than get frustrated and distracted by the parts that they did not understand. They might not have got near to fully comprehending the poem, but they did understand that finding a poem difficult is not the end of the world, nor a reason to give up thinking about it. They learned that it is legitimate to like parts of the poem, even if you are not sure what those sounds that you find so enticing actually mean."

Here, for the record, is a selection of the poems shared by Sean and his class:

John Agard	'Where does laughter begin?'
Allan Ahlberg	'Please, Mrs Butler'
William Blake	'The tyger'
Valerie Bloom	'Duppy Jamboree'
Charles Causley	'Early in the morning'
Emily Dickinson	'A slash of blue'
Richard Edwards	'Keep well back'
Max Fatchen	'Isn't it amazing?'
Eleanor Farjeon	'Cats'
Robert Frost	'Stopping by woods on a snowy evening'
Julie Holder	'Chips'
Gerard Manley Hopkins	'Pied Beauty'
Wes Magee	'What is the sun?'
John Masefield	'A ballad of John Silver'
Beverly McLoughland	'Lemon moon'
Spike Milligan	'On the Ning Nang Nong'
A A Milne	'When I was one'
Adrian Mitchell	'What to do when you find a poem you like'
Ogden Nash	'The duck'
Judith Nicholls	'Riddle'
Brian Patten	'Schoolitis'
Jack Prelutsky	'Black cat'
James Reeves	'Grim and gloomy'
Michael Rosen	'The Michael Rosen rap'
Christina Rosetti	'What is pink?'
Willie Russell	'Sammy'
William Shakespeare	'Full fathom five . . .'
William Shakespeare	'The witches' song' (Macbeth)
Shel Silverstein	'Magical Eraser'
Alfred, Lord Tennyson	'The Eagle'
William Makepeace Thackeray	'A tragic story'
Kit Wright	'Acorn Haiku'

No selection of poems will satisfy everyone, of course. Nor should we ignore the customised aspect of Sean's, it is directed at particular kids in a particular situation as appraised by a particular classroom teacher. As such, outside commentators should know their place. It seems to have worked for Tom, however, and it is not hard to see why. The predominant tone is light hearted but there is considerably variety in style, tone and mood – including a smattering of non-contemporary verse. The emphasis on present-day poets, however, lets the children know from the start that poetry is a living medium; also it provides up-to-date models for their own verse writing which are neither too formidable nor too bland.

Models, yes – not templates. The question of tone of voice arises here – always problematic for adult writers intending a child readership. Anne Harvey quotes with approval the attitude of James Reeves who 'did not feel equal to write poems for children until he had been writing adult poetry for over twenty years'. She adds 'Could this, I wonder, become law?' Let us hope not and be glad it never was. Otherwise, Robert Louis Stevenson (1995) would have been prosecuted for *A Child's Garden of Verses*. In fact, the sort of adjustments and modulations that a children's poet makes are no less complex, subtle and necessary than those of a children's novelist…and we have Barbara Wall's (1991) study *The Narrator's Voice* to demonstrate that far more is required of the latter than the mere refusal to 'condescend'. So let us give the children a variety of voices to experiment with, reminding ourselves that poetry's capacity to be numinous, and spine tingling, is only one tool in its kit. It can be mad, bad and dangerous as well. Also, it can cope with reality, however harsh:

> I have just discovered
> a hole in the floor of my car.
> I say 'my' car.
> It was my mother's.
> She died…

Michael Rosen's superb low-key meditation on his mother's cancer in a poem called 'Bodywork'.

However, I would not suggest that Tom should read this yet. At some stage, nevertheless, he will realise the truth of Wallace Stevens's comment that poetry is 'a response to the daily necessity of getting the world right', a definition which is splendidly agnostic about the what and the how of doing this. Why, it even permits humour – that *bête noire* of the Grantchester School of Versifiers.

Also, real poetry takes risks. It involves the sort of playing that is a serious business. Tom found this out by getting to verbal grips with his strawberry. Sean gives this report on the writing of 'The red thing'. See Hattery:

> "We started by looking at a Wes Magee poem which vividly describes the sun: 'The sun is an orange dinghy sailing across a calm sea' (from 'What is the Sun?'). In discussing the poem it felt natural to explain what metaphors and similes were. The best explanation I could provide was that they both made 'pictures with words'. We attempted a class composition about the moon in this style. The children found the idea very difficult at first but, after much discussion, eventually many interesting images emerged, including the following: 'The full moon is a capital O.' 'The moon is a lightbulb in the sky.' 'It is a white boomerang thrown into the sky.'
>
> In a later session, wanting to introduce imagery in another context, I asked the children to choose a classmate and to 'make pictures with words' about them. Many of the poems focused on physical appearance:
>
> > Claire's hair is as soft as a rabbit's fur.
> > Allan's ears are as round as a ball.
>
> > When Jeffrey
> > runs he
> > is like
> > a rhino.

Other examples used imagery to give a very perceptive view of their classmates' characteristics:

> Jack is a waterfall fastly falling off rocks.

> Elvin is a big black rock.

Jack was rather a blur at times; Elvin did have a rock-like calmness to his nature.

Some children took the idea of envisaging a friend as something else and really flew with it. This was written by a child with English as a second language:

Martin is calm as a sun
He is floating in the sky...
He has not got no hair
He's got a yellow face.
He has no body.
He's boiling down at us.
What's the matter with him?

When I introduced the strawberries as objects to write 'pictures in words' about, the children understood immediately. They still needed lots of opportunities to discuss ways of doing this, however. I want to emphasise the role of talk in the success of all these activities. Thinking, discussing and questioning together provided individuals with the confidence to value their own ideas. This had gone on all year, helping them to define what they had read, what they wanted to write, and what they had written.

The children were asked to think of at least three pictures of what the strawberry looked like, smelt like, felt like, sounded like (if they thought it made a sound), and finally – for obvious practical reasons – what it tasted like. At this stage it was important for the children to work on their own, in silence, interrupted only by my sharing with them examples of good work. Paired and group writing are vital, but so is the opportunity for children to work alone, not least to demonstrate to themselves what they are capable of. Silence allowed the children to concentrate intently on creating their own strawberry, seen afresh in different ways:

It looks like a star
with a beanstalk

It is a
face with freckles

It feels like
a dog's nose

The quality of the children's writing was vastly improved by their increasing grasp of redrafting skills. When their first draft was complete they worked in mixed-ability pairs. I asked them to listen to their partner's poem, to say something positive about it and to try to suggest something that could be changed. This could involve adding words, taking some away or switching some around. They then negotiated where slashes were needed to indicate line breaks. All these ideas were being regularly modelled for the children when we redrafted our class poems and in my conferences with individuals.

Tom was thrilled with the quality of his poem – as were all the children – and the class book that we made was a very popular read. Their poems show what children can do when given the time to look and think. I shall never look at a strawberry in the same way again."

Now we have come full circle. What, for me, is most pleasing about the response of Tom Hayes, aged 7, apprentice reader and writer in Rotherhithe, is the likelihood that he has been inoculated already from the sort of anxiety about verse displayed by Dickens's Tony Weller in *The Pickwick Papers*. Charles Causley quotes this in his introduction to *Poetry Please!*

'Tain't in poetry, is it?'
'No, no,' replied Sam.
'Wery glad to hear it,' said Mr Weller. 'Poetry's unnat'ral; no man ever talked poetry 'cept a beadle on boxin' day, or Warren's blackin', or Rowland's oil, or some o' them low fellows; never you let yourself down to talk poetry, my boy.'

This is an opinion that Tom would not share. As for his future, who can tell? With luck, it will include Addlestrop and Arnos Grove, Omar Khayamm and Miss Hubbard, dads with gurgling stomachs and yes, daffodils – together with more and more verse of his own. Tom is out of Sean's hands now. He has got a long reading and writing road ahead of him. Surely, however, he has made a wonderful start, in that it sounds like he is saying, 'Hey, poetry!'

References

Agard, J. (1997) *Get Back Pimple*. London: Puffin Books.

Causley, C. (1996) *Poetry please!*. London: J. M. Dent.

Dixon, P. (1988) *Grow Your Own Poems*. Basingstoke: Macmillan Education.

Hamlyn, S. (1998) 'Children's Poetry: the real or the rubbish', *Carousel* spring, 10–11.

Harvey, A. (1998) 'Children's Poetry: the real or the rubbish', *Carousel* spring, 10–11.

Mitchell, A. (1993) *Thirteen Secrets of Poetry*. London: Simon and Schuster.

Rosen, M. (1981) *Wouldn't You Like to Know*. London: Puffin Books.

Rosen, M. (1985) *Quick, Let's Get Out of Here*. London: Puffin Books.

Stevenson, R.L. (1995) *A Child's Garden of Verses*. London: Penguin Children's Books.

Wall, B. (1991) *The Narrator's Voice*. London: Macmillan.

Wright, K. (1981) *Hot Dog and Other Poems*. London: Puffin Books.

Chapter 17

The role of drama in the literate classroom

Suzi Clipson-Boyles

The standards of children's reading and writing have always been high on the agendas of schools and governments. Most parents also hope and expect that their children should become literate. In the past, these concerns have been predominantly concerned with acquisition, achievement and literature (Street 1994) and have ignored the fact that literacy practices in our society spread far and wide beyond the reading and writing of fiction. Stop to think for a moment about the multiple applications of the written word in our society. A journey on the underground, watching television, a visit to the shops or even a tour around a farmyard will reveal vast varieties of print instructions, labels, logos, advertisements, packaging and so on. The literate classroom should aim to provide a multidimensional mirror of literacies in the outside world, so that children have opportunities to encounter, use and create the printed word in different ways for a wide range of purposes and audiences.

Recognising the vast prominence of print and other semiotic systems is an important step towards creating an effective language environment in the primary school. The acknowledgement of children's own literacies, and those of their cultures and communities is also a vital part of the process, building outwards to develop their experiences into wider realms (Heath 1993). In this way, their existing deep levels of knowledge, skills and identities are extended rather than ignored. Exploring a full range of literacies can provide children with a broad understanding and experience, enabling them to make well-informed choices. This is more likely to result in high achievement in literacy than narrow models of transmission in which children are expected to adopt imposed practices which are totally alien to themselves and their world.

Drama is an extremely good means of providing experiences which contribute towards meaningful models of language development and learning. It can be used in many ways to offer encounters with a wide range of language and literacy systems. These can provide opportunities to teach skills, to provide contexts within which those skills can be practised, and to empower children as decision makers and users of language and literacy. However, before examining actual examples of how this might happen, let us look more generally, first of all, at the place of drama in the primary curriculum.

Drama in the primary curriculum

The twentieth century's two most significant education acts have each had a powerful impact upon drama in primary education. The first, in 1944, set in motion a post-war enthusiasm for self-expression which was harnessed in the 1950s and continued to develop into an experiential approach to learning during the 1960s and 1970s. The second, in 1988, introduced a National Curriculum which resulted in virtually eliminating drama from primary schools.

However, in the mid-1990s, drama was embedded firmly into the revised order for English (DfEE 1995) and became the focus for scrutiny by OFSTED inspections. This led to a slow but steady revival after a decade of virtual extinction. As with most spiral changes, it has emerged in a newly adapted form which has been referred to as new wave drama (Clipson-Boyles 1997). This approach goes a long way to resolving past conflicts between those who have seen drama as a purely experiential child-centred activity, never repeated or rehearsed, and those who insist that theatre arts and performance should be included as a distinct curriculum subject in the education of young children. Such contrasting views have not always been helpful to the cause of primary drama, often being perceived as opposite, and usually irreconcilable, points on a spectrum as illustrated below.

The primary drama spectrum

Educational drama <————————————————>	Performance drama
child centred	audience centred
spontaneous	planned
unrepeated	rehearsed
process oriented	product orientated

Educational drama was about providing experiences for children through which they could develop ideas and understanding of themselves and their worlds, both real and imagined. The process was the all-important feature. Performance drama, on the other hand was seen as the development of theatre skills for the presentation of an end product and was centred exclusively within the performing arts.

Rather than continuing to regard these features as two extremes, new wave drama identifies them as complementary, and sometimes interwoven, features of a drama curriculum. Just as experiential drama can sometimes feed into performance activities (e.g. an improvisation might be developed into a scripted scene to show to an audience of parents in assembly), so can performance skills and knowledge of theatre arts contribute towards children's experiential learning (e.g. sustaining a role during hot seating). In this way, the true richness and diversity of primary drama can be recognised and employed for maximum impact upon children's learning and development.

The extent to which the emphasis on process or product connects or overlaps depends very much on the way of working, and this in turn will depend upon the learning objectives of the activity. There is no single assumed way of teaching drama. Instead there are many different ways of working, so let us now take a look at the choices of drama modes available to teachers when planning for a literate classroom.

Modes of drama

Drama need not always happen with the whole class at the same time, and it does not always require a large space. A 5 minute improvised interview situation with six children in pairs as preparation for writing an imaginary report is just as much a part of the drama curriculum as a full-scale presentation of scenes from 1940s' Britain. Drama can happen using:

- different group sizes,
- different group compositions,
- different time spans,
- different spaces,
- different planned outcomes,
- different levels of teacher input and
- different styles of teaching.

Clearly it is beyond the scope of this chapter to provide a fully comprehensive guide to planning drama. This can be found in more detailed specialist drama books. However, it is important that you begin to develop an awareness of the main drama modes available to your teaching repertoire. Table 17.1 summarises the most commonly used teaching approaches with examples of how these might be used in the development of literacy.

Table 17.1 Different drama techniques with literacy examples

Approach	Description	Example for the literate classroom
Role play areas	Designated area of the classroom with props, costumes, etc., to encourage role play	Using telephone directories and catalogues, form filling and phone messages
Dynamic duos	Improvisations of interviews, telephone conversations and other work in pairs	Interviewing a character from a story
Hot seating	Character in role (either teacher or child) to be questioned by class	Children research a history topic and prepare questions for a 'time traveller' (possibly teacher in role)
Writer in role	Writing activity taking place in an imagined situation, writing from the perspective of another person	Writing as a politician to explain the plans for a local park
Reader in role	Reading activity taking place in an imagined situation, writing from the perspective of another person	Spontaneous improvisation of response to a letter which the teacher provides (e.g. news of a competition prize)
Guided action	Children improvise to teacher running commentary	Exploring a desert island after a shipwreck which may lead to writing a message in a bottle
Spontaneous improvisation	Exploring a situation without any forward planning	Discovering that the house has been burgled: make lists of stolen items, write a statement
Reconstructed improvisation	Revisiting a spontaneous improvisation to reshape it for presentation to others	An alternative ending to a particular chapter from a story
Simulation	Creating a pretend experience within which the children will role play and improvise, often discussed extensively beforehand	Recreating an event after research in non-fiction, CD ROMs, etc.

Script work	Writing scripts after improvisation or from stories	Reading a newspaper story then writing a script to present certain events from the story
Teacher in role	Can be used in different situations, e.g. to answer questions from the children, to share a problem for them to help solve, to participate in guided action, improvisation, simulation, etc.	Teacher in role as parent of a character from a story, asking the children for advice about how to deal with the characters situation
Tableau	Create a still scene of characters	Presenting three scenes which sum up the action or atmospheres from a story or poem
Mime	Representing through movement and expression, but no speech	Creating a nursery rhyme for others to watch and guess
Radio	A range of programmes can be explored, helping children focus on language, expression and fluency	Rewrite news items from the paper to be read aloud, interviews and comments about the report
Video	Using models from film and television to create videoed presentations	Making an advertisement for an invented product
Freeze frame	Still scene which can happen in the middle of action (to be discussed) or which comes to life after a countdown to action	A scene from fiction which comes to life as the characters
Puppets	A vast range, from sticks with a cardboard face to string puppets, can be used to retell stories and create new ones	Puppet characters from known books
Masks	Helps the less confident to take on another character	Used especially for retelling the Greek myths, etc.
Dance drama	Movement with sound presenting story or poetry	Composing sounds based on the moods of a piece of writing
Performance	Preparing drama for an audience	Exploring a play, e.g. *A Midsummer Night's Dream*, improvising scenes, using contemporary language with some of the original vocabulary, presenting a rehearsed summary version of the play

Drama offers contexts for learning which could not normally be part of an every-day classroom environment. It can transport children through time, across seas, into space and into the worlds of fantasy. This is a wonderful resource for teachers to have at their fingertips! In addition, drama can offer much to the shaping and development of collaborative and social skills. High motivation, longer periods on task, and the more effective retention of learning are also positive outcomes of working with drama.

Despite the temptation to expand on all these wonderful advantages of drama in the primary curriculum, we are looking specifically in this chapter at the role of drama in relation to language and literacy. Therefore, we shall now go on to examine how drama can provide multiple purposes for reading, writing, speaking and listening. We shall also consider briefly the place of theatre arts and drama within the agendas of the literate classroom.

Teaching language and literacy through drama

Drama is a requirement of the National Curriculum within the programmes of study for English where there are 16 explicit references. Some of these are theatre oriented (e.g. the reading of plays, or the response to professional performances) and some relate directly to language skills (e.g. speaking for different purposes in role play). It is also possible to see drama as a teaching approach to other requirements of the document. For example, reading and writing for a range of audiences could take place as preparation for, during or as a follow-on from a drama activity.

Likewise the National Literacy Strategy (NLS) states that drama has an important role to play in developing outcomes from its reading objectives and many of the literacy activities required by the NLS can be supported and enhanced by drama (DfEE 1998).

Drama has three main parts to play in the development of language and literacy:

- to provide frameworks for learning about, using and discussing language as required by the curriculum for English and the NLS;
- to provide language learning contexts in other subject areas;
- to develop communication and performance and critical appreciation skills, within theatre arts.

Each of these should encompass an integrated approach to language learning, where speaking, listening, reading and writing are inter-linked in useful and meaningful ways. Here are some examples.

- experiences as stimuli for writing and/or reading, e.g. improvised interviews between reporter and victim of a burglary, leading to report writing;
- play contexts for practising skills in role, e.g. travel agent's role play area, reading brochures and completing forms;
- simulation of situations requiring reading and/or writing, e.g. research from non-fiction before preparing an air raid experience;
- developing spoken language as a starting point for writing, e.g. improvisations of a scene to be developed into a script for others;
- providing a context for reading and/or performing aloud, e.g. reading a poem while others mime;
- reading and interpreting play scripts, e.g. time-limited task to interpret stage directions and then a 'perform' workshop session, reading from the text, to the rest of the class, with movement;
- comparing language in different situations, e.g. presenting a short soap opera extract in a different genre.

Drama and literature

The place of literature in primary education is not just about teaching children to read stories and poetry independently. It should also involve discussion, critical listening and a range of reading and writing experiences. The exploration and analysis of literature and poetry required by the NLS can be assisted enormously by drama. Interactive and experiential activities can offer real opportunities for burrowing beneath the surface features of texts and beyond. Not only does this help children to develop as active and critical readers, but also it deepens their knowledge of the workings of texts and their authors which they can, in turn, bring to their own writing. Here are two examples.

Key Stage1 The Snow Maze *by Jan Mark (1993)*

Having read the first three chapters and discussed the rhyming taunts of the children ('Joe's mad. Joe's sad. Joe's bad. Mazy, crazy, lazy Joe.', etc.), possibly writing these onto a flip chart and asking children to change the onsets, the activity then turns to an examination of character motivation. Explain to the children that you will pretend to be Joe and they should be kind children, helping him to solve his problem with the unpleasant children in the story. Stress that you want them to ask Joe as many questions as possible and then to try to help him to solve his problem. Using a prop or costume to differentiate between in role and out of role (e.g. a baseball cap or an anorak, leave the area and return in role (see hot seating, in the previous section)). Remember that you can redirect the questioning if it is not sufficiently deep, e.g. 'How do you think I felt when I hid under the table?' 'What do you think I should do with the magic key?' When the hot seating has reached a conclusion, return to normal and discuss the outcomes.

Key Stage 2 The Iron Man *by Ted Hughes (1986)*

Read Chapter 1 of *The Iron Man* to the whole class. Discuss the author's use of language, are in particular the atmosphere of the scene and implied threat which is created by the actions of the Iron Man. Also discuss why the author might have chosen to include the interactions with the gulls (rather than humans) at this point in the book. Next, divide the class into six groups and give each a different role and information relating to that role. Examples might include ministry of defence workers who wish to destroy the Iron Man, scientists, local residents, etc. Having set up the classroom as a meeting room (probably all the children on chairs in a square around the edges of the room) establish signals for in role and out of role, and let the meeting commence to discuss what should be done about the Iron Man. You will also need to select an appropriate child to chair the meeting. You will be in role of Hogarth, using the opening paragraphs of Chapter 2 of *The Iron Man* to guide you about your sighting of the Iron Man. After the role play, ask the children for their views on what events they think would take the story forward in an interesting way.

Drama, theatre arts and the literate classroom

It is perfectly appropriate to include a theatre arts strand within the English curriculum for the following reasons:

- Performance activities can include relevant oracy skills.
- Performance appraisal can include relevant critical skills.
- Reading and writing scripts are valuable language activities which should be placed in a practical drama context.
- Reading and watching the work of professional playwrights are important parts of the literature curriculum.
- Theatres also offer a range of other texts (e.g. programmes, posters, reviews) which can be used in the classroom.

Providing children with opportunities to watch and critically to appraise the performances of others (as required by the National Curriculum Order for English) can offer models of language which they can emulate in their own work. Likewise, theatre visits are also valuable tools for developing the boundaries of critical response.

Drama, non-fiction and real world texts

Language and literacy are not limited to literature alone. While fiction, poetry and drama texts are an important part of the cultural and multicultural past and present, these represent only a proportion of texts with which adults engage in their daily lives. It is important that the literate classroom reflects this, both in the range of texts available to the children and in the variety of genres within which they are expected to write. Drama offers contexts for learning by creating situations to give their writing a real purpose.

The NLS prescribes a broad range of genres in addition to fiction and poetry. Table 17.2 shows some examples of how such texts might be integrated into work beyond the Literacy Hour using drama.

Table 17.2 Drama and the use of non-fiction

Year, Term	Text	Drama activity
Year 1, Term 1	Signs, lists, labels	Children creating an office in role play area
Year 2, Term 1	Explanations	Whole-class guided action of an event; write an explanation of each section on a frame chart using *because* as the main conjunction
Year 3, Term 1	Non-chronological reports	5 minute dynamic duos as parents and teachers discussing pupils; follow-up writing of report writing about their best friend
Year 4, Term 1	Instructions	Role play as safety officers in a super-market; brainstorming the dangers; designing safety posters for staff and customers
Year 5, Term 1	News reports	Groups of five to create special report television news feature on selected event (improvise, reshape, script, perform or video)
Year 6, Term 1	Diary	Follow-up writing to an improvisation such as the evacuation of a village in the path of a volcano

As with all good teaching, it is important to plan areas of focus when using drama. The teaching points and intended learning outcomes should be made explicit in prepared plans and should be clear to the children as well as the teacher!

Multiple literacies and drama

The wide variety of uses for print in our society, mentioned briefly at the start of this chapter, can differ in five essential ways:

1. purpose or function;
2. intended audience;
3. text format (outer framework);
4. vocabulary and construction (inner content);
5. contexts in which they are used.

In order to consider the importance of extending literacy and language so that the multiple literacies of society are included, it can be helpful to look more closely at texts and contexts which are not always featured in the traditional curricula for teaching English:

- community languages: scenes with translations and/or discussions about language;
- comics: freeze-frame strip cartoons followed by writing speech bubbles;
- television programmes: exploring dialects in soap operas;
- shops: role play corners with associated writing activities;
- cartoons: using as model for personifying different animals;
- advertising: look at examples, then design and sell a product;
- home life: home corner with reading and writing opportunities;
- work places: improvisations and role play with real texts and writing tasks;
- street language: thematic rap as part of performance.

Drama across and beyond the curriculum

Such planning should also take place in other subject areas. The teaching of language and literacy is not limited to the curriculum for English, and the literate classroom is one in which the teacher does not merely build on chance language encounters but proactively plans language and literacy learning into other curriculum areas. Cross-curricular topics such as gender, multicultural and health education can also generate useful contexts for language and literacy through drama.

Summary

Literacy encompasses more than mere technical approaches to deciphering and creating codes. Literacy consists of a complex set of practices which have social and cultural implications. Acknowledging this rich and diverse nature of literacy, and its inextricable links to communication, can assist teachers in providing contexts for learning in which children not only develop strong skills and high levels of achievement but also become discerning and confident users of multiple literacy practices.

Drama is an excellent way of providing such contexts. It offers many approaches which can be adapted according to the teaching and learning required. It is a pedagogy which should be part of every primary teacher's repertoire, and the wonderful responses from children observed during drama activities can only serve to reinforce this view. If a classroom is to be truly literate, it should include drama as an integral part of its total curriculum.

References

Clipson-Boyles, S. (1997) 'Drama', in *Implementing the Primary Curriculum. A Teacher's Guide*. Ashcroft and Palacio (eds) London: Falmer Press.

DfEE (1995) *Programmes of Study for English*. London: HMSO.

DfEE (1998) *Literacy Training Pack*. London: HMSO.

Heath, S. B. (1993) 'The madness of reading and writing ethnography', *Anthropology and Education Quarterly* **24**(3), 256–68.

Hughes, T. (1986) *The Iron Man*. London: Faber and Faber.

Mark, J. (1993) *The Snow Maze*. London: Walker Books.

Street, B. (1994) 'What is meant by social literacies?', *Language and Education* **8**(1–2), 9–17.

Index

academic achievement 107
accent 115–16, 117, 121
accuracy 19
active learning 86, 108
activities for learning 13, 16–17, 31, 135–6
    see also games, multisensory learning, role play
affixes 112
alliteration 111
alphabet awareness 13–15, 16
analogy 6, 16–17, 32, 116
Arabic 100
assessment 14, 118
audience 133, 139
auditory memory 13, 16
aural phonic dependence 31
authentic materials x, xi, 139
autobiographical writing 55, 57

Bangladeshi families 100
Bengali 100
big books 1, 2, 38–40
bilingual learners 99–100
bilingual speakers 117
bilingualism 28
blends 31, 32, 33, 34, 35
book sharing see shared reading
books x, xi
    big books 1, 2, 38–40

collaborative learning x, 1, 36, 108, 136
community languages 99
competence model (Bernstein 1997) 19
composition 5, 73
compound words 111
comprehension 38
connectives 93
connotation 107
consonants 31, 32, 33, 34, 35
    see also onset
context 108
contextual cueing 32
contextualisation 96
Cox Report (DES 1989) 114
critical skills 137, 138, 139
cross-curricular project 52
cross-curricular topics 140
cultural awareness 58
cultural diversity 14, 99, 103
Curriculum Matters 1 (DES 1984) 114
curriculum subjects 92

decoding skills 17, 31, 33
demonstrations 2
developmental psychology 2
dialect 115–6, 117, 121
dictionaries 34, 108–9
discussion see talk
drafting 34, 83–5
drama 133–40
dual-language stories 103, 104

editing 7, 8
education acts (1994, 1998) 133–4
educational success 107
English as an additional language 8
enlarged texts see big books
environment for learning x, 1, 13
evaluation 50, 118–20
examinations 33, 94
experiential learning 134, 138
Extending Literacy (EXEL) Project (Nuffield Foundation)
    92, 94

fiction 37–44
fluency 19
frames see writing frames

games 12, 13, 16, 32
genre 5, 7, 77, 93–4, 95, 139
grammatical development 106
graphemes 33
graphophonic knowledge 4
group work 5–6, 8, 53, 58, 61
Gujarati 99

handwriting 31, 32, 33–6
hearing loss 13
historical fiction 52
History National Curriculum 53
homonyms 15
homophones 15

illustrations see pictures
improvisation 135, 136
independent reading 8, 108
independent writing 15, 31, 94
inference 108
instructions 93, 94
integrated approach 137
involvement 4, 12

Key Stage 1
  drama 138
  phoneme identification 15
  phonics 31
  punctuation 18
  reading longer texts 31
  shared reading 1–5, 66
  shared writing 5–9
  sound-symbol correspondence 15
  word level requirements 17
  writing for SATS 73
Key Stage 2
  drama 138
  fiction 40–44
  language study 114–21
  literature: shared discussion 58
  programmes of study:
  history 53–4
  reading 52
  shared reading 66
  standard English 114–21
  writers' workshop 74, 77
kinaesthetic learning 14
Kingman Report (DES 1988) 18, 114
knowledge about language (KAL) 100,114

language
  censuses 99
  development 106, 133
  environment 133
  Language in the National Curriculum (LINC) project 114, 115
  investigation 121
  patterns 8, 93–4
  study 114–21
  styles 117
  variety 114, 115
languages 99, 100, 110
large-format books *see* big books
learning difficulties 96
learning outcomes 139
learning styles 14
letter-sound correspondence 4, 11, 34
letters 8, 14, 32–5
lexicography 109
linguistic diversity 99, 103
linguistic principles 24
listening skills 12
literacy 9, 17, 137, 139, 140
  other languages 101
Literacy Hour 38, 58
  literature teaching 65–71
  punctuation 28–9
  story structures 88
  writing 76–7
literacy strategy *see* National Literacy Strategy
literary competence 40–1, 66
literary models 79
literate classroom ix
literature 42, 139
  curriculum: World War II texts 52–7
  debate on models of teaching 65–71
  drama 137–8
  see also poetry

materials see resources
medical problems 13
metalanguage 16, 81, 120
metalinguistic awareness 28
metaphor 111, 116, 130
methodology 14
miscues 32
mnemonics 14
morphemes 11
morphology 109, 110, 112
  see also morphemes
motor skills 33, 35, 36
multilingual word processing 100–101, 104
multisensory learning 14, 33

names 110–11
narrative 8, 39, 55, 68, 79–89
National Curriculum 125
  assessments 31
  drama 137
  English 138
  History 53
  language study 114, 115
  level descriptions 120
  poetry 125
  punctuation 19, 24
  reading 45
National Literacy Strategy (DfEE 1998) x, 2, 7
  composition 37, 73
  drama 137, 138, 139
  handwriting 35
  literacy, definition 120
  Literacy Hour 121
  literature 58
  phonic skills 11, 31, 32
  spelling 35
    teaching debate 66, 68, 70, 71
  vocabulary 109
National Literacy Strategy Framework for Teaching see
  National Literacy Strategy
National Literacy training materials 38
National Writing Project (1989) 70
NLS *see* National Literacy Strategy
non-fiction 139, 91–7
novels 39–40, 41
Nuffield Foundation: Extending Literacy (EXEL) Project 92

OFSTED (Office for Standards in Education) 50, 134
onomatopoea 111–12
onset 15–16, 31, 32, 34, 35, 112
oral skills 12, 96
oral work *see* talk
overhead projectors 7

Page Composer 102
pair work 5, 131
Pakistani families 102
Panjabi 100, 101
parental involvement 100, 102, 103–4
phonemes 11, 12, 15, 32, 33, 34
phonics 11–17, 31, 50, 70
phonological awareness 12–13, 32
phonological development 106

pictures 58–64, 68
play *see* games
poetry 115, 116, 118, 121, 123–32
prediction 2, 4
prefixes 112
prescriptive trends ix
print 4, 32, 33, 133, 139
pronunciation 15, 33
   Received Pronunciation (RP) 33, 115, 116
proof-reading 8
punctuation 18–29
puppets 12, 136
purpose 133, 139

Qaida (Urdu software) 103
QCA (Qualifications and Curriculum Authority) 31, 32

reader response 37–40, 58–64
reading xi, 17, 43–4
   independent 8, 108
   literacy hour 65–71
   reading aloud 41–2
   shared 1–5, 35, 58, 59, 66
   silent 45–51
   see also fiction, genre, non-fiction
real texts x, xi, 139
Received Pronunciation (RP) 33, 115, 116
records 76
redrafting 7, 8, 75, 131
regional variation 116
register 93, 116–7
response see reader response
Responses to Curriculum Matters (DES 1986) 114
resources 13, 16–17
rhyme 6, 70
rime 15–17, 31, 32, 112
role play 12, 116, 117, 135, 136
roots 11, 112
rote learning 107, 109
RP see Received Pronunciation

SATs (Standard Assessment Tests) 41, 73, 79, 125
SCAA (School Curriculum Assessment Authority) 79
scaffolding x, 2, 81, 94
script work 136
second language learning 99
self-correction 32
semantic fields 109, 110
sentence level 5
shared reading 1-5, 35, 58, 59, 66
shared writing 1–2, 5–9, 17, 66
silent reading 45–51
slang 117-8, 121
slow learners 49
social groups 117
social skills 136
software (Urdu) 102, 103
sound-letter relationship 11
sound patterns 11, 12
sound-symbol correspondence 15, 32
sound system 31
specialist teachers 13
speech therapists 13

spelling 6, 15, 31–2, 33–6
SSR (sustained silent reading) 45–51
Standard English 114–121
stories 1, 7, 41
   dual-language 103, 104
story grammars 80
story structures 79–89
suffixes 112
Sylheti 99
syntactic patterns 35

talk x, 42, 62, 76
teacher as role model 48
Technical Vocabulary list 121
text interaction *see* reader response
texts 1, 5, 8, 39, 70
   structure 93–4
   types 81, 140
theatre arts 134, 138
thesauruses 34
training materials 38
transcription skills 5, 7, 36
transfer of skills 99

Urdu word processing 99–105

visual patterns 32, 35, 36
visual representation 82
visual strategies 31–2
visual support 13
vocabulary 32, 139, 106-12
vowels 15, 16

whole class teaching 29, 35
word families *see* semantic fields
word level work 5, 17, 106–12
word processing in Urdu 99–105
word relations *see* morphology, semantic fields
World War II texts 52–7
writers' workshops 73–7, 99
writing 34, 43–4, 135
   developmental stages 31
   drafting 34, 83–5
   frames 81–97
   handwriting 31, 32, 33–6
   independent writing 15, 31, 94
   National Writing Project (1989) 70
   non-fiction 91–7
   processes 9
   shared writing 1–2, 5–9, 17, 66
   story structures 79–89
   writers' workshops 73–7, 99

zone of proximal development 2, 5